# Essays on Performance Writing, Poetics and Poetry

## Volume 1

*Also by John Hall*

Between the Cities
Days
Meaning Insomnia
Malo-Lactic Ferment
Couch Grass
Repressed Intimations
Else Here: Selected Poems
Apricot Pages (A Novella)
Couldn't You?
Thirteen Ways of Talking about Performance Writing
The Week's Bad Groan
Interscriptions (with Peter Hughes)
Keepsache: a companion selection to Else Here

Writings towards Writing and Reading
(Volume 2 of the present collection)

# On Performance Writing

*with pedagogical sketches*

Volume 1 of
Essays on Performance Writing,
Poetics and Poetry

JOHN HALL

with a foreword by Larry Lynch

Shearsman Books

First published in the United Kingdom in 2013 by
Shearsman Books
50 Westons Hill Drive
Emersons Green
Bristol
BS16 7DF

www.shearsman.com


ISBN 978-1-84861-317-1

# Contents

Glosses on or for Performance Writing

*Part Two: Pedagogical Sketches
on Arts Teaching and Interdisciplinarity*

This volume is in memory of Dartington College of Arts and is dedicated to the graduates and colleagues whose intellectual company has been so important to me.

# Author's Preface

This two-volume collection includes most of the essays—sometimes taking a very broad view of that term—that I wrote for publication between 1978 and 2013. These dates might deserve some comment, since there is no earlier collection and I had been publishing as poet from 1966. The 1978 "essay" was a memorial piece for John Riley (2: 210–215)*, following his murder. The only other one published before 1991 was on Peter Riley. (2: 225–232) Before that there had been a review or two and one aborted longer essay on an individual poet, but no sustained practice of thinking—and sharing the thinking—through essays.[1] I am sure that this isn't wholly a matter for autobiography and has much to do with the conditions in which certain kinds of poetry and certain kinds of teaching occurred in the UK at the time. Though fired, like so many at the time, by the polemical use of prose by, among others, Ezra Pound and Charles Olson, I certainly did not think of the academic essay as anything like a close cousin to poetry, and the teaching that interested me did not, to my knowledge, have a discursive network of journals and conferences. The difference in 2013 is striking.

There is another way of putting this, though. With very few exceptions, these essays were produced in response to invitations and, in my case—and this probably wasn't unusual—the invitations were few and far between until the 1990s. The invitation in 1984 to write on some recent publications by Peter Riley came from John Welch, as editor of the *Many Review*, a poets' journal belonging to the unrefereed world of small presses rather than to academic publishers or one of the stables of journals operated by commercial presses. I was used to responding to Peter's work in the epistolary modality of *I-you*, where responsibility to the addressee is self-evident, and was anxious about the third-party triangulation of a critical essay, where lines of answerability are much less clear-cut. Awkward as this switch felt, its benefits to me were also apparent, and an ambivalent sense of productive discomfort remains with me still when addressing specific writers who are my contemporaries. I am implicated

---

* References to essays that are included in the two volumes appear in brackets with the number of the volume followed by a colon and page number(s).

in their work, otherwise I would not be interested in responding to it, and the implicatedness is specific in each case. Sometimes it feels as though this must addressed within the writing; at other times, that it should be set to one side within the established protocols for critical distance. Carried in the etymology of the word *essay* is the prudent humility of the notion of trying something out rather than disseminating completed thoughts or fully formed knowledge from an authorised position. We all know the image of the teacher as the *one supposed to know*, often a seductive role where special domains of knowledge are marked out in advance or where a charismatic initiator starts changing the lines around these. But what is it that writers and performers know? (And what do their writings and performances know?—a different question altogether.) What *should* they know? What is the source of any authority they do have?

Having used that word 'critical', with its etymological trace of *judgement*, let me say too that I am not interested in the stance of judge-critic within these essays, whether it take the form of consumer advice or pronouncements on fitness of texts for some supposed canon. Of course, acts of judgement or discrimination take place all the time outside or before the essays. I write about those I admire. This implies countless exclusions but by no means accounts for all the omissions; in many cases, it means only that there has been no invitation. I am well aware that as a consequence the collection lacks balance in some obvious respects and is far from representing a full sketch of either my own interests and admirations or of the contemporary scene of writing that fits either category of poetry or of performance writing.

Some years after the pieces on two unrelated Rileys, a third Riley—Denise—came up with the next invitation, to contribute to a book of essays by poets on writing rather than on the written. How could I do this in good faith, except through further discomforts of autobiographical meditation, since I was not at the time "writing"? I could not be more implicated in the response. The resulting piece—'Writing and Not Writing' (2: 15–23)—fills out the pairing of two broadly different modes of engagement within these essays: the mode that is an extension of acts of reading of specific texts and events and the mode that attempts to understand the implicit values in such acts and the necessary acts of writing that enable them. I hope that some of these essays combine both modes. Others, I know, separate them out.

The motives and energies for all of these essays undoubtedly come out of my own sometimes related and now long combined practices of poetry and teaching. I was lucky enough to work for many years at Dartington College of Arts, an institution that assumed a close relation between teaching and arts practice and whose small scale put practitioners from different disciplines into close conversation with each other. Its emphasis on contemporary practice also posed a number of conceptual and pragmatic challenges, traces of which will be found in the following pages. I'll do no more here than name two of these that had a very considerable impact on my own thinking. The first is the notion of context and its inseparability from text: from 1976 until about 1990 I was preoccupied with pedagogic issues posed by a course called *Art and Social Context*. The second is the notion of performance, and all its morphological variants, very much including performativity. When a pragmatic understanding of writing is developed in the context of fine art, music and theatre—especially non-scripted theatre—this is very different from the understandings relayed and developed within—or just outside—the domain of "literature". Out of these convergences emerged something we ended up calling Performance Writing. The essays in Part 1 of Volume 1 take up this enquiry, which is still very much alive.

There are two volumes because it turned out that by 2013 I had produced more of these essays than could comfortably fit into one. There was also a logic, though an uncomfortable one, for the separation here applied, between those essays considering the idea of performance writing, together with loosely related pedagogical issues (Vol 1), and those explicitly addressing poetry (Vol 2). Because I suspect that the two categories of my essays have until now mostly been read by different people within different discursive contexts, I am hoping that this division is seen as no more significant than a separation into parts within a single volume. A number of the essays could have been placed in either.

I have made no attempt to edit out the original purpose and context of the individual essays and am aware that this has at least two effects that may be unfortunate at times: one, that explanations are sometimes provided which would seem wholly unnecessary to one set of readers; and two, that some essays repeat what has already been covered in others. I hope that readers will be understanding and that the repetition may even be helpful for some.

❧

My thanks go to all the editors and publishers who first made these essays accessible. Details appear for each essay in the endnotes. Many other debts will become apparent from within the essays themselves. My own essaying is increasingly collaborative, even when not explicitly so, in the sense that I am aware of relying more and more on conversations with others to prompt and shape thoughts that I wouldn't otherwise have had, at least in the form they have taken. Performance Writing has been a collaborative venture through-and-through: the intense conversations with Dartington colleagues from across the disciplines that took place as we transformed the initial proposition of "performance writings" into a persuasive field of practice and study were among the most rewarding of my teaching career. Subsequently I was privileged to work closely with Caroline Bergvall, who not only took on the main burden of putting the proposition into practice as an undergraduate teaching project, but also, from the outset, of establishing its significance way beyond any one teaching institution or, indeed, any one part of the world. Her own practice played no small part in this, as did the articulacy and intelligence of her accounts of the field. My own pieces that deal directly with Performance Writing would be more profitably read alongside writings by her, and also by Ric Allsopp, and cris cheek, among others (see, for example, 1: 149–150). Other names will be found within. My thanks go to all colleagues and students over the years at Dartington College of Arts, whose company as thinkers and artists has been so valuable to me. Volume 1 is offered here as my own thanks to, and memorial for, that extraordinary institution.

Particular thanks go to Simon Murray for generously allowing me to include our jointly written essay (1: 164–181); to Larry Lynch for instigating this collection and for his editorial encouragement and support in preparing the essays for the press and for giving precious time to writing a foreword; to Marianne Morris for offering to write the foreword to Volume 2 and for turning her attention to this the minute the ink was dry on her fine PhD submission; to Jaime Robles for giving me the benefits of her experience and judgement in page-setting; and to Kerry Taylor for her invaluable range of advice.

John Hall, April 2013

# The Quiet Ear of Conversation
## a foreword by Larry Lynch

When circumstance requires an introduction, or a "placing" of his working identity, John Hall goes for this: "Poet, teacher and essayist". The last of these is the principal concern of this two-volume collection. In considering the context and cohesion to these essays, though, the other two also need to be in play, for it is in the various touch-points and overlaps between the three, as ways of thinking and contiguous fields of activity, that the critical energy of his essays can be located. It is in the complementary circulation of the practices and intellectual commitments of writing poems, teaching, and critical exposition and commentary, that certain social imperatives and forms of attention become tangible, such that a diverse collection produced over the course of more than three decades can be read as a coherent (albeit complex and meta-linear) narrative body. The three terms also serve a more prosaic chronological function, in that his adult life thus far can be appraised as a series of "phases of intensity" that follow the order of the activity types he chooses to define his working life.

Fundamental to Hall's work are two conjoined activities: listening and conversing. These specific modes of attention, and the particular qualities he brings to them, temper his approach to poetics, pedagogy and criticality. I've opted for "listening" in part due to its co-dependence on and with conversation, but also as a multi-sensory (so as absolutely to capture "looking") supplement for an expanded sense of reading. I want the idea of a finely-tuned prosodic ear working with a more general, less specialist or exclusively literary ethics of attention that takes other voices seriously and regards both as key to a socially valuable intellectualism.

"Conversation" can bring with it both "discourse" and "dialogue", which is fine, but it also assumes a certain sociality predicated on a permission-giving that upholds the value of inclusion, and resists the imperatives of canonical power-play and institutional propriety.

These two modes of social engagement seem to me to provide a texture of cohesion and collective intelligibility to a body of work otherwise marked out by a multiplicity of subject and objective and a frequent interdisciplinary bias. As ways of thinking, and of activating thought in context, they found an early and enduring home in his work as a teacher. Whilst practice as a poet tuned his ear to grammar and prosody (matters which a number of these essays address), teaching opened it to a broader field of intellectual responsibility by locating questions around the social currency of knowledge (knowing and not knowing) within the wider fabric of his work. It's appropriate then, that "teacher" is the central term in Hall's self-defining triplet, and that teaching is the activity that shapes and informs his essaying more than any other. Here I mean "teaching" to encompass activities ranging from direct engagement with students to the design and development of curricula, not to mention all the conversations that efficacy in the full range demands. Specifically, it takes in his time at Dartington College of Arts (DCA) between 1974 and 2010, and his earlier years as a school teacher. Volume 1 of this collection derives from this work. Some of the essays are quite explicitly about teaching (for example, 'Arts for what...',1: 164–180 and 'Designing a Taught Postgraduate Programme...', 1: 195–207). Some are "of" teaching, in that they were written for a student audience ('Thirteen Ways...', 1: 23–41), or by invitation take up a pronounced teacherly agenda, as in the 'Grammar for Performance Writers' trio (1: 53–74). Others—I'm thinking of the sequence of 'Glosses' (1: 146–161)—demonstrate a care for terms that draws on etymology and both specialist and everyday usage. All the essays in Volume 1 either tracked, or were subsequent to, an extended period of pedagogic enquiry that took place at Dartington from the early 1990s through to the college's closure in 2010, around the emergence of an expanded field of writing practice that became known as Performance Writing. This is nicely charted in the first three pieces of Part 1 of the first volume. The work in Volume 2, though less emphatic in its relationship to educational contexts, is nonetheless indebted in its modes and methods to the particular pedagogic imperatives and ways of processing practice that evolved at Dartington and in Hall's work as a teacher there.

The primacy and enduring vitality he finds in conversation was cultivated through his own experiences of being taught, and of engaging in peer group exchange, as part of a burgeoning community of poets. Whilst reading English at Cambridge he came under the tutelage of the poet J.H. Prynne, a relationship that drew him into a wider context of poetic activity that resulted in his participating (as poet, reader and correspondent) in *The English Intelligencer*, a poetry circular edited by Andrew Crozier and then Peter Riley. Although not included here (some have been recently collected in Pattison 2012), his first prose commentaries appeared in the *Intelligencer*, and can be read as a precursor to the celebratory essays on poems and poets that constitute the latter part of Volume 2. Indeed a number of these essays address the work of writers also involved in the *Intelligencer*, such as Peter Riley (2: 225–237), John James (2: 116–131), John Riley (2: 210–224), Douglas Oliver (2: 163–193) and Lee Harwood (2: 96–97, 103–111). The longevity of these friendships and the conversations they supported add weight to the huge value Hall places on both in their capacity socially to enrich the critical attentiveness of reading. Note also, that almost every essay in this collection was prompted by an invitation, often from a friend and invariably either in response to, or in advance of, conversation. I often think that were the essay to have only one purpose for Hall, it would be to punctuate the contexts of other (past and anticipated) occasions for talking.

Supervisions with Prynne and the critical energy surrounding the work of *The Intelligencer* were both highly conversational initiatives, and both entailed the granting of a close and attentive ear to the practice of writing. The idea of a practice (the doing rather that the done of writing), particularly one's own, as the object of sustained critical attention, was an informal proposition at Cambridge, taking place outside the curriculum, if not sometimes the university. *The Intelligencer* was not a university initiative and it would seem that Prynne's allegiance to any sense of curriculum was (at least in Hall's case) highly flexible. It needed to be, for were it not for his intervention, Hall would most likely have left university prematurely and disappointed. Struggling to reconcile his own emergent values with those he perceived, at the time, as belonging to institutionalised learning, the generosity and expansiveness of Prynne's teaching and responses to his poetry made his time in Cambridge productive and affirmative. The practical intensity of their conversations and the relative social and intellectual plurality of *The Intelligencer* poets countered his youthful disdain towards a knowledge economy that seemed to trade too much in the entitling of access to "what ought to be known", and seeded some attitudes to education, teaching and the handling of knowledge that find their way into his essays. This time compounded in him a deep-seated belief in the social value of learning, but with an educational health warning firmly attached to the then (and still?) prevalent strain of "fully authorised knowledge" and social exclusion manifest in many teaching institutions.

Much of what Hall found informally productive and enriching at Cambridge was to become formally structural and systemic at Dartington, as were some possible correctives to what had troubled him in the former. 'Arts for what...' (1: 164–181) and Designing a taught... (1: 195–207) offer a historical background to Dartington and outline some of the key approaches to pedagogy developed there. The significance of the Dartington project can be summarised in terms of "practice" and "knowledge" and their variable relatedness. This could be recast as "making" and "knowing" and their social and pedagogic possibilities, when taken on in a heuristic doubling rather than the more normative dualism of either/ or. I emphasise the importance of Dartington not because it subscribed to any singular, codified methodology (although it is true that over time certain approaches and values became engrained), but because it provided a distinct educational context for the thinking through and developing of arts pedagogy as a set of methodological propositions and questions, rather than as being rooted in disciplinary convention and cultural inheritance. It is this notably idiosyncratic set of permissions that determined the capacity of Hall's teaching practice to cultivate not just *what* he essays on (as is the case for many academics), but more important than this, *how* his essays do their work and *why* he favours certain modes of exposition before others.

Dartington developed a critical ambivalence to any sense of knowledge as a given body and as being necessarily proper to the advancing of a particular field of practice or enquiry. Rather than asking, "what ought we/I to know about what has been done in X?" the question would be, "what do we/I need to know about (and for) what we are doing in X and how do we/I need to know it?" This stance significantly shapes the way these essays work. Received wisdom and assumed academic meta-narratives have no privileged place or propriety, so the object or point of study needs to be listened to very carefully, on its own terms; any singularly knowing didactic voice loses currency, as the grounds for an authoritative reading become decidedly shaky. Hall's essays are alert to these conditions. They read as though asking, "what does this work need to know, or ask us to talk about"? More than, perhaps, "what do I know about this work"? Or, "how might this work fit within the wider critical scheme I bring to it"? This is where his capacity as a listener becomes critical. To answer the call of the work's processes, material features and routes to meaning requires attention that is both close and open. Openness to what might not be known and to an axiomatic engagement with what is materially "there" engenders modes of attention and ways of reading that look to hear the substance of work: quite literally, what has been done, and then, what it is doing. This approach, which often brings to mind Gadamer's commentary on Paul Celan's poetry (Gadamer 1997), can be seen in many of the essays that attend to a specific poem, artwork or text. There's a brief but clear example of this in one of his two commentaries on Prynne poems (2: 203–209):

> But first, let's *look* at it very briefly. There is a column of text, occupying the full length of the page but only about half the width, left-justified, ragged right, with noticeable but not extreme variation in line length. There are no markers of sections or stanzas. Only the last full-stop comes at the end of a line. There is a title. What I see looks like a unified thing, long and thin and joined up.

The same essay continues through a simple (though far from simplistic) take on what the poem is doing:

> Here's a literal reading of the scene in the poem. Some children gather—or have gathered—to watch the "I" of the poem mend a lawn-mower. "I" narrates some of the process of fixing the mower and reflects on the children, not as individual social beings but as instances of genetics; as messages and as carriers of internal messages; as reliant on the pumping mechanisms of their hearts, as reliant on what they don't know. No speech is cited. By the end of the poem the mower works.

Hall's frequent recourse to a kind of "first principle" approach to reading and commentary is reminiscent of the Practical Criticism developed at Cambridge in the 1920s (Richards 1929). Prioritising the immediacy of the work's substance, and resisting the potential hijacking effect or critical foreclosure incurred by the supplanting of wider theoretical frames, are qualities often aligned with this method that he holds onto, but develops through a distinctly Art School sensibility. Hall's criticism (and teaching) combines direct and uncompromising attention to the primacy of the work, with openness to the discursive productivity of knowing and working with that which is unknown (and in some cases unknowable), and to taking on an expanded set of arts concerns as absolutely part of the fabric of a text. I'm thinking here about his tendency to work into poems (and other kinds of text) from the perspective granted by their material, spatial and visual construction. This can be seen in the first of the two excerpts from the essay on Prynne cited above, but also in parts of the essay 'Eluded Readings' (2: 24–45), a text which also talks through poems and poem sequences as units of visual organisation in page-space as well as openly taking reading pleasure in lacking knowledge. The theme of the page is itself discussed in the two connected pieces, 'Reading (Il)legible Pages' (1: 80–92) and 'Reading a Polished Page' (1: 93–95), the latter adopting an overtly interdisciplinary stance in carrying the concept of the page and its reading into the context of the photograph and its frame. This essay, despite its relative brevity, is a critical one. It would certainly have been written in close hearing distance of his poetic practice, which has, for the last 15 years or so, included making an extensive body of visual poems for domestic photograph frames and settings. In this sense, it reads very well alongside the much longer (and similarly practice-led) piece 'Time-Play-Space' (2: 60–71). The two pieces gather and foreground a trio of themes—context, interdisciplinarity and performance—that temper Hall's thinking, and both reveal a developing preoccupation with reading as a contextual and situated mode of performance manifestly caught up in the exegesis of material *space / time / play* in visual textuality and language enactment.

Context, interdisciplinarity and performance: these themes could stand as the principal headings in a Dartington typology, and they certainly orientated Hall's work there and the expository writing it often prompted and always characterised. At Dartington the question of context was reified to the status of a fundamental conceptual and compositional determinant: to ask who and where an artwork (of any kind) is for and to what possible ends was fuel for teaching and wider conversation. A particular scheme of contextual thinking is the way these essays sketch the contingent relationships between specific texts and other social practices. 'Making it new' (1: 123–132) and 'Do Not Ignore' (1: 115–122) both, for example, make a point of reading and processing textual and linguistic material through its social context; and not simply the social context in which the work takes place, but the ways in which the socio-political implications and functions of language and writing reverberate within, and augment the work itself, weaving texts and the ways they are encountered into a wider fabric of lived experience.

Behind this is the idea that properly to engage a practice, it is necessary to be alert to the conditions that grant that practice its aesthetic and social currency—that is, amongst a broader set of socio-cultural factors and other practices. Look to the trio on grammar (1: 53–74)), and note how music, dance and the performance of breath are alluded to as means through which to think language.

Hall's involvement in these approaches to pedagogy, along with decades of interrogative exposure to arts disciplines other than his own, has brought to his primary concerns of writing and poetics a developed acuity for critically enlivening aesthetic, conceptual and compositional dynamics in textual and poetic practice that are more usually treated as incidental or secondary. This is certainly the case in his work on the visual, on sound and prosody ('Foot, Mouth and Ear' (1: 133–145)), and on situatedness ('Not Showing' (1: 75–79)), but is most significant perhaps in his critical negotiation of ideas of performance into the literary domain.

This process is largely framed by the development of Performance Writing and is not one Hall undertook alone. Conversation and collaboration shaped the development of the field and remain its abiding dynamic, central to which is the "question of performance". 'Performed through' (1: 61) begins: "the term 'performance' is an invitation to debate rather than a fixed term with an easy definition". This interrogative stance helps open up performance (and subsequently performance writing) as an expanded field of practice and enquiry. In his critical work, ideas of performance relate primarily to a broad sense of embodied and temporal activity, further expanded to take on the uses of the term by Austin (1976) and Chomsky (1965). Just as these essays frequently ask that texts be considered as things that *are*, in material and visual terms, they also ask that they be engaged with as things that have been *done* (in their writing) and that are in the process of *doing* (in their reading). The seminal 'Thirteen Ways…' (1: 23–40). 'Arts for…' , and again, the 'Grammar for Performance Writers' essays, present this perspective clearly, and set-up a range of approaches to reading and thinking about writing that are re-played in other pieces.

In these essays Hall's social and pedagogic commitment is rendered through the stuff of language, writing and textuality; matters that have themselves been subject to notable change in their means and contexts of production and dissemination over the course of his essaying. The increasing dissolution of disciplinary boundaries and the rapid emergence of new writing and publication technologies have seen the environments and contexts within which writing happens and texts take place alter more, perhaps, in the last 30 years than in the previous 300. Such a profound evolutionary surge has challenged writers, and those who discourse on writing, to expand and reimagine the practical and critical instrumentation and framing of their endeavours, so as to take-on the textual and contextual implications of a radically new and emergent literary landscape.

Hall's essays negotiate and open-up approaches to reading and developing writing in relation to these changed literacies and textual modalities. This is an undertaking that asks for an advanced set of conversations and a corresponding capacity for listening to practice through an expanded range of contexts and constructions. In particular, Hall's essays put the idea of performance to work, releasing it from the strictures of disciplinary specificity. It becomes an effective critical instrument or methodological device for thinking about reading and writing as things that are *done* (in bodies and contexts), and about texts as things that take place in material time and space. There is no canon of study or set of standardized critical approaches for this work. Rather, it requires modes of engagement and critical tactics that are openly responsive, contextually mobile and interdisciplinary in reach. The means and modes of criticality and commentary engendered by the development of Performance Writing have folded back into Hall's readings and responses to poetry, accounting, in part, for the distinctive features of his work on poetry for the page. Taken together, the essays speak of a vital dynamism and social commitment in respect to the activities of writing and poetics, enlivened by the quiet ear of the practitioner and the conversational drive of the teacher.

Larry Lynch,
April 2013

# PART ONE

# On Performance Writing

# Thirteen Ways of Talking about Performance Writing
## (a lecture) [2]

1.

Composition and performance: in your own work, in your own subject area, what is the relation between the two? Which is thicker in the mix that is your work?

Does this come with the medium or the traditions of the form or is it a decision that you yourself have made about how you want to work?

This morning I had to put a tie on (Not this morning as you can see; I mean the morning on which I wrote that clause—last Wednesday in London). Because I don't wear ties that often I was very aware of what my hands were doing, of the thickness or density of the activity. I was not only putting a tie on—I was aware of performing the act of putting a tie on. That led me to think of two different approaches to a tie being put on in a performance.

In the one, an actor puts a tie on in performance as a representation of the fact that the character he/she is impersonating puts a tie on at that moment in the story. The act may give density to the narrative or to the character. That depends.

In another, the doing up of the tie is *the* point, is in no way an optional piece of business. An example could be a clown exaggeratedly struggling with a knot. As a spectator to this second performance you will probably find that you own hands are wanting to lift to where your own tie would be, drawn into the density and complexity of the act. Or even drawn across in imagination to the performer's tie, to help, to complete the performance.

Think of the relation of composition to performance in these two examples: in the first, the performer had to bring in a real-life skill, simply and casually, in order to perform a score; in the second the performance itself is most crucially part of the composition, perhaps *is* the composition—the placing of part to part which constitutes composition shows us in this instance that doing up a tie in performance is itself composed of separable moves, sequenced and juxtaposed.

I want to hold on to this idea of density. The components of performance are not equally pre-composed; the components of your composition do not equally decompose. Where is the thickness?

Writing can be all composition—all, as it were, done beforehand— invisibly decomposed into performance—no thickness left. Or it can retain its thickness, drawing you in to the act, as it were, of language trying to do up its tie; not because it doesn't know how to, but because the thickness of language gives us from time to time a thick sense (a sense with density, like thick paint) of the medium in which—or, perhaps, better, against which—we perform our lives.

2.

For the first minute or two—and a minute is a long time in any performance—of Man Act's Dartington performance of *Jimmy Messiah*, no words were spoken in the performance space. There wasn't silence. There was noise: sonic noise through (I was going to say "from") the sound system; visual noise from the smoke machine; the physical noise of narcissism from the male body of the performer, Simon Thorne, cocky and strutting, even when performance words were spoken.

How was this absence of words written?

I have just written words back into the absence, after the event.

How was it written before the event? Or to put it another way, was there a writing event before the performing event, which prepared for the performance of no words?

How do you write no words? Would it help to ask a musician for an answer to this question? Or a visual performer?

A performance writer needs to know how to write no words; needs to know words, to know no words.

A performance writer and a performer—and they may be one and the same—need to know the duration of no words. How do you measure the absence of words in a performance? In what medium or dimension does performance time exist? A writer measures time on the heart-beat (the pulse), on the breath, on the held breath. A performance writer needs to know how long before a performer blinks.

3.

X is a performance writer

she writes pages and she writes performances

she performs writing

she forms writing which informs performance

what is it to perform writing?

she performs the act of writing

quite simply, she writes

imagine that there is a performance of X in the act of writing

or you, perhaps, in the act of writing

how do you perform this task?

Could you take another body and direct it to write
just as you write—that is, to move into and through writing just
the way that you do?

And if you did—the same thick fingers around the same pen, say; the
head at precisely the distance from and angle to the paper that you
take—could you direct that body to write what you write?

You who are a body, could you direct yourself to write
precisely in the way that you write?

Is it you who writes what you write?
It is certainly a body out of which you say "I" which writes what you
write.

As you write, did you say yes it is most certainly I who writes?

The I who says so and the I who writes is the same I;
there is no spectator here;
no performer watching herself write;
or watching the about-to-happen of the writing leaving this I-who-writes,
going out through the fingers into another space,
from where it can look back as though to say,
now I am the writing that *you* wrote.

A moment later—really just a moment that it takes you, dear writer,
to become dear reader—
two "I"s squint and split and are caught in a parallax of close separation.

And this is just the page. Because the writing then hovers on the edge
of a space which is the place of performance.

It is about to become topical—which means of its place.

The performance writer writes the space between the writing
and the performing,
where the writing is always about to leave to become something else;
where the I is about to become at least another I,
whoever's I that is, however many eyes there are.

4.

Y writes a page that becomes a book

when he performs that writing the words are on the page, which he has written, are in the form of the performance, inform it and are transformed in it

his performance cannot be contained by or in the words; the breath that inspires his words (quite literally)
the respiration which he so robustly modulates, breaks through, is held *and* suppressed

his writing is up against the physical hurt of talk; it makes you know that it takes all of a body to pass through the controlled slimness of these fingers—

of course it is not adequate, of course so much gets lost.

between a sigh, a scream, a gasp, a gag and a laugh—
(these are not words—are they written?)
there are words talking of simple things.

check out the names of things.

write the names of things quietly.

you may perform a spell against madness.

what is it that makes people write?

5.

Z saw the words that came out of her hands

she saw that once they were there

on the fabric or on the paper or on the post cards

from that moment on they were there to be *seen*


she saw that she had made something

and that she had made something that passed beyond itself, swinging

from garments on a line, say, but linking messages one to the other,

suggesting stories of personal violence


she saw that she had made something

that in controlling she couldn't control;

in putting her words out into a space

which others moved in and out of

there was a performance space in which these others had to perform,


caught in a narrative of swinging things and meanings.

6.

*Performance Writing*

*Writing performance*

*Written performance*

*Writing in performance*

*Performance rites*

*Writing into performance*

*Performing writing*

*Writing performing*

*Performance in writing*

*Performance Writing*

7.

Is performance a noun pretending to be an adjective—
i.e. is there a kind of writing which is performance writing?

Or is it an ordinary noun, followed by a verb
in the form of a present participle—
as in "performance running" or, tautologically,
"performance performing"?

More likely "writing" is a gerund—that is to say,
the noun form of the verb;
an action caught as a thing

8.

This is a lecture about Performance Writing in a series on the definings of the practical subjects taught at Dartington.

It is a defining, not a definition. Like "writing", "defining" can best be treated as a gerund, catching the present tense of the verb up into a noun, without losing the continuous dynamic of the verb: the process of the act of defining. If the process were to end in resolution we would move the defining into definition. We would know.

We won't.

This is a lecture. A lecture is a reading—it comes from the Latin word for [RED] "read" (sounding like the colour; rhyming with bed; i.e. past tense). What gets read in a lecture is, of course, writing. These two words, these two activities, are folded into each other, like the inside-outness of socks before they go into the washing machine.

I am performing a text which I wrote. Only when I look up and break away from the text will I be talking (talking is not the same as reading aloud)—but only just talking; my talk will be no more than a moment of improvisation—a cadenza, if you like, held in place by the strictures and structures of script(ure)—of the written.

Meanwhile, Caroline and Melinda are performing the act of writing. They write in front of us. They write writing while I write talking and talk writing in a written talk about writing.[3]

9.

Two ways of coming at the notion of "defining":

First, that the thing is already well established and just needs defining, perhaps through a process of collecting examples of practice and commentary and identifying the defining characteristics. This is how dictionary makers go about their task: meaning of terms is deduced from actual usage.

This won't work for Performance Writing.

The second sense is not to do with finding or refining a definition or arguing with long-established ones; it is to do with *making* a meaning. Defining is the whole process of constructing a subject.

Here at Dartington we are helping to make a meaning which many writers—and others interested in writing and performance—were beginning to find necessary.

And this leads me to another set of two:

I.   For a few thousand years (that's all) writing has been brought to bear on the business of performance, in the process transforming what performance could be. Historically this has produced many different kinds of related writing: epic narrations—sung or declaimed, poems of all kinds, play-texts, song writing, opera librettos, texts for radio, film and TV, writings as scenographic elements within or on the skin of performance space, various forms of graphic titling and text production. Developments in computer technology open up new possibilities by the month.

This is a vast field of performance modes, all needing different writing modes. You could get lost in it easily. And neither in terms of performance nor writing (for these are inextricably linked for performance writing) is there anything stable about any of it.

For Performance Writing the size of the field poses one of the defining questions: are there general issues for the ways that writing and performance have related to each other, and could relate to each other, from which new writers could most usefully learn?

Let's try answering with some more questions. Trying to answer them—through practice and theory—is one way that Performance Writing will define itself.

*What is writing?*

*What does / can writing do?*

*When writing does not treat the page as its destination, where does it go?*

*To what extent is it useful to think of writing as a notation system for performance behaviour which disappears into performance (transformed from writing into performance exactly like a musical score)?*

*And to what extent can (and does) writing retain its quality as writing right through into performance? In other words, are there performance forms which are precisely the performance of writing?*

II.  Which brings us back to the second *two* and the business of naming or adopting a name, which is not the same as defining, though it contributes to it.

Recently a number of writers have found that their practice has moved away from a happy fit with any existing names. I am thinking particularly of the kind of work where a writerly text is activated into performance—the poetic text into performance—but this is by no means the only kind of work.

It is useful to think of four points of origin, four departures away from the security of a name:

~ *from poetry or a poetic text*
~ *from theatre and related forms of dramatic narrative*
~ *from visual art, including performance art*
~ *from sound composition or words that lurk near music*

The stress is on the preposition "from". In this context this should be called a post-position not a pre-position. "From" here means both "out of" and "after".

Performance Writing is founded on the belief that these four (which are already in themselves very varied) converge in crucial respects and that the place of this convergence is the one from which to view the future of writing in its relation to performance.

10.

We are trying to define Performance Writing. I say "we" (On Saturday 12th November 1994, I wrote down, in inverted commas, "we" in order to "say" it on Tuesday 22nd November which I can now call today). When I wrote "I" and "we"—for it was I who writes both, as you will have noticed—I was in a house with two others who are close to me, with whom I am close. But they weren't the "we" I meant. Writing is a means of casting forwards into an anticipated "we". This now today is the "we" I anticipated. When "we" works it is a powerful word, few more powerful; it is a social word, obviously; a political one, always.

The present tense I used when I wrote "I say 'we'" was an anticipatory present tense. I did not say, for example: "at this moment I am writing that I shall say 'we'". I anticipated a present; that is to say, I tried to make it.

Performance Writing will always try to make a present, to make itself present through performance. Through Performance Writing writing has presence in space and time.

SO, to return and repeat (and wondering what turns in a "so" when it is used as a hinge or a join like that): "we" are trying to define Performance Writing. What could I possibly mean by "we"? I mean that I hope that you are too (that when I wrote that sentence I expected to be hoping that you would be too); otherwise I don't know what we are doing together in this room.

My writing prepared for this performance, which is only present to you if you take yourself up somewhere into a "we" that I, and—for this moment perhaps not you—have shaped.

My writing prepared for this performance.

11.

Caroline is performing writing. "is performing" is a form of the continuous present tense. In her present activity she draws on a past which gave her knowledge of writing—that is of language, of letters and a world. Writing always reaches back, otherwise it would never reach anyone else. It reaches back in order to reach forward.

On the screen is an other writing. (On the screen is another who has written). This other writer is hidden before (a preposition in time and space) the screen. You were expecting me to say behind.

A screen is something designed to substitute one appearance for another: i.e., like nudity, to show and hide at one and the same time. A screening is a showing and a hiding. Does it show to hide or hide to show? A question which is on a hiding to nothing; nothing, of course, doesn't need to be hidden.

On the screen is writing, writing away all by itself now, thanks to Random Access Memory. In the continuous present, now is the future of a past mark. Each *now* becomes another now. The memory has also been transferred to the disk drive. Now that I have told you, I can say "we" in the next statement: to remember we need to remember that it is in memory.

The computer is a time machine: a machine designed to manipulate and defeat time through the most abstract abstraction of forms of knowledge. Writing is no more and no less than this: a technological process designed to manipulate and defeat time, operating in terror of loss of power through loss of memory. Writing creates the conditions it sets out to repress.

I write because I do not trust myself to tell through speaking; because I don't trust myself to remember, because I don't trust myself to perform. As I write I suppress one set of stories in favour of another. Or I write because I don't know who will speak or who will remember, or who will remember how to speak, who will perform.

WE (this is a different "we" now)—we write because we know that our people has lost its memory of what and how to perform. Otherwise their performance would be written in memory, and none of us would challenge the stories these memories remembered.

And if our people has lost our memory then there probably is no people and we can know why there is a certain desperation about all written performance.

But what do I mean by memory here? Well, for example, you wake up in the middle of the night in a familiar room. You want to turn the light on. Written in your body is a memory of exactly where the switch is. You reach out in the dark and your hand alights on it gently: click; this is the oral tradition at work.

When there is a people and it remembers, the stories are written in its body.

12.

3 senses of writing:

*the act of writing as in the act of dancing*
*the generic category which includes all such acts*
*scripture or literature: that which has been written*

Writing and the written: Performance Writing is writing and not scripture.

Writing has been written all over the place and on all sorts of things, using many kinds of materials and technologies.

This lecture was first written with a fountain pen into a lined A4, hard-back book which cost me 81 pence. I wrote it in sections, which were intended to sound as sections, with pauses and turns (strophes) between. I wasn't sure at the time of writing how much detail I might want to change. I was sure I would want to perform the sections in a sequence other than the one in which they were written. So I transcribed one form of writing—through the process of reading, of course—into another, through a so-called "word processor". Writers are word-processors; machines aren't. I had to key this in. Having done so there is no reason why it should ever reach a page. But it did. And soon, through computer technology, we will not have to key in through our fingers but will be able to speak writing, talking into a machine which recognises the sounds we make as words which can be transcribed.

MEANWHILE (compare this "meanwhile" with that earlier "so"), writing is everywhere, on and in all our buildings, on and through screens, through windows, in lights. We inhabit a written environment; this means that we can't help performing writing.

13.

"Performance" implies a contrast with the enclosed and secretive world of the page of a book or of the bureaucratic statement of a notice.

I don't know whether those old-fashioned things, letters (as in royal mail) are examples of Performance Writing. I think they are. What is the difference between a telephone call and a letter? How many performances that you have seen include a telephone conversation?

Performance Writing: all word writing that finds its way into performance or, through words, provides the memory of performance for the purposes of re-performance.

Performance Writing can start with the tools of the writing trade. You can go away and write a performance—a song, say—in your room; get it all readably down on paper and then later set about performing it or getting someone else to.

Or Performance Writing can emerge out of a fuller process of devising, which might well be collaborative; a process, at any rate in which there is a dialectic of performing and writing, a shuttling to and fro between modes for the purposes of each.

Or Performance Writing can emerge as a set of compositional materials— perhaps among many others—in a written space, which might be painterly or sculptural or performic—in the sense that written words may themselves move about as performers in space.

We could, of course, be much more literal than that but that would be to attempt a definition and this has been a defining. The lecture ends; the defining begins.

# A note on Performance Writing
## at Dartington College of Arts

An undergraduate degree under the name of Performance Writing ran at Dartington from Autumn 1994 to the Summer of 2005. The spirit, though not the full name, survives (in 2007) in the current degree with its generic name of Writing and its optional inflections of "Contemporary Practices" and "Scripted Media".

From 1999 until the time of writing there has been a Masters (MA) in Performance Writing and there have been research students whose research is into "performance writing".

The following were all part of the core team for at least some of the time: Ric Allsopp, Caroline Bergvall, Barbara Bridger, Jerome Fletcher, John Hall, Peter Jaeger, Mark Leahy, Brigid Mc Leer, Redell Olsen, Alaric Sumner, Aaron Williamson; with significant contributions from: John Cayley, cris cheek, Helena Goldwater, Larry Lynch, Claire Macdonald, Deborah Price and too many others to name here.

Early on there were two Performance Writing Symposia—one at Dartington in 1996 and another, *In the Event of a Text*, in Utrecht in 1999. Caroline Bergvall started a series of colloquia called *Partly Writing* in collaboration with colleagues in other institutions. So far there have been four gatherings.

# Performance Writing 1994–2004

## a talk [4]

I think I know why I have been asked to give these few words. It is because I was in at the beginning and can talk a little of the history and first motivations for starting something called Performance Writing at Dartington College of Arts. I am not going to try to talk about the work in the exhibition. You can see that for yourselves.

Back in 1992—more than ten years ago—we made the decision at Dartington to add a writing degree to the portfolio of courses. Writing was already happening as part of the existing courses in Music, Theatre and Visual Performance and we didn't want to displace this. We wanted, though, to design a frame for a range of approaches to writing that made sense of what else we did at Dartington and of what was happening to writing in the world at large and more specifically in its relation with other arts practices.

I was asked to convene a planning team. This was before e-mail (at least at Dartington) so I put out an old-fashioned paper memo: would anyone like to join me in designing the details of a degree to be called, we thought at the time, "performance writings", deliberately asserting the plural. At a very early stage I asked all staff to suggest what texts and works they thought should be in the course bibliography. The team that was formed included a composer, a musician-theatre maker, a live artist, at least one poet, an arts manager, a specialist in adult education, and had as its consultant, because at the time he was mostly working away from Dartington, the current Director, Ric Allsopp.

We wanted, in the broadest sense, to address the writing that might be about to come and neither of the two words in our title—performance or writing—was a term we wanted anyone to take for granted. Our approach was predicated on the assumption that writing has a history. It changes. And this history is as much to do with what writing *performs* within a society as with what *forms* it takes. For example, walking around Exeter today I was reminded, as though a reminder were needed, of how ancient sacred and bureaucratic inscription has been appropriated and transformed for the purposes of capitalism. The city is a place of words of desire (as is the "country" though these words are largely invisible—internally audible perhaps) and every home and place of work is filled with text, sounded and/or seen. Already in the early 90s it was becoming clear that paper, ink and pen—for some time the conventional tools of a writer's trade—would not in any simple way be superseded but would themselves be changed through the emergence of new environments and technologies of writing. Printers still use ink but a computer screen or projector doesn't. There is now a writing in light and a writing whose substance is digital and therefore transformable into different media.

So we were recognising two related questions: that the material practices of writing and the environments in which writing occurs were changing and that behind this was a whole set of questions about changing uses of textuality in social life—you could say, how texts are *lived* or even how texts live us. I use the word "question" because we wanted from the start a practical approach to writing that was driven by questions and not by taught solutions. Every act of writing is a partial reply. We caught something—a moment in the changing history of writing—with this approach, that has attracted international attention. The first undergraduates were recruited in 1994 and graduated in 1997. Some of their work is here in the exhibition. In 1999 we added an MA award. At last count we had twelve research students working in—or in relation to—the field. Some of their work can be seen here in this exhibition.


30th April 2004

# Performance Writing:
## Twenty Years and Still Counting [5]

With the convenient selectivity and time-shuffling of retrospection, I have been trying to think back to the factors that helped shape or constrain the idea of Performance Writing when it was being developed as field and degree course at Dartington College of Arts about twenty years ago. I have been doing this in order to try to assess what might have changed, might be changing as I write, or might be about to change (though if something is palpably about to change then you could argue that it is already changing). One rather loaded way of putting this is to ask whether the idea of performance writing was of its time and has— or soon will have—run its course. There are two obvious ways in which this might occur and two others worth mentioning. The first, which is a familiar one in the worlds of arts and organised knowledge, is that an initially pioneering and productive development is widely adopted into a mainstream and no longer needs its separate name. The second is that the conditions that gave rise to it might have changed in ways that render the proposition redundant. A third is that in some way the proposition has proved plain wrong or destructive. And finally, a name which is suggestive rather than precise could have been appropriated, and thereby transformed, for different, perhaps narrower, purposes.

Though I shall try to touch on three of these possibilities—the exception being the third, whose elimination will be implied in almost everything that follows—I hope that I can be forgiven for not trying too hard to join everything up. I take my justification from the figure of a constellation, according to which quite separate stars can, through knowing perception, be seen as though they form a higher level unity: a figure "traced on the face of the sky" (OED), such as Orion or the Plough. Performance Writing was the consequence of just such shared acts of discernment, connecting up a number of emerging and established practices that include, or at least have a bearing on, writing, together with ideas emerging out of the conceptual practices of philosophy (broadly understood) and social sciences, especially those branches where either language or performance have been found to be conceptually useful.

The imaginary (OED again) figuration of constellation can become fixed and lose its initial suggestiveness, giving way to the assumption that there really is a singularity for which the name Orion or Performance Writing is no more than a label.[6] I think we always knew that there must never be such a *thing* as performance writing.[7] It is not and was not a nameable practice or even a fixed set of practices. It was instead from the start intended as a name for a set of dispositions towards textual practice and enquiry, motivated by questions requiring both practical and speculative answers through writing and performance, their various interconnections, and their embeddedness in political economy, technology and practices of everyday life. Put at its simplest, Performance Writing recognised that practices of writing far exceeded the "literary" in a number of ways that perhaps fall into two broad categories: as significant elements or potentials in supposedly non-literary arts and cultural practices; and as having pervaded most aspects of contemporary sociality and citizenship. In literate societies, selves, necessarily performed through language, are increasingly so through language-as-writing. The "media" have always been social, though the forms of sociality vary significantly; since the social is always constituted out of inter-subjectivity, forms of sociality shape subjectivities. Only a reductive determinism would explain this solely in terms of the "media".

"Consumers" of consumer capitalism are required to be literate: to be able to consume text both as commodity and as means and desire towards other consumption.[8] Since consumer capitalism has until recently mostly been assumed to require the conditions of parliamentary democracy, literacy is also required for participation as *citizen* in the self-regulating order words of social cohesion. (Deleuze 1992: 79) Consumer-citizens ("we") are now increasingly required also to be producers of textuality, not only to inscribe themselves in the registers of official membership with more than a thumb-print, but in order also to buy the new devices that manage the circulation and reciprocation of text (and with the increasing capacity to combine text with image and sound). The last two decades have seen a remarkable change in these respects in ways which will no doubt be covered in other essays in the journal. It is enough here to say that the conjoined development and commodification of so-called digital technology is the clearest recent context for rapid changes in the performance of textuality in social life. A technicist response, though exciting enough in itself, would never be enough.

When contemporary pedagogic institutions refer to the "cultural industries", they usually do so, without the guidance of Adorno, to refer to a(n uncritical) responsibility to train future employees for, and to contribute to research and development in, organisations that either manage symbolic goods such as music, film, TV programmes, "knowledge" and "information", or produce the equipment on which such symbolic exchanges come to rely. If these "industries" really do "produce culture"—and how could they not?—then the responsibility remains to engage with the cultural consequences which, by definition, will extend beyond them. According to any useful definition, "culture" shapes actual lives in their interactions with each other.

Far from being overtaken by events, then, the need is all the more urgent for an approach to writing that concerns itself practically with the changes in the textual environment that the "cultural industries" respond to and generate; this was perhaps the most ambitious feature of Performance Writing's early aims. This is far from a plea for priority rights for "digital writing" or "e-literature". That would be to pre-empt *before* writing a question that for performance writing needs also to be a question *through* writing. There is no reason to presume that questions posed by new technological developments can only be addressed through those technologies. A technology, being inseparable from the human relations it mediates, obviates or extends, is always more than a combination of hard- and soft-ware. But these technologies are not of the same order as the machines that threatened the livelihoods of the Luddites. They are now technologies of everyday life, irresistible, inexorable, reshaping economies and discursive environments and therefore inevitably also re-shaping discourse. Writers want and need to be in there. Of course. And motives will range from the opportunism of those responding to pioneering opportunities through to direct political or ethical engagement—and not just through critical commentary—with what it *could be* to live these cultural changes.

✍

Historically, education has tended to keep relatively separate a critical engagement with the performativity of general rhetoric from the pragmatics of direct involvement in specific rhetorical practices. An obvious example is (was?) the assumption that literature can be studied without the need to make it. Cultural Studies, invaluable in its time, and highly influential on Performance Writing, often lacked a sense of the very practices that its mode of study might suggest as appropriate.[9]

Like so much at Dartington, the performance writing enterprise was pedagogic through and through, but never as a pedagogy whose purpose was to transmit the known. Most of those who planned it or participated early as teachers or students thought of themselves as practitioners whose task, through both practice and pedagogy, was to make sense of an emerging world rather than to conserve an established canon or at least its formal properties. An option that did not occur to us at the time, but which could no doubt be made attractive to some senior managers in higher education, was a version of performance writing conceived as preparation—even training—for careers as writing specialists within the "cultural industries".

I have been slipping between the terms *writing* and *textuality*, perhaps with the idea that writing is verb and practice, and textuality the general outcome of all writing, a second or third nature that weaves through the world as the already written, reactivated every time an act of reading or textual memory takes place. Textuality is produced and reproduced through writing and reading, its material and aesthetic forms proliferating without any sign of decay.

For PW there were from the start other provocative and related pairings of terms: speech and language (Saussure 1974); orality and literacy (Ong 2002); voice and graphic mark (gramma) (Derrida 1976, 1981); constative and performative (Austin 1976); competence and performance (Chomsky 1965). It is easier to think of the performance of language as oral, as speaking, with writing perhaps as a preparation or substitute for or record of such speaking, but from the start we did not want to treat these as part of a dualism.

Derrida's notion of *trace* suggests something left over from an earlier process. Contemporary recording equipment can retain an archival trace, in a form that the particular technology permits, of any act of language whether thought of as writing or not. In a supposed contrast is a valuing, in a technological era of blatant mediation, of the ephemerality of unrecorded live performance, leaving only a network of memory traces—including motor memory in the bodies of the performers—and tangential commentary. The written is notionally not ephemeral: that is the point. But the acts themselves of reading and writing are live, and without those acts the written is no more than archived potential for renewed liveness. The notion of *live writing* remains a productive and exemplary problematic.[10]

From the start, performance writing had what-is-writing questions built into it, as ontological more than taxonomic. How could it not? It was being formulated, as a paragraph above indicates, in the wake of the twentieth century's so-called turn to language, and in particular in the recent wake of Derrida's programmatic transformation of that turn, from language understood as founded in speaking, into a turn to writing (Derrida 1976, 1981).[11] Until quite late in the planning process for the degree course, we ducked deciding between an approach founded on a taxonomy of forms and a responsibility for the Idea that provided the logic for the set. We did this by adopting the plural form of "performance writings". We dropped the *s* when we became aware that the plural might also invite an itemising of the singularities as permitted members of a restricted set; that the empirical and desirable plurality did not preclude a general "competence" of Writing and that there was no writing without performance of some form. Performance was now understood not as *kinds* of writing but as a frame for the consideration of any writing. Just possibly, in doing so, we also provisionally designated performance writing as any approach to writing that made a point of not being sure what writing was in relation to what it did. This move also had the effect of leaving the project open. Behind all this, "Language" remained the grand abstract singularity, with its body of literature growing by the day.[12] Wherever there has been a "turn to", though, there can be a turn away, just as soon as a conceptual or epistemological paradigm stops being useful.

In 2012 are these matters now settled? Of course not. Are they still productive for writers? I would say that they are, without doubt, but in a pedagogic context there are the obvious risks. What continues to be needed is active (performative) *thinking*. This requires engagement with bodies of theory and help in how to engage with them without being lured over into theoreticism. The moment that there is a slide from engagement in thinking to the teaching of bodies of thought, a discipline, in a bad sense, has been formed. If Performance Writing were to become a thing or a conspectus of solutions, the project would be over.

I've already put to use an important sense of the term *performance* in PW when I invoked Chomsky's distinction between a general competence and the actualisation of such a competence into specific acts of performance (1965): in Searle's lexicon, out of Austin, a "speech act"; for performance writing, an "act of writing" (Searle 1969; Austin 1976). The relationship between the two is, of course, dynamic or dialectical: performances don't only draw on competence; they also sustain it or augment it or transform it. It probably works for my particular purposes to see this as a recursive chain in which performance at one level might become competence at another. Competence does not lie only in the bodies of performers (Chomsky's speculative linguistic organ, for example), but also in social and technological relations and mechanisms, in genres and established forms.

A challenge for PW was always to ask: what is this general competence if it is not to be defined by the specific requirements of specialist writing practices. I shall leave this question hanging, except to say that the idea of a dutiful writing for an existing mode of performance, where there is a template for such writing and a powerful set of expectations that feed back into the act of writing, is of little interest. I should say that when generic expectations are consciously included in acts of writing—so that the writing puts the genre "rules" to work at the same time as it stands outside them in some way—then the interest grows. An obvious example is the designation of the page as a particular kind of performance space, comparable to a stage or a screen, for certain modes of writing, rather than as the taken-for-granted destiny of all literary writing.[13] Within this logic, any practice, genre or mode can become relevant. Some of us from the outset saw the idea of PW as belonging to a general poetics (and indeed poets played a significant part in the formation of the field).

In a time of stable genres and stable textual environments there would be no need for performance writing. And it seems that, for some, the genres that matter *are* stable, and that the changing spaces are primarily threats to or opportunities for modes of distribution.[14]

Dartington College of Arts is not the topic of this article, only a significant case study or symptom, as the institution which instigated and developed the innovative idea as an academic field. Dartington as an autonomous institution is no more, having been merged into University College Falmouth in 2008.[15] How much did PW need the very specific conditions of Dartington? And if it did, are equivalents likely to be found again? What, at great speed, were some of these conditions?

·   Dartington emerged as a teaching institution out of a few decades of subsidised arts activities of two different kinds: international modernist practice (Kurt Joos, Mark Tobey, Michael Chekhov …) and what might now be called participatory practice (Imogen Holst). Both streams—those of avant-gardism and of ethical responsibility—were sustained, not without conflict.

·   It was small, specialist and practical, with specialisms combining music, theatre and visual arts. It offered no conventional humanities degrees and certainly not English Literature.

·   Writing was taking place within these disciplines as elements of practice, in different ways and with different emphases.

·   Collaborative and individual disciplinary boundary-crossing increasingly took place.

·   The College won respect from funders for its unconventional approach and was supported despite the high unit costs resulting from its small size and its practical approach.

·   It attracted many teachers and students who would not have been at home in conventional institutions and would not have applied to them.

·   Many experienced it as not only a place to teach or learn but as an opportunity to participate in a collective project.

Following the merger into an institution that, whatever its past, was now responding to the opportunities and conditions of Cornwall's entitlement to "convergence funding"[16] in ways that probably merit the term "business-facing". At the time of writing, though PW is no longer available as an undergraduate award and an MA based in the Arnolfini Gallery in Bristol has been terminated, there is still a significant doctoral and post-doctoral research programme. So the end of Dartington's autonomy has not marked the effective end of Performance Writing, even locally. Looking further afield, a very quick search on Google gave 144,000 results on 16th November 2012, with most of the results on the first two pages being highly relevant.[17] The term seems to have a growing currency beyond Dartington, Falmouth and the Arnolfini and by no means only among alumni and past teachers.[18] There have been significant parallel educational developments, for example, such as Goldsmith's *Art Writing* or Royal Holloway's MA in *Poetic Practice*. Rachel Lois Clapham's *(W) reading Performance Writing: A Guide* (Clapham 2010) is another example, as is her collaboration with Mary Paterson on *Open Dialogues*. (Paterson, no date) The Arts and Humanities Research Council's (AHRC) well funded *Beyond Text* project, though now closed, could offer more support at research level. (*Beyond Text*, no date)

Projects like Performance Writing tend to rely on two categories of support: the institutional patronage of teaching institutions, which only works when the educational aims are valued to the extent that they are incorporated into the curriculum and/or in research programmes; and arts funding. The next few years will be testing on both counts.

PW was conceived as an inter-discipline rather than a discipline: a constellation whose figure could change when viewed from different angles or in a different time. Inter-disciplines have a way of congealing into disciplines, often for very pragmatic reasons. PW's energy and purchase have relied on its interdisciplinary status. The term *inter-discipline* implies that it is indeed disciplines that are in interaction, and that these are fixed and official, whereas PW has drawn on and attracted those who find themselves on the margins of disciplines and practices, often defining their own practice as in contrast to or in flight from the current conventions of their discipline. (1: 182–194))

How disciplines—or any of the institutions of knowledge and practice—assign writing a value and a place in their systems of classification, how they set certain modes as default and—formally or informally—proscribe others, has been of concern within Performance Writing as one of the contextual factors that might shape the inside of writing from an outside. Disciplines change; the needs for margins change; inter-disciplines change and are perhaps of their nature short-lived, at least as inter-disciplines. Even so, I cannot myself see, given continuing and interconnected technological, social and economic change, a time when a project much like Performance Writing will not be needed. The question is more: what forms of support will such projects receive, and from whom.

# Sentenced to
## *(grammar for performance writers: 1)* [19]

This article is intended as the first in a series that engages with grammar as an awareness of syntactical function and structure within the process of writing. The series will be interested in what writing *does*, how it performs itself within the structuring and generative rules of grammar. The most localized writing decisions—syntactical choices and particular uses of parts of speech—are assumed to contribute to the totality of written performance just as much as so-called content. Because the sentence is usually taken to be the largest unit of speech or writing in which grammar realizes itself, the series starts with some thoughts about the sense of the sentence in writing.

It is possible to speak or write without using sentences but it isn't easy and it is more readily done in the cool of writing than in the heat of speaking. The sentence is there as the quite unconscious shaping principle, guiding the way in which one word can flow—or not—meaningfully from another.
In school we were taught—if we were told anything on the subject—to connect the sentence with the idea of completeness: something was finished when you reached the full stop. It was usually implied that what was completed had something to do with meaning or with logic, that it was a completeness that had to do with more than the given mechanics of language. For most of us, I don't think that it was ever very clear. As a schoolteacher, I found it helpful to ask pupils to attend to their own breathing, and to think of sentences as something to listen for if they wanted to understand where one sentence had ended and another begun. This was useful because it helped to locate sentences as physiological experiences and to feel them both as units and as a continuity: each pulse of breathing leads surely to the next.

The sentence is there as a kind of tune or dance routine; once you start you know where it should go or is likely to go, not in terms of meaning or proposition, but in terms of rhythm and function—you feel the trajectory which is being set up, how things will fly or lean. The end of any sentence proposes itself the minute it is begun or even anticipated: seldom as a precise semantic sequence, word by word, but as an organisational and sonic template, a pattern or space which is likely to be filled. This does not mean that you keep faith each time with the initial promise; but if you don't you and your listener both know what you are *not* doing.

So, a sentence is a set of expectations, initiated in general by that great abstraction "the language", and more specifically almost always by the earlier sentences in a sequence and, most importantly, shared by speaker/writer and hearer/reader. How difficult it is not to finish someone else's sentences for them.

In this are two very simple points. 1) Sentences belong as much to the listener/reader as they do to the speaker/writer. We prepare empty sentence shapes in readiness for the meaning of others; we are not passive; we have rights. If it doesn't come the way it should, we experience tension or surprise, discomfort or pleasure. 2) The way a sentence feels as though it is going to go is part of the experience of that sentence whether it goes that way or not. Anticipation produces the image of a sentence before the actual sentence is played out.

I shall test out the experience of sentences in four different passages, all taken from larger contexts (two play-texts, a poem-sequence, a song).

The first is from that moment in *King Lear* which launches the main plot. (Shakespeare 1963: 1.i.19 ff.) The father wants his daughters to use a rhetoric of daughterly love to bid for (his) territory and power. When Cordelia answers with her "Nothing, my lord", the grammatical form of her reply—its syntactical status—owes itself to his elaborate question and its confident expectation of a full (fulsome) reply. "Nothing, my lord. / Nothing? / Nothing". Syntactically, it is complete, an answer, a sentence. But it is incomplete too, in that it is completely context-bound, syntactically, semantically, psychologically. It can be performed as almost not a sentence. Of course, it is psychologically incomplete. Minutes later Cordelia speaks eloquently about separation,[20] with rhetorical confidence in the form of address (of which one symptom is in the firm anticipation of the end-points of her sentences). This latter is already both psychologically achieved and syntactically finished. It begins "Good my lord" and that brings us to the end of the prosodic line. *Good my lord*. The phrase positions both of them in relation to the sentence to come, the sentence which is already given and which will be finished. It *performs*[21] an acquisition of power and the right to dispose the "you" in the distance of controlled speech. What a different "you" this is from the earlier "Nothing, my lord" in which "my lord" could be left out in performance provided intonation carried the sense of dependent incompleteness.

This incompleteness is already much more than she told us in an aside that she would say: "What shall Cordelia speak? Love, and be silent". The clear, double self-imperative: a grammar of self-evident love, a grammar of silence because the grammatical registers in play already do allow truth. Already she is speaking *to*, using the grammatical devices of specific address. How shall Cordelia speak to the one who demands a reply? She won't. She does haltingly. Then truthfully and clearly. These are grammatical and psychological transitions.

> Because of this business of completeness—fullness, Gestalt— there is always in language use at every moment the possibility of failing to complete, of refusing to complete. *Nothing, my*. There is also always available the virtuosity of control, knowing from the first word how the whole thing will end, like Milton with his blank verse. Or, not like Milton, letting the sentence appear to go, but knowing all along how the field is set, so the play of syntactic order is just there, just, all the time. In writing, the punctuation of control is marked not with the full stop (the period)—you're going to hit that anyway. It is in the inner hinges, commas which separate clauses and hang them together; or colons which signal, semi-colons which segment. Keeping your balance in heavy traffic, that is a different matter. Dashes, parentheses, digressions and pullings back—the feeling that punctuation conventions are not quite up to their task.

The sentence can't help itself but be a rhythmic entity. That is to say, the traffic is all going somewhere and all you want to do is cross the road. Word order and standard grammatical inflections of words might lend themselves to repeated rhythmic patterning, to the sense of pre-shaped templates operating below the level of meaning. Do you play with or against the expected? If this structural unit is also a rhythmic unit— and it is—what is its tensility? Here are some of the variables that you play with: length, tempo, rhythm, tight/loose, simple/complex structures, extensiveness of noun and/or verb phrases, cadence/end-marking... Why? What is at stake? Performance writing is nearly always written in a space other than that in which it is performed. There is the writerly voice, perhaps, and the performic voice, a bi-vocalism, which is always there even if the two voices are separated by no more than the deferral of time. This is true even of lyric forms where we are supposed to trust the authenticity of the I who speaks. (The "you" of "I love you" is almost certainly historical in the moment of performance; at least you hope so if the poet's/performer's mind is on the job.) Whose words are "Nothing, my lord"? There may be two subjects behind the subject of the sentence, ensuring that the theme speaks beyond its narrative containment. The two voices can set up two expectations of the shape of a sentence, one perhaps nestling the other. In the quoted passage from *King Lear* there is very evidently a conflict between grammars—between grammatical stances within the world—and very evidently too the context (the author? the text?) favours one of them. Cordelia's way of speaking is the one to trust.[22]

The following fragments are from more recent texts (the earliest being 1961). Here's the opening of the first section of J. H. Prynne's poem-sequence, *Not-You* (1993; 2005: 381–408):

The twins blink, hands set to thread out
a dipper cargo with lithium grease enhanced
to break under heat stress.

The prosodic line provides a form of punctuation on the page (which means for both eye and ear) which is offset from where the instinctive clause analysis would place it. That first comma—the sentence could finish there, but there is more to come with a chain of clauses linked with participles (adjectival verbs—"set", "enhanced"). That's a double control. This sentence promises sanity. Unlike this, from page 16:

Her pan click
  elb
second fix
  for them
pencil
    breather park
over
  talk a small to

These are fragments of sentences, an alternative prosodic and visual syntax, holding off a reader's attempt to fill out. The choice of words—the lexical clues—together with the syntactical fragmentation—suggest tone and rhythmic potential (that is, the rhythm of imaginary completed sentences as well as the broken but tight rhythms we are actually given). Do you, as reader/listener, abandon your expectation that these are part-sentences, that the performance of a sensible listening posture can be maintained? What do you do? These questions assume that you have available to you, in your hands, as you answer, the whole text of *Not-You*.

The other book on my desk, Beckett's *Happy Days* (1963). Almost anything of Winnie's will do for the purpose:

> And now? *(Long pause.)* The face. *(Pause.)* The nose. *(She squints down.)* I can see it... *(squinting down)...* the tip... the nostrils... breath of life... that curve you so admired... *(pouts)...* a hint of lip... *(pouts again)...* if I pout them out... *(sticks out tongue)...* the tongue of course... you so admired... if I stick it out... *(sticks it out again)...* the tip... *(eyes up)...* suspicion of brow... eyebrow... imagination possibly... *(eyes left)...* cheek... no... *(eyes right)...* no... *(distends cheeks)...* even if I puff them out... *(eyes left, distends cheeks again)...* no... no damask. (Act 1, 39)

As written, we have two parallel, interdependent, discursive lines: the dialogue and the "stage" directions (instructions for director or performer). Both lines float their syntax in an event—a sequence of actions which are more than speech—that continues, that the italicized line in a sense produces. The directions form a sequence of elliptical sentences, not quite imperatives, since they prefer the third-person approach of the novel to the second-person address to a performer.[23] What Winnie says is at most a long sentence, full of suspensions, figurative near repetitions and distractions of the speaking *I*. When the theme is the narcissistic one of the *I* behind the *I*, the subject of the sentence and its theme remove all constraints from each other. So there are two sets of sentences and yet the organizing principle looks beyond language it seems, at times, only to return to it. And another language form, which is not sentence-based and which favours nouns, is at work: the list, most specifically the inventory with commentary. Estate agents' talk. Even if there was anyone there to interrupt they wouldn't, loose as the sentence-form is. The sentence leads us back to the person who speaks and what she speaks about is an objectified version of herself, so the *I* appears in at least two different grammatical functions within the sentence. There is perhaps even a third, if we ask to whom she is talking. In the context, this is ambiguous since she appears to be talking to herself, though Willie's presence conveniently socializes the talk. Meanwhile the directions bypass the performer (who is not, as already noticed, their addressee) and address instead the director or the reader of the published script, in a very different form of address.

Writing (I mean any writing; writing-in-general) identifies discrete units in the flow of speech, usually conventionalized ones which are not available to the ear alone (letter, word, phrase separators, sentence). The smallest character on the keyboard punches a dot on each side of the recognized syntactic unit. Speech is *meaningful*, even or especially in its incoherence, and writing is *orderly*. Conventional graphic notation ("grammatical" writing) insists on dovetail joints and finish, none of the blurring, sliding and abandonment to silence or physical gesture that live utterance allows, where the buck can be passed from code to code, always an alibi available or a continuity to override the end of something being joined. The full stop has fragile authority once it has to leave the page. Where to put the full stops in speech in any way which does not attempt to mimic the orderliness of rhetoric? The difficulty does not mean that sentences are the fantasies of writers. All sentences which start also end somewhere, not necessarily completed in script, but held back possibly, in play.

I listen to the remastered CD of *Fresh Cream* (Cream 1967), to 'I'm so glad', credited to Skip James. The "lyrics" are not provided to give notational clues. So, let me try. First, let the musical (poetic line) avoid the issue of grammatical punctuation:

> I'm so glad
> I'm so glad
> I'm glad
> I'm glad
> I'm glad

Second, sentences … but how many? (I'm avoiding exclamation marks; they are intonational markers not grammatical punctuations.)

> I'm so glad. I'm so glad. I'm glad. I'm glad. I'm glad.

But, no, when I hear the song I don't hear five sentences. I hear the latency of five sentences but not five manifest sentences. Or is it the other way round?

> I'm so glad. I'm so glad. *(There is definitely repetition, with reinforcement.)* Then *(but not quite)* I'm glad I'm glad I'm glad. *(Both repetition and complex statement. Recursive gladness. Gladness in infinite recess. Gladness seeing itself seeing itself glad. A melancholy narcissism of gladness, hedging the bets on the sentence.)*

We need a Derridean device for the notation which wobbles between conjunction and disjunction:

> I'm so glad. I'm so glad. I'm glad t̶h̶a̶t̶ I'm glad t̶h̶a̶t̶ I'm glad.

or

> I'm so glad. I'm so glad. I'm glad (•)I'm glad (•) I'm glad.

All my examples used the already written and/or the already performed to try to get at the grammar of the writing. This is certainly a problem of methodology. It is difficult to get at the phenomenology of sentence production, at the impulse which adds word to word. Even so, I hope these remarks help any writers reading them to consider where they are when they embark on a sentence; with what timing, what balance, what aggression, what insouciance perhaps about the risks involved. The circularity of the sentence means that it is always finished as soon as started (even perhaps if aborted); its linearity on the other hand gives narrative and drama to the performance of any sentence. And it is all at the start, all to do with the syntactic expectations set out at launch. If all the earlier sentences have been completed in predictable maps of circle and line, if listener\ reader is not being pulled into an answering enactment of the structure and tension, then expectations, well then

# Performed through

## (grammar for performance writers: 2) [24]

The term "performance" is an invitation to debate rather than a fixed term with an easy definition. In this paper I want to work from two different understandings: (i) writing *as itself* performance; (ii) where the performance is an event that is larger than, more than, writing, and the writing's concern is with its relation to the whole which constitutes the performance.

What do I mean by "writing as itself performance"? I would like to hold to one side a special case of what I could mean: for the moment I do not mean the acting out—the display—of the act of writing either in events that everyone can call performances without any sense of problem or its ritual use at key moments in civic or judicial procedures or ceremonies, such as the signing of the register or of the treaty or of the big cheque. All such cases belong as much in my second category, where writing is part of something more than itself.

I am taking the term from Chomsky. In Chomsky's pairing of competence and performance, the latter plays the role of *speaking* (*parole*, the act of speaking) to Saussure's *language (langue)*. In both cases we are talking about the particular, a very particular actualisation of the potential of a system or even "organ". When anyone speaks or writes in a language that I know, they put into play, they render actual and material, a system of possibilities that I share (more or less). According to communication theory that enables me to "understand" what they are saying. Of course. But more than that, my ear must follow the dance of their tongue. There is a physical mapping of attentions, one on to the other, as word follows word, as each grammatical unit fits itself to the next, so much so that at any time the grammatical journey can be hijacked, as listener becomes talker, as reader pushes into the traffic of writing. I like to think of this idea of "performance" as very literal, as taking place slowly, through time—in the case of writing, letter by letter, literal by literal.

Because speaking and writing are often simply instrumental, hurrying to perform some other task, this performance is automatic, unconscious, losing any sense of itself *as* performance. For the story teller or the joker or the poet this is never so. For the ever careful literalist, this can never be so. Personally I am not interested in any writing—*as writing*—that does not actively engage me in some way in this process of actualisation. Talk, too. I like that phrase, to hang on your words.

In my second sense of performance, there are different kinds of actualisation implied: the actualisation of writing as part of the larger performance or the actualisation of writing into performance. In this sense of performance, to which performance theory has given its attention, the performance is a structured social event, in which time is in some way publicly orchestrated. Various forms of the individualisation of cultural experience make the distinctions difficult to sustain. A short footnote in de Certeau's *The Practice of Everyday Life* reminds us that even reading from the page can be ceremonial:

> Theresa de Avila considered reading to be a form of prayer, the discovery of another space in which desire could be articulated. Countless other authors of spiritual work think the same, and so do children. (1988: 26)

Reading is the form of performance to which writing for the page aims itself. There are other forms of performance which writing serves or participates in, in which the page is only a stepping-point, or a by-product or a record or not relevant at all. In each case I am interested in an articulation of writing with and into this notion of performance and the way that the forms of articulation have a bearing on the grammar of writing.

Grammar concerns itself with the way language operates *as language*, with those structural features of a language which enable the system of the language to be actualised in speech, writing or thought. In Saussure's terms, how *langue* can become *parole*; in Chomsky's we are talking about the process by which *competence* can produce *performance*. Grammar is concerned with the *how* rather than the *what*, with mechanism and structure, or functioning of part to part within language, rather than with semantics. In this respect grammar is a formalism. But it is only because the *how* and the *what* are never finally separable that structure and mechanism are important.

As an internalised operation, most of us are unconscious most of the time of this sense of autonomous function. It is so internalised it is as though it speaks through us. In its generative aspect, it is a set of rules which enables us to speak, rather than one which inhibits us from speaking. As social behaviour, it is also, of course, subject to the sometimes inhibiting pressures of the normative. This is Hélène Cixous on the subject:

> This mystery is easier to convey through music than through writing, because music is not subject as the text is to the fearful imperatives of language that force us to construct sentences with grammatical correctness, to attribute genders properly: writers of fictional texts are called to account. (148)

For a writer—for one who shapes language for special purposes, who manipulates words and their inner changeableness and who breathes through them to make them work—function and meaning are never fully separable. How you function is what you mean. And in any case, meaning is too laden a term for many writers, implying a direction of semantic intention somehow separable from the play of words (or as I shall be saying later, play of those other activities set in motion by the words or alongside them).

This takes us back to the two different senses of both performance and function. Neither banishes meaning; they are just attempts to recognise the complexities of the way that meanings are actually traded. The first looks at the moment and manner in which linguistic potential is actualised into speech or writing; the second sense of function raises the troublesome questions: whatever their own internal functioning, what do speech acts, including writing, get up to in the world? The social function of a sentence might not be what it would appear—when taken out of context—to "mean".

Sometimes we just call this irony—the way you might insult me to make me feel better about myself. I have in mind, though, rather than the devices of irony and deliberate ambiguity, that wonderful phrase of Edward Sapir's, "the caress of small talk". Whatever else they appear to be saying, all I know is that your words are stroking me.

Because some take exception to the term "function" and have a distaste for functionalism, I shall put this second sense of function differently and move us closer to the idea of "performance": not, what is that sentence "saying", or even how is it constructed, but what is it *doing*?

Of course, what it seems to be saying and how it is formed are inseparable from what it appears to be doing. Together they make up an ensemble, either reinforcing each other or not. A sentence will do nothing unless it is heard. A sentence by someone already defined as ignorable will still do nothing, even if it is heard, however it is shaped, whatever it is "saying".[25] Sentences don't do anything in isolation. A caress, for example, can be experienced as an invasive irritation.

The clause, "With this ring I thee wed" only *does* marriage (is performative of the marriage union) if all the other circumstances of performance are right—including most significantly that there are first and second person pronouns present who both make evident that they mean what is being said. The inversion of phrase order is important, lining up in order of ceremony the ritual object whose localised, highly concentrated ("this") power reinforces the performative power of the linguistic statement. The grammar of the words used in a "real" marriage ceremony and the grammar of those used in a mimicked or represented marriage ceremony can be identical. The subjects of the verbs, though, viewed as social beings rather than as linguistic entities, have a very different status. It is not the grammar but the frame which tells us that one mimics the other. Or you could almost say, taking the larger view, that the grammar of social process is very different in each case. Pronouns are not that cheap and changeable.[26]

Performance writing always poses questions of relationships between writing and its frame, writing and other symbolic and/or expressive practices which together form the ensemble of a specific practice. Inevitably this raises questions of hierarchy, even a hierarchy of grammars. I myself would look for the answer in the politics of collaboration rather than the philosophy of language. The specific answer in the case of each performance piece has implications for the burden of grammar; in what medium, over all, are the parts of writing suspended?

Perhaps the first, and most lasting of the questions of relationship— and of difference—is the one between writing and talking, between the practice and production of each, and between the written and the spoken. I have already started by referring to a third position between writing and talking—which is the loud reading: the script which isn't hidden. I recall a poet saying years ago that he would not read from a script at a poetry reading since only a bad poem is not easily recitable from memory. For most of the other poets reading on that occasion it was obvious that the page was the space of composition, the detailed memory pad of the poem and the reading had to stay true to the page, not supersede it. I believe that in many readings, especially perhaps recorded ones, you can hear the page. It provides the frame for the point of origin of the sentences and for the cohesion between them. It keeps them in line and refers to an authority more stable than the emotional logic of the speaking bodily presence.

Again, there is the crucial difference referred to here between the written-spoken and talk: writing is mostly an individual, monologic practice (though it doesn't have to be); writers do it, on the whole, on their own. Sadly there are many forms of talk where the same applies: the talker assumes, or is given, authority to be the only one who really talks. But talk is essentially dialogic; when we think of talk we think of people talking to each other. In speech, actual social speech, grammar is situated in exchange, can be cut short, outstared etc. Meaning is generated dialogically as much by the speech of an other as by the enunciative momentum of the speaking subject. The generation of speech/writing carries the sense of the other, of another, of others, whether or not an actual other is present. There has been considerable emphasis since Lacan on the emergence of the *I* through language. I need hardly say that the image of *other* effected through grammar is every bit as important since language is the very condition of the social or—more simply—of the sociable. This other may be you or may be she or he; if love enters the field of pronouns we are in real trouble.[27]

The next two categories have in common that they both apply to signifying fields which are primarily visual. This might remind us of the close relationship between the word grammar and the Greek word for a letter. Parts of speech are inevitably still there, of course, but we are reminded that the fundamental part of writing is the letter-form together with the letter-sized space and other forms of punctuation.

First, a relation between writing and architecture (or more broadly between writing and the design and organisation of space) is both more and less than visual, since it has to do with habitation, work and movement, with reading as casual, monumental or environmental, not as prayer but as surround. We expect here to find writing at its most laconic: grammar fragmented but solidly relocated in architectural sentences. The proper name, the logo, the motto, the slogan, for example. This spatial placing of writing does not keep it in one line. The lines of architecture or organised public space lead in all sorts of directions. Writing is put into space where, if it achieves linearity, this is just one line among others and you can keep returning to it.

Secondly, between writing and the practices of fine art: drawing, painting, sculpture, installation, performance art. Grammar is diachronic; it functions through time. It sets up lines. It propels forward. The time of writing corresponds to the time of reading/hearing; at least there is a fit, which time-based performance attempts to reinstate. In those media which arrest time—the photograph, the painting, the sculpture, for example—the time of viewing bears little relation to the time of production. In these contexts, the power of the sentence can be broken, and individual nouns and phrases can be suspended in a visual space.

Thirdly, a relation with sound structures, many different relations within sound structures, from the setting of words with music, through pieces which use words as the material with which to make a sound world, to poetic work which moves through the lexical layer of language into the phonic substance from which meaning is shaped. At one end grammar defers to a form of prosody; at the other grammar is the merest suggestion that the sound we hear belongs to language.

Fourthly, a relation between writing and gesture, writing and movement, writing and a choreography of behaviour. The minute that writing is just a means to another end it could be that something else— another form of notation perhaps—could do the job better? Or is it that the gesture, the movement, the action, is overlaid on the written and the layering of the two is the performance? In writing with this kind of purpose there is likely to be a pull between the need for complete sentences that comes from linguistic grammar and a sense of movement which corresponds to the phrase, which is a sketch, a suggestion.

Fifthly, a relation between writing and different traditions of and attitudes to performance. I have in mind here scripted performances, performances in which (usually) performers speak, in which there is a grammar for the speaking of performers and a grammar for the notation of the performance other than their speaking. There is an extraordinary delicacy about the grammar of stage directions. Their purpose is that of instruction, like a recipe book:

Simmer the diced potatoes in the stock until tender.

The verb is in the imperative mood. Simmer. There is, of course, a "you" involved. The two "the"s situate the two nouns in the here and now. That's from *The Soup Book* by Carolyn McCrum (1978). Whereas this is from Max Frisch's *The Fire Raisers* (1962):

Biedermann has to sit down on a drum, sweating.

"Has to"! The obliqueness and tact of this! Playwrights become novelists of the present tense. Presumably they avoid the imperative mood out of deference to directors and actors and find themselves instead in the present indicative, through the use of mood and tense making an absence present in the wished-for (wished for because writing a play does not mean that it will be put on) re-presentation of drama.

There is a variation on this from the (film) script of *The Graduate* (Karton 1983):

We move with MRS ROBINSON and BEN out of
the sun room, into the hall, up the stairs and along
the hall to the doorway to ELAINE's room.

We is the camera, we is the audience in collusion with the makers, shuffling along in a sentence, whose string of prepositional phrases mimics the journey through the house (out of, into, along, to, to). The first person singular narrative is one thing; the first person plural—when it feels this literal (as against some grand collectivised we—quite another.

In each of these cases, writing has a relationship with at least one other expressive, symbolic or aesthetic "system", each with its rules, conventions and procedures for the generation, production or transformation of—let's take a short cut here—"texts". Each "system" has its dynamic repertoire of possibilities, born of constraints. To speak loosely, each has its grammar, affecting the grammatical options of the writing.

But I don't want to use grammar *too* loosely and want to hold a distinction between grammar and composition or grammar and discourse or even grammar and rhetoric. For linguists, as far as grammar is concerned, the sentence (with its parts of speech) is everything: every language user has to negotiate the sentence, even if only through finding devices for avoiding it.[28] But any actual use of speech or writing is always more or less than a sentence. As discourse—as something made from the texture of language for the purposes of expression, communication or deferred or amplified presence—the status of the sentence is very different. Any discourse can be less than a sentence, is usually more. There are other conventional units apart from sentences, which are units of discourse rather than grammar—for example, paragraphs or verses or "speeches" in the turn-taking conventions of dialogue.

The aspects of grammar most likely to reward the attention of performance writers include at least the following:[29]

- as always, the sentence—most notably length and complexity and implied rhythmic and syntactic entity

- personal pronouns and the other linguistic signs of non-linguistic presence (the "shifters", such as "here", "over there", "now")

- conjunctions, most notably "and" and "because" but also "but" (and, of course, "or")[30]

- prepositions, especially in terms of what they do to time and space

- nouns and their relation to surfaces and substance

- proper nouns and their domestication of the world

- abstract nouns and attitudes

- all the different behaviours of verbs through mood (indicative, infinitive, interrogative and that key mood for performance instructions, the imperative); voice (active/passive); and tense, with its mixture of temporal and ethical inflections

- the use of adverbs in performance scores—the qualifier of a verb transferred over to another performed action—slowly, angrily, lightly, etc.

The reward, if it is to be a reward for writing as it relates to performance, will only occur if the attention comes through into the ways that speech and writing are actualised as events and take up the activating presence within events.

## Summary/argument

1. Grammar is a fundamental characteristic of language. All writers—and indeed all talkers—use it.

2. Grammar is a dynamic playing out of part to part and part to whole where the substance is language and the whole is a sentence

3. The parts of grammar are not individual words with dictionary meanings but parts of speech: categories like nouns, verbs, prepositions, which perform different functions in sentence formation.

4. Writers aim themselves, in the playing out of composition, at wholes other than sentences which for convenience we can call texts.

5. In the case of texts which are wholly written, there is correspondence between grammatical decisions and compositional decisions. Sometimes these will be the same.

6. In the case of texts or compositional wholes which do not end up as pieces of writing, there is still a correspondence between localised grammatical decisions and the compositional whole.

7. All grammatical events take place in social space, which they in part effect and always affect.

# Missing Persons: Personal Pronouns in Performance Writing

*(grammar for performance writers: 3)* [31]

> If I or you should chance to be
> Involved in this affair,
> He trusts to you to set them free,
> Exactly as we were. (Carroll 1993: 109)

In this brief meditation on personal pronouns I want, in the context of a journal dealing with performance, to keep in mind three different conditions in which pronouns operate, all of which have a bearing on performance writing: spoken exchanges, writing, and performance. The pronouns which interest me most are the first and second persons, *I* (or *me*) and *you*. The proximity of *I* and *you* implies an exchange that is both grammatical and more than grammatical: a relationship of persons. I want to suggest a tension always there between the grammatical and the extra-grammatical. Because pronouns together with the other "shifters"[32] always refer speech acts back into the site in which they occur, it makes a considerable difference how that site is staged, what kind of site it is.

A concentration on the first two persons singular makes the absence of the third conspicuous. I shall take this up. There are a number of significant issues which I shall do no more than acknowledge. For example, there are the various motivated evasions of first person singular including *we, you, one*, any one of which merits an article on its own. I shall say nothing about the *she/he* problem.

Let me start with everyday speaking. Here pronouns could seem the most necessary parts of speech. They are the ones that seem to embed us, warmly even, in the action of exchange. *I* is used by the person talking to refer to her- or himself. *You* usually refers to the person being addressed, the one at whom the talk is aimed and who is needed for the talk to be dialogic or conversational.[33] *You* is the one expected to reply, though perhaps not in words, whose lack of reply is itself a reply.[34] In conversation there has to be a second person even if only to provide the pretext for a monologue. And do we know who is meant to be *you* (at any one moment, because only *I*'s talk can sustain the condition of being)? As soon as more than two are gathered around speech there can be doubt. For one thing, Standard English has shed the thou/you distinction. To sort out any doubt we go, as observers or participants, for contextual clues, since any actual discourse is polysemic—there are always multiple grammars involved and the different grammars inflect each other. For example, in a vague, easily imagined context, someone is talking as *I*. There are three others present. The speaker's body, and her look, angle themselves subtly towards one of them: this must be *you*. Or perhaps the speaker keeps her eyes on the floor because she cannot bring herself to reveal the intimacy of a *you*. Or again, in oratorical confidence, her eyes sweep the company as she pluralises—perhaps even communalises—the occasion. In English, the pun is irresistible: if *I*'s eye aims at you then *you* it is.

If there are only two present and they keep replying to each other, then each takes a turn at being the *I* of discourse and while that one is *I* the other is *you*. That's dialogue. If there are more than two, then anyone present can become the temporary *I* of shared discourse and everybody else can become an unvoiced *I* of the not (quite) spoken. I can think *I* and know it. You only know that I am thinking *you* if I 'say' it. *You* belongs to *I*.

Anyone spoken of in the third person is treated as not there.[35] Apparently Arab grammarians called the third person the 'absent person'. Emile Benveniste called it the 'non-person' (1971: 197). The *I* and the *you* of speech are both in speech and mark its outer (utter) limits: the actual mouths from which these words come address the person of the other across a space, even if it is the space of telecommunication. When these mouths say "here" and "now" they mean the same here and now, or at least ones whose relativity is evident. *I* and *you* , as words, belong to speech every bit as much as *he* and *she* do. They are all parts of speech, pronouns all, but *I* and *you* do not refer in the same way as *he* and *she* do. *I* and you mark the poles of discourse itself, the terminals through which language can become discourse, can situate speaking subjects in relation to each other. They are not in any simple sense pro-nominal. They don't stand in for names, for nouns, the way *he* and *she* can. They can also act as indices for either the anonymous or the unnameable.

Benveniste's notion of subjectivity posits a *speaking* subject and not a *writing* subject. "Language.... institute(es) a unique but mobile sign, *I*, which can be assumed by each speaker on the condition that he refers each time to the instance of his own discourse. This sign is thus linked to the *exercise* of language and announces the speaker as speaker". (220)

This is a "condition" that both writing and performance can challenge (or avoid). Except where writing is being purposefully performed in front of our eyes as an act of writing—and wherever this occurs presence is being "performed" as well as writing—there is at the very least a temporal, and probably also a spatial, gap. A person behind the text—the grammatical subject of utterance tied as an *I* to flesh with a joined history—can only be inferred from and in the text. In place of the joining of body and utterance is the other body, the corpus, the text as itself an inscribed body, to which the reader brings her or his body and asks perhaps: what was my speech to which this text is the reply? The reader has had to go missing from her or his own time zone in order to encounter this text from which the writing *I* has already gone missing (except as the textual trace of written *I*). The only *you* the reading *I* will find is also in the text.[36]

The reader of this text will be aware of the slipperiness of the topic that is opening up here. Interactive texts can mimic the conditions of speech events, though with a different delay. And many texts invite a reader to play the part of the empty position marked *you*. In his tongue-in-cheek 'Personism: a Manifesto' Frank O'Hara "invents" a literary "movement" in which poems and telephone conversations could substitute for each other: "The poem is at last between two persons instead of two pages. In all modesty I confess that it may be the death of literature as we know it." (1972: 498–9)

Despite this example, literature and performance are at best oblique forms of address. Gertrude Stein's comment on this obliquity was to say, "I write for myself and for strangers". (1966: 78) The place of the text and the place of performance are places where a "for myself" is a gift for strangers. If there were a pronoun for it, a special *person*—an indication of an address for no one—then, and only then, could we talk of texts and performances as "forms of address". Up till now this pronoun is at best a pure negativity, the *Not-you* of J.H. Prynne's poem sequence of that name (1993; 2005: 381–408) or is signalled through a slipping around between pronoun forms as a search for that place and a keeping empty of the pronoun reference. Beckett's *Not-I* is "mouth", is not a name (1984). The play dramatises—by which I mean offers a psychological account for—the failure to mouth "I".

Beckett's *Not-I* doubles as literary text and performance text. As performance text, "mouth" is a part to be "acted", to be impersonated on stage; the presence which is forwarded is that of the text/performance, now legally controlled.

What then of the bodies of "live" performance? There may be speaking mouths situated in the same space, addressing each other across that space, constituting a to-be-witnessed *I-you* exchange. Or a performer or "the performance" might appear to address the audience directly. Is there then a *you*? Can I reply? Does a body lean towards me or an eye single me out? Can the discursivity of the performance text be, as it were, a speaking subject? Am I friend or stranger?

There are troublesome categories of performance where performers manifestly or ambiguously perform themselves. The recent solo performances of Nigel Charnock for example appear to work through an autobiographical excess of the performing *I*. In contrast many poets feel themselves to be the unavoidable excess of a performed text.

> The strange convention of the poetry reading ushers in a theatrical self with a vengeance, the performing I bringing her accidents of voice and costume and mannerisms to flesh out a starved text, married and reconstituted with it in fullness before all eyes, like wartime powdered egg soaked in water. Inside this show and working against it, the borderline inauthenticity of the lyric "I" gets relieved only inside the performed I's speaking, where everyone, you hope, finally sees the truth of the matter—that it isn't you. (Riley 1997: 80)[37]

The performance company Desperate Optimists play out ironically this "borderline inauthenticity" as part and parcel of a method both of construction and of performance. They work in between the theatrical conventions of im*person*ation (the mask found in the text) and the ambiguous lyric duplicity of live performance where the body insists on bringing its history back into the text. There are forms of direct address (deliberately disingenuous) to the audience. The performers on stage address each other with the names that are known to be their off-stage names. The pronouns can't settle between two possible sets of referents. Signs of authenticity—of the kinds that are not offered in conventional scripted theatre—playfully, sardonically at times—reveal their inauthenticity. I may feel I am about to be interpellated but the *you* passes safely by, leaving me as it were precisely to one side.

The density of a full performance text can draw me into that missing pronoun position where I am beside the text and not staring at it, where I might take myself up into the texture of its discourse. A theatre is a space of discursivity and not a speaking subject of discourse. The audience can only be constituted as a *you* by that discourse and there is a problem, in any case, with plurality because a you needs to be able to turn into an *I* for dialogue to take place. *I*s speak. *We*s do not. *We* is always a figure of *I*'s speech.

Readers and witnesses are strangers, with moveable relations to the persons of the text/performance. Even lovers and friends are strangers when they read or witness. A reader, dear reader, is not a *you* except by virtue of deliberate rhetorical devices. Likewise audiences. An audience for a text or a performance consists of strangers. Let's call it (*us, you*) the fourth person, witnessing an event whose central exchanges it is excluded from, the shadow of the missing first person who "wrote" the piece.

# Not showing
## (*On Writers and Public Space* Partly Writing 1) [38]


### A.  A note on two chosen items [39]

1. Ian Hamilton Finlay: 'Evening Will Come' (Poster print, approx. 18 x 80 cms) (1998)[40]
2. J.H. Prynne: *They that have powre to hurt; A Specimen of a Commentary on Shake-speares Sonnets, 94* (2001)

Prynne's text is a term by term philological commentary on the famous sonnet. The sixth section of the commentary responds to the last phrase of the second line, "most do showe". The section, difficult to excerpt, starts as follows:

> 6. "most do showe": to attempt clarity across fragile links, it may be affirmed descriptively that what is most shown is a *thing* (proxy for "the thing that", "that thing which"); and that the thing is probably capable of being performed or done (an act or pattern of acts), by virtue of its being withheld as what would or could otherwise be done; and that the probably wilful not-doing of the thing re-phrases (probably) the *none* which is not done or willed to be done; which in turn is probably the end result of a not-exercised "povvre to hurt" which if *done* would inflict harm, probably upon vulnerable others; of whom the implied speaker is probably one, if not in this immediate context (or as he would deem himself) the principal one. Use of the probability-marker here indicates that, although the logic feels tight, it is full of incessant small gaps which constrain the making by the reader of assumptions matched to the supposed mood of the implied speaker. (20)

Underlying both choices of "item" is a growing interest in interrelations between genre, textuality and sociality, very much including where these take place within or penetrate private and/or domestic spaces. I am not sure that the term "genre" quite extends to this last term, "space"—those virtual ("cultural") and concrete places where texts utter and mutter themselves. Where these "items" are repeatable events or acts, transformed through dis- and re-placement, perhaps we need to add to the terms of Bakhtin's enquiry into speech genres (1986) some of the conceptual apparatus developed by Halliday (1979) for considering situation: is it, for example, the "place" or the "text" that sets or adopts the rules of political and ethical engagement.

I choose the Ian Hamilton Finlay print because I have lived with a framed copy in two different houses for well over twenty years, its blueness available to any passing, the white letter forms beckoning from time to time towards the lyric or narrative suggestiveness that they never resolve and which I have never tried to outwit through the acquisition of interpretive knowledge. It (the "image") and they (the words) are another opening into and from the hallway. Recently I have produced my own framed texts to engage in the dynamics of domestic space and its multiple cultural entailments.

The Prynne text dazzlingly does to the Shakespeare sonnet exactly what I have for years withheld from doing to the Finlay one. Prynne tracks the multiple ambiguities of the power-relations of not showing, and of prior utterances which at one and the same time disambiguate and sustain ambiguity. One clause in particular from the extract provokes thoughts about the missing parts of partly-writing:

> ...but not to be aware of what is not given would deny these omissions their force of meaning.

How does a text shape silences not only textually as withheld spaces in socially acknowledged utterance, but also interpersonally, so that that silence and its commands might shape an unpredictable number of social spaces, and ideationally, so that the inflections of silence are read off in relation to the harm they negotiate? There is a broad category of the already uttered which remains latent for re-utterance; we could talk first perhaps of genres of memory and then afterwards of closed books in shelves or of images which merge into the environment. Every day, it seems, the modalities of latency and of re-invocation shift in response to new technologies for social memory and new textual behaviours to go with them (*or is it the other way round?*). Finlay's blue belongs to writing, in part, and is an old technology. When does not writing at all—not *showing* text—belong in and to writing? Within the frame or the page there is always included a not-writing—a withholding in order to find purchase.

## B:  Intervention in Session 2
(Interfaces between "private" and "public" processes)

I have said in my material for the web (above) that I have a growing interest in interrelations between genre, textuality and sociality, very much including where these take place within, or penetrate, private and/or domestic spaces; and, allied to that, in the implicit rules of engagement for different forms of rhetorical exchange. In the UK at least, it would seem to me, even choosing to operate through poetry is a proud or foolish act of withholding.

The title for the session would seem to me a useful heading for any discussion about that social and cultural entity, the person ("subject"), the private citizen of recent democratic politics.

The two terms, "private" and "public", rely on each other, of course; even the OED can't talk about one without the other. It is a very public notice on the door which reads "private". What constitutes privacy is, as it were, a public decision.

Private is the space hidden from public view—legally protected perhaps even from zoom lenses—or it may be a privileged space (those who are privileged live, of course, by private law) where access to the public is restricted. Which doors can you enter freely? Which ones do you knock on? Which ones do you not even think of entering?

The private may be a place for all of the following: grief; loss ("bereavement" is there in the etymology);[41] protection from exposure of shameful acts; where face can be prepared and repaired; where there is asylum from the rigours of public face (what Shakespeare was so good at catching in his plays about public figures).

There is individual privacy and there is the relative sociable privacy of being among friends, lovers, family: special forms of trust define sociable privacies: the difference between weeping into a pillow and weeping on a shoulder.

I would make a distinction between "private" and "secret". Everybody sort of knows what goes on in private just as everybody has private parts. There is no breach of etiquette in swapping notes about the private, provided conditions are right. The secret on the other hand relates to the confession and is governed by a contradictory impulse to conceal and show, perhaps to find a form of showing that can enter the public domain and the same time find a journey around shame or through a prepared and manageable version of same. Categories of the private are subject to the same contradictory charge: three different performers on last night's *Top of the Pops* wore clothes that ostentatiously displayed the concealment of their pudenda, flaunting the very shame that was being protected.

The private that is not a secret is often up against another form of shame: quite simply that it is not worth saying; the banality of private life should be kept from public view.

And as to the public, let me limit myself to three distinctions: (i) "in the public domain"—i.e. available to anyone to see, if they so wish; (ii) needing public attention, as in an audience of paying customers; (iii) participating in public affairs.

Perhaps contemporary poetry is powerless to operate in the latter two. It is not enough to speak on a topic of public concern; it is necessary also to speak in a place—a topos—with a face endowed with authority for such speaking, and with a specific rhetorical competence too, of course.

So what to do? The lyric has become the mode of the private citizen, whose walls still carry emblems of proverbial wisdoms. The lyric is a mode exiled from the exchanges of external power. Or, if not exiled, a curtain has been drawn, in a sensual exclusive arrogance.

And, of course, as Gramsci so clearly explained, there is no one topos of power exchange in a capitalist society:[42] the *res publica* is dispersed through multiple topoi and traffickings. Dispersed texts mark moments of symbolic exchange. The cheap book, the telephone, e-mail, the net, TV, radio, CDs, all of them are welcomed into the privacy of the domestic space and are busy re-configuring it all the time. These spaces are no longer saturated, on the whole, with the Book, but with the multiple murmurings of forms of personalised public address. Some are ephemeral and pass through like currents; others are latent—that is available but closed when not being used; others—and it is an ancient tradition—are open and on all the time. These are interfaces, with moving mouths.

# Reading (Il)legible Pages [43]

What is it to read a page? But there are so many pages, so many readings. Is there always a resistance from a page? Is a page always both resistance and lure? Or can you pass through or over it, skimming off its layer of language to re-embody it as speech or ineffable lived experience? I am going to take a special case of resistance, that of illegibility, to help ask the question. It may not be such a special case.

## ~~illegible~~

I have found it very difficult to get this word ~~illegible~~ ~~ineligible~~ ~~intelligible~~ to behave consistently, to be intelligible as a fixed sign in the space of a page for which it is eligible. There is a seemingly irresolvable jostling for a place with at least these two other words, and a third (fourth) comes in derisively with an elegant clarity that is nowhere legible in its form. There is this jumble of "i"s, "g"s and "l"s that are the same at the beginning and end but confused in the middle. Fig 1 is a kind of graphic representation of a version of this jumbled hearing.

Fig 1 (Photo: Nicky Matthews-Evans)

In this example the three words accept the conventional rule of horizontal line and have also been drawn to same length ("stretched to frame"). It is easy to see that there are three "g"s; less easy that there are three final "e"s; very difficult that there are three initial "i"s. Looking at it again I find that *intelligible* wins out over the others. Perhaps Perhaps this is because I want it to. Fig 2 sticks to the rectilinear grid implied by a lineating page and enabled by the operating matrix of a

Fig 2 (Photo: Nicky Matthews-Evans)

computer "page" but slightly separates the words vertically. Is this more or less legible? Is the word sandwiched in the middle now lost? This word is "illegible" and this word is illegible (to me, who put it there).

# inelegant? / ineloquent?

Fig 3

The software on the computer I am using finds "inelegant / ineloquent' (Fig 3) perfectly legible as both "editable text" and as "image". Any text whether legible or illegible can be read as image, but the overlaid words are illegitimate in the computer's domain of text recognition. This can suggest three overlapping categories: text operating primarily to deliver (optical) character recognition (by humans and machines); text as *legible* "image" (in speech marks to allow room in "image" for tactility, spatiality, mobility…); text operating as image-of-text.

## in / il / ill

There is something else unsettled about these words: an ambiguity of the "in" (or transformed "il"). In two of the three words it is a morpheme for negation (just like "un" in "unreadable") while in the third it is not "in" at all but an eroded "inter" with a spatial force of *between* or *within*. I can't get rid of this prepositional and adverbial force from the other two. Everybody knows that "illegible" means that you can't read it; but is everybody quite so sure that it doesn't also acknowledge a performative (transformative) of *into* legibility or an uncovering of what is lurking *within* or *between* legibilities, another order of legibility.

There is also the syllabic pun of *il / ill*, suggesting two states of legibility: *ill legibility* and *well legibility*. Searchers for legibility will always find something that they can read, to the extent that filtered or suppressed legibility is often a lure into reading, if a modified and resisted reading, or a reading that finds another circuit or flow. According to Harley[44] reading is, at least at the level of word recognition and at least for literates, "mandatory". Confronted with writing you don't choose whether or not to read. If your reading is blocked what do you do?[45]

But you do choose, do you, to open a book? When you do open a book what you see are pages. And on those pages?

## Page, book and text

*Page* is a term in a set of at least three, the other two being *book* and *text*. It is the middle term: a page is in a book; text is in/on a page.[46]

Actually it is not quite as simple as that. *Book* is standing in as a term for any generic form of folded or fixed assemblage of pages, such, for example, as a newspaper.

And although *writing* is still perhaps the primary association with page, "text" must be supplemented with "or image/text or image and text". Images on pages nearly always have words in close proximity. When those words are captions they are expected to be efficient, instrumental, deferential: it is the materiality of the image that counts, not theirs.

## Book

A "book" is a fold containing pages. The minimum number of pages in a book is four (including the covers). Because a book is a fold, for a reading to take place somebody has had to unfold it. A contemporary adult reader expects to do this herself. When a book—as most of them are—is a manifold, then there are many turnings. Each opening is also a closing. Every closed page is, as such, illegible. Most of the pages in the world are closed and therefore, as I write, illegible. I take it that every reader is from time to time overwhelmed by the thought of all these illegible pages.

It is easy to feel superior as a reader to some forms of illegibility but only some.

## Page

Most pages are now made of paper. When you fold and unfold a book you touch paper. You might even run your finger along the line just ahead of or below your reading.

So a page is a surface to be handled, touched and stroked. Each page is also a space and a view. As a space it is a site where objects are (or could be) placed (composition) and where movement takes place between them ("reading"). The objects are marks. Even an empty page is scanned, perhaps felt. On an empty page there are no legible marks. This does not mean that an empty page is wholly illegible. Its textured surface, its size, its shape, its colour, can be read. Momentum from immediately preceding reading might project on to it an imaginary spectral text. It can behave with the doubleness particular to a screen: screening off and ready for a screening.

There are different kinds of empty pages. Some are there to be filled. Some are places of transition, pause, rest, or an extra fold, like a wrapping asserting the value of the filled pages between. Others are blank because that is what is written on them: nothing, white on white.[47]

For a sheet (of paper, especially) to be a page, it must either be written on or available for writing; it must also either be in a book, have come from a book (what severance!), be going to a book, or otherwise mimic in its configuration what is to be found in a book.

There is no such thing as one page since a sheet that becomes a page is double-sided. To talk of a single page is to insist on forgetting *the other side*. The other side might well be an *under* side, or a *back* side. I am not sure what difference it makes to know that this is blank.

## Page as three "field vectors"

Each page, whether filled or not, is a complex force field that is a dynamic of (at least) three vectorial fields. For brevity I'll call them lineating field, framing field, mapping field.

### Lineating field

Within a top-to-bottom, left-to-right, writing system, the page's association with text privileges the top left hand corner. This is a quite specific privilege like the GO square on the monopoly board (Fig 4.): it marks a starting point and a new lap. In this space the privilege of beginning and end of line is played down: all marks are presumed equal unless explicitly signalled otherwise (as headings or footnotes, for example). The space of the page is already a kind of strip-field, with a left edge as a place to re-start and a right to drop and return. Faced with a filled page no reader can do it all at once. The best thing you can do is to try not to stumble as you move from left to right and then down, left to right and then down, with your eyes making their saccadic jumps only slightly ahead, aware of peripheral (illegible) textuality above and below. (Harley 2001: 142) The waymarks are the

Fig 4

83

graphic characters belonging to writing, all of which also face right. To sustain this particular lineating vector the marks will all be clear and recognisable and in all other ways will follow the rules of written language. There is, as it were, a gate at top left and another at bottom right. This page is something you pass through. But then you start again even though in some respects it is a new field. A "real page-turner" is a book which suppresses the sense of re-starting, of repetition. Though the lines are visually in parallel, procedurally they are in series and the series is hardly interrupted by the turn of the page.

How welcome the gaps and indents are, when they come—those spaces inscribed not with letter forms or even punctuation marks but with empty characters placed there by way of space bar, return key, tab key, or by lifting the pen momentarily off the surface.

Lack of graphic clarity in this kind of page will stall or crash a reading, provoke obsessive decipherment or just encourage you to skip. This is page in a relay of pages. Everything moves forward. You can always go back to get a better run at it, use the momentum to guess your way through.

Andrew Powers is one writer who has recently exploited relative contrast to pick out a secondary text and leave the faint tones of the original text difficult to read (Lama Lobsang Darjy and Powers 2003). Tom Phillips has of course taken varied and extreme approaches to the same principle in his continuing work on *A Humument* and its related texts. (Phillips 1997). Forced Entertainment have used selective obliteration in their textual version of *Speak Bitterness* (Forced Entertainment 1995).

**Page as frame**

The page's framed character, usually reinforced with a margin, organises the space quite differently, playing up its relationship with pictorial space and with conventions of composition that are to do with containment, rather than with passage, with a mirroring back of held foveal vision rather than with the mobility of a traveller's searching gaze, with scanning rather than forwarding, with marks that form visual constellations rather than with linguistic tracks. Sequence of engagement is relatively open and it is quite possible to look at writing without reading it—in fact to recognise that writing is just a particular way of making marks on paper. It may be enough for marks to look like writing.

The term constellation is intended to suggest that not all marks in the framed page are equal—blocks, graphic edges, swirls, implied centres, patterning, all these will establish a viewing or reading hierarchy that is not the same as in a lineated sequence.

In the page as a frame it may not be at all clear what is signal and what is noise.

When the framed page is a formal determinant within textual genres, the page is then not just where writing happens; it belongs to writing.

At this point let me remind you that I am suggesting that all three vectors are at work within any page, with their relative force varying in readerly expectation and textual realisation. Lineated reading has now such a strong history that many pages are divided into grids of visual frames, to be read from top left, as in the set of ideograph-like figures made by cris cheek using his tongue and various dyes (Figure 5).

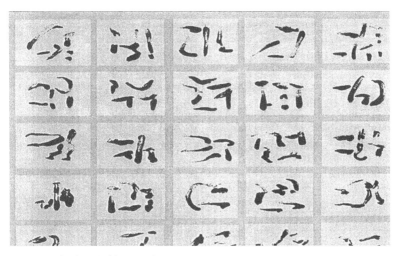

Fig 5: cris cheek in Cobbing and Upton 1998

### Page as map

And thirdly, mapping: the rectangular plane of the page provides axes and co-ordinates for mapping position, movement, orientation, time. As a map the page is a space allowing for the remembering or anticipation of specific locations, or journeys and connections other than the lineated or constellated ones: a graphic or textual item with its own specific co-ordinates. As an illustration, when you are looking for a particular phrase or sentence in a book you have read, don't you recall that it is, for example, on the left (the verso), about two thirds of the way down? Perhaps *searching* always treats pages as maps.

A page as a map doubles as a record and as a notation. Mark and position of graphic marks on the page are indexical, have a motivated analogical relationship with something else: a metrical line, for example, an indicator of the relation of breath to reading (for example, Charles Olson), an indicator of direction of a walk (Richard Long or Hamish Fulton) or movement through enclosed site (Bergvall 1996), "notation" for improvised performance (Bob Cobbing), directionality of thought or historical overlay (Susan Howe). Any form of indentation from left margin or wrapping of line before the right marks the space of the page as cartographic.

The strictly lineated page is a prose page. There are variants, such as the list-page or table-page. In a prose page, tempo is carried within syntax and morphology—with lexicon, type-face and line-spacing playing parts too—not as markers but as features of variable resistance internal to the process of reading. The length of the line is also significant but this is a decision of page-width and margin and is probably made by the publisher.

A mapped page may even be concerned in mapping morphological and syntactic features, breaking and shaping words and grammar to re-reveal their parts, perhaps to transform the part they can play in "speech". It will use spatial configuration

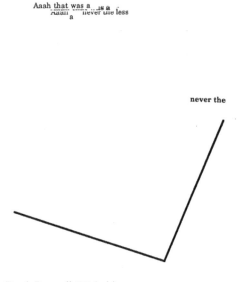

Fig 6: Bergvall 1996: 44

to map tempo or to complicate time in a trapped angle between the time of concatenation and the space of composition. In a mapped page there is more than one syntax at work, more than one morphological set. Letter-based—literal? grammatical?—writing can treat each individual character as a morpheme within a grammar that may not ever be fully actualised.

## Text

The three vectors are different ways of talking about anticipations and realisations of different logics for patterns of marking. *Marking* on pages is usually done with ink and provides the *figure* to the *page's* ground. And in this context I am talking specifically about those kinds of marks that are available as the graphic means for writing, and, also, those marks that sufficiently resemble writing to suggest through their presence that writing may be the topic if not the means of the marks (see Fig 7).

Let's rehearse something about the recursivity involved in alphabetic writing whose destination is a page.

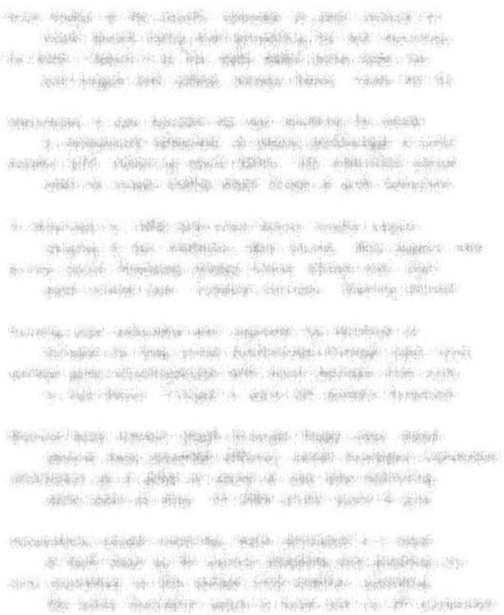

There is a surface ready. This will act as ground. It may not yet be a page. It may be a sheet. It may be a screen. This surface must be fit for the purpose of legible marking—not too absorbent or too resistant, too rough, too crumpled, too dark, too bright. There will be the means—equipment and materials—for applying marks to that surface. Each mark will contrast with the surface to which it is applied and will stand out from that surface as figure to ground. Too much or too little contrast—both of these disturb reading.

Fig 7. A map of prosodic form: it is most certainly a poem that has been rendered "illegible".

The precise shaping of each mark is already itself marked with a history of association—in other words these tiny "meaningless" elements that are used to set language in motion are already written all over with "meaning".

These marks of writing, these letters, punctuation marks, numbers and other related symbols, that can currently be shaped by hand (usually using an implement) or relayed through a keystroke, relate to the soundedness of spoken language. This is not at all exact. For one thing their grapheme-phoneme relationship is not in all respects fixed. And for another the correspondence relies not on actual sounds and fixed character forms but instead assumes zones of differentiation within systemic set of visual signs belonging to graphology and of sound signs belonging to phonology.

Fig 8 shows a range of drawings of the letter "s" currently available in the top part of Adobe InDesign's font set. As a form of marking, writing lies anywhere on a continuum between being a species of line drawing and a species of stamping—in other words applying the already-drawn. It is never a case of drawing what you see or hear. It is always a matter of re-drawing drawings that have set purposes in a given writing system and of doing so in a context where different modes and styles of drawing operate too as registers of affect and differential social exchange ("In your best handwriting...").

Fig 8

The word "drawing" catches very well the cursive movement of a hand over paper. It will not do for the punctiveness of cuneiform or the soft percussiveness of computer keyboard writing. This latter if of course a form of clip-art. The drawings are already in memory. Choose the style (font) and select with a stroke. You will not see that I hit the keys in anger from an impression on paper. You will not witness my tentativeness, verging on the illegible. If I want you to see my anger I shall need to represent it as a deliberate supplement. I shall choose tentativeness as sign, perhaps by doing no more than damping the contrast between figure and ground. Gesture of a hand mark is brought back in as a simulation.

These graphic marks are crucially members of combinatorial sets. They are added together, usually in horizontal lines, to make syllables and words, using conventions of spacing or of joins that preserve as well as possible their differential status ("rn" not "m", for example). Legibility counts on the integrity of the letter form—its size, shape, density, contrast with ground, spacing, stylistic consistency with other letters in the set.

Using unfamiliar or ineligible combinations (consonantal strings without vowels, for example) will block sounding and frustrate word recognition.

Writing has come to rely on punctuation—crucially on word spacing—but also on parsing markers—switches at clausal or sentence joins. Punctuation marks are enablers of reading but do not have the status of graphemes. To produce an illegible page, strip out all punctuation including word spaces. Alternatively treat punctuation marks as belonging to their own exclusive combinatorial set (for example Bergvall 1996).

Where there is writing—or something that looks like writing—there is always something to read. Resistance in one layer might re-route reading to another.[48]

## Legibility of text

In alphabetic writing systems, basic legibility relies on grapheme-phoneme transfer: that individual graphemes can be recognised and discriminated from within a written-language set *and* recognised as indices of phonemes that are thereby activated as though they belong to the sound shapes of spoken language.

Below or to the side of this base, there can be: recognition and discrimination of graphemes with no or limited transfer; recognition that there *are* graphemes on the page (see the cheek example above) but without information for full discrimination and transfer.

At a higher level, the grapheme-phoneme transfer has to be effective enough for the sequenced combinations in the graphological modality to activate transfer on to a parallel modality of phonological combinations, leading to the articulation of syllables. This doesn't mean that you have "understood"—you may be effecting this transfer in a language that you know just well enough to sound in your head but not well enough to be at ease with its lexicon and grammatical construction. There may not, in other words, have been a phoneme-morpheme or grapheme-morpheme transfer. You could at this level produce a homophonic translation but not a literal one.

Fluent legibility (reader *and* text) produces further and further transfers into semantic exchange and, most importantly, into pragmatic engagement with the text's world and the world of the text.

## Textual transactions

I have been treating legibility and illegibility as sets of conditions affecting transactions of readers with marks on pages, where the marks either belong to or gesture towards writing.

A will to read has to be in play for the terms to have any sense at all. Obviously a given text can be seen to meet conditions of legibility without being legible to *me* because I don't know the language, the writing system, am unfamiliar with the handwriting of a person, place or time, or am simply not practised at coping with a wide range of letter forms. Parties to the transactions of reading are not equal. An easier solution would be to describe legibility as a condition of a text rather than a condition of relationship with a text. But there's no legibility—and therefore no illegibility—without readers.

"Legibility" could be the term for the textual condition where the graphic marks are performing their linguistic function without in any way drawing attention to themselves. They simply(!) carry a reader's desire into the text as though this were a wholly paraphrasable domain. They provide a signal whose "noise" is not even noticed by a reader absorbed in narrative or argument or some instrumental transaction that is the context of the message. The "message" is the text and the graphic marks are the channel or perhaps operating code, no more visible than the computer languages that provide a deep structure for the "user-friendly" interface.

There are variations to these neutral conditions. One is that the code can be degraded, be very noisy, and you struggle to listen to the signal through all the noise. Another is that the signal is so noisy you shut it out, you don't bother. Another is that you find yourself treating the noise as the signal.[49] And here we may have differences between illegibility, the representation of illegibility, and a readerly code-switch, that looks for readability in a different part of the message (Hayles 2002: 50–51). Finally—and I have Jakobson's definition of the poetic in mind here (Jakobson 1960)—the elements of the code might themselves become the message through phatic display, hyper-legibility.

In all but the condition of neutral or "ideal" legibility, a reader's desire encounters friction at the very moment of activation, is obstructed, distracted or refracted by any questionable status of the mark-page relationship. Consciousness of legibility is already a kind of il/legibility, is a material reminder of the material processes of reading and as a force cannot ever mark an absence of meaning-affect-effect. You can always walk away but already something has happened. A mark that belongs to writing is always a mark or trace of utterance as well as an instance of a writing system. As sign of utterance it will always provoke some form of psycho-graphological reading, however casual. A sign has been left and this already implies a Someone; perversely this someone may have tried to obscure the very sign they have left; there may have been later sabotage; the sign might be a sign of obliteration of the sign. Who knows, illegibility in some cases might be the paranoid gesture that repeatedly reveals the site of a crypt it thinks it is thereby hiding (Abraham and Torok 1994). In others, of course, it is strategic activism within the politics of textual interaction.

## PS: Some types of illegibility

A different essay could start at this point and set out to try to read some pages in which illegibility is at issue. (And indeed I shall attempt in a separate note to comment on the contribution to this issue by Tanja Dabo.) Instead I shall finish with a sweeping set of gestures towards different kinds of symptoms of and different strategies for il/legible texts. I am not in this context including those experiences of unreadability that can be produced by syntax, vocabulary, unfamiliar encyclopaedic reference or an unrecognised performative function. Instead I am seeing illegibility as inadequacy in or "damage" to the material features of a text—the ink, the letter forms, the paper, for example.

## Page

The page itself, the paper, as one side of a two-sided object, is vulnerable to many forms of damage: burning, crumpling, tearing, cutting and re-assembling and shredding and re-assembling (TNWK—see Fig 9), folding, spillage, cup or glass marks, gluing up, pasting over, sealing, deterioration through exposure to heat, light, damp. Most poignantly a page is vulnerable to loss, to being lost.

## Graphic marks

Overprinting, scale of characters (too small or blown up beyond definition), degradation or poor definition; (partial) erasure; obliteration; distortions; use of letters, words or lines to make drawings (including collaging of text-parts to form non-linguistic shapes (Jaeger in Cobbing and Upton 1998); a refusal to respect the usual rules of combination; interruption of "technotypographic layout with a kind of gestural semiotics".[50]

## Interventions between the two

Many of these forms of production of illegibility are quite specific to the writing machine (Hayles 2002) current and available. Much of the typewriter art of earlier decades took procedures, forms and effects from the fact that a typewriter was designed exclusively as a writing machine. Anyone who had used a typewriter could look at typewriter art and feel her hands shadow the the movements of paper and carriage in a need to change orientation and positioning. Or else the cutting and pasting would be literal and not the metaphor of PC terminology. Distortions could also be achieved through moving a sheet on a photocopier. Now this can still be done on a scanner bed but there is no need since the same effects can be produced through the use of software. Again we have a move from reading gesture to reading representation of gesture.

Could all these be talked about as no more than the production techniques for "new" kinds of cultural commodities[51]? Or are they "signal vacations" (Joanna Drucker in Cobbing 1998), games played within the instability of written language, or acts of revenge against the written where it has appeared most stable? Or instances of remappings and reinterpretations of the human body through its cybernetic engagement with texts? (Hayles 2002, p. 51) Or acts of avoidance—holdings or foldings back within acts of writing from what is too appalling to be written? There are so many pages, so many illegibilities.

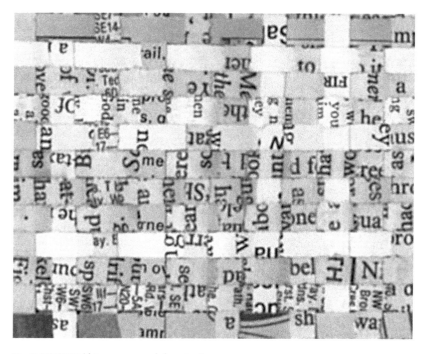

Fig 9. TNWK (things not worth keeping)

# *Reading A Polished Page* [52]

A rectangular photographic space, itself a surface, offers another surface whose clearest outlines are the edges of the frame. Intruding on to this surface is an arm, severed by the frame edge, holding a rag and appearing to press this on to the surface. This arm, the rag, a smear of white paste, darker areas of stain—all these are outlined within the frame, altering a sense of what constitutes pure surface, how such purity could be attained. Outline differentiates—divides up a surface into things that might interact. Pure surface? Would that be an absorption of everything visible into the same?

I am looking at two versions of a photographic image by Tanja Dabo, one of these on a flat computer screen (23 x 33 cms on the screen), the other on photographic paper (24 x 36 cms), with an acetate overlay. Both of these versions are as it were on the way, are part of a process towards publication on a folded page. The one on my computer screen must have been scanned in. In this one, the arm comes in from the top left. In the paper version, the acetate marks up the outlines that can be found on the surface and tags the islands and peninsulas, seas and lakes so formed, with capital letter signs of "G" and "M". A handwritten note on another piece of paper explains that these stand for "Gloss" and "Matt". Decisions about the degree of lustre—usually global ones for photographs—here lead to another set of internal contrasts, adding perhaps a narrative possibility of transformation from one to the other. I must allow these instructions to transform my viewing. I must filter the surface of the photograph as it appears, in a deliberate act of perception that imagines change. The printer received these as instructions for processing and I assume that we can all now see, on its folded page, the result of these instructions.

The Gs and Ms provide an orientation for the photograph that has the arm coming in from bottom right. What decision of dexter and sinister will the printer have made?

The image is in monochrome. It is prepared for a journal that does not use colour images. Even so in 2004 a monochrome photograph of this scale carries the sign of art. The frame divides into two, left and right. This is not the division produced by matt and gloss or dirty and clean.

The hand reaches half way across. The rest is surface where stain and lustre provide contrast.

The arm is a reductive metonym (synecdoche) of a person who is doing something with this rag. I read it as a woman's arm. Is this, perhaps, the shape of the finger nails and of the wrist? Or is it more because I still expect it to be a woman's hand that presses a rag to a surface, unless that surface be mechanical or part of a process of construction?

The only way to avoid collusion with an act of severance—with a frame that asserts its exclusions over and above its containments—is to imagine the missing body. The hand is a right hand; the rag-holder is right-handed. Her head is not in the way. I assume the surface is horizontal, like a worktop, and she stands before it, keeping everything out of the way except that arm. I experience an imaginary strain as I identify with this assumed posture, so forcibly represented off frame. But also I can't help identifying with the camera position and find that this is where my / her head should be. Maybe that is the source of the strain. And isn't that area below the hand bright?

If the orientation of the image has the hand coming in top left, then this is another body, over the other side. The camera's angle of view meets the rag-holder's imagined angle at a diagonal. Why should this be?

Just before it is cut by the frame the arm provides the darkest area in the photograph. This may not be so. Maybe that stain or spillage, diagonally across, is just as dark.

Half of the photograph can be read within a convention that aestheticises texture, surface, even dirt, that appropriates the object-world into a formalism of surface, light and shade. The other half could almost belong to the same convention, in a more extreme variant, where not just the object-world but also human work that takes place in it is appropriated for these aims. But because it is an arm, and because the hand presses into a rag, and seems to have been doing so enough for the rag itself to press back up between those fingers, the frame does not provide that rectangle of contemplation this convention requires. The outer frame insists, to my viewing, on violence—a violence of a severed body part, of severance from authority—from an author—of the work suggested in this image.

Like so many still images this one too seems to hover on the edge of narrative or portraiture, perhaps both.

This is a photographic image by Tanja Dabo. I know, in my viewing, though I have never witnessed them, that Tanja Dabo makes performances and that many of these have taken the form of meticulous polishing, in at least one case of a whole gallery floor. I have held back this knowledge in my account so far. But now it comes flooding back in. The image itself is a metonym of performance. A person acts, works, makes and removes marks. Marks are both stains and assertions of presence, smears and spillages of a has-been-here. They can be both polished up and polished away. Where varnish or lacquer add shine as a layer to a surface, polish acts in a combination of abrasion and fill. In a perfect shine there is nothing left to fill.

There are no words in this image. I mean this literally, though words might form on a viewer's lips. But here it is in a journal issue called On The Page. And my account comes out of a conversation with the editor that encourages me to read the image as illegible. Have all the words been polished away? Is this sometimes what photographs can do? How long can words be kept away? Could anybody, seeing this image, not find themselves "reading" it? If such a reading happens, is it "spoken"?

# Two Textual Collaborations[53]

I am going to be talking about two recent projects, both collaborations and both leading to the potential for an open set of outcomes. I do so in the context of a series of research seminars taking place in a community of practitioners, where the difference between a research seminar and an exchange of notes and reflections on practical processes is not always clear. People in the arts are always researching, in the sense of finding out for yourself: how to do things, what happens if you do them this way or that way, source or reference material for the task, who else has worked in ways that might be instructive? In doing this we are unlikely to be driven by the wish to make a distinct contribution to the international knowledge pool of some putative "subject". Also, as artists, we are often knowingly caught between the technical (all the *hows* of our trades), the discursive (the commentary and argument that provide an environment for our trades), and the world or context our work cannot help but refer to and engage with.

So in what follows I will be making no claims for contributions to knowledge and certainly not for innovation. Rather, I hope that by talking in some detail about two different processes and reflecting on them in relation to the outcomes, I might contribute to a continuing conversation about collaboration, a term that can be seen as at the heart of Dartington's ethos, and as standing in contrast both to an individualism that will always want to single out an author, and a dirigisme—sometimes the same—that will assume that work involving more than one person will always need to be directed, conducted, led.

My examples are simple. Each, on the face of it, involves only two people.[54] Each was motivated by the wish of these two people to work together on a process with an unknown outcome rather than towards a known end that would benefit from complementarity of skills. In each case, both participants are poets and so the collaborations are "textual", though I shall complicate this later.

A collaboration can be motivated by a wish to access another named practice or different abilities and angles of approach within the same practice or in the borderlands around it, such as, for writers, typography, computer know-how, book-making. And quite apart from skill—knowing how to—there is the attraction of having access to other kinds of knowledge, through differences in lives lived, through different reading, through different cultural experience of all kinds.

I could put this differently, and perhaps add to it by numbering some different motivations, which are not at all intended to be either/ors: (1) a desire for conversation-like exchange *within* the work; (2) a curiosity—an envy perhaps—about the way another poet does things and a wish to get close to that; (3) a wish to work with *difference*, with the tension of ill-fit; (4) a wish to avoid the lyric responsibilities of sole authorship. I shall mostly leave these as speculations, in the air, hoping that from time to time you will recognise them in what follows.

Themes about process that will emerge are all obvious and familiar: basis of trust, divisions of labour, rules of engagement, degrees of autonomy, editorial judgement, communication through the work, communication about the work.

I'll talk first about a collaboration with Peter Hughes, poet, painter, small press publisher. We had known of each other's work for some years and had corresponded from time to time on specific issues, such as his generous editorial and publishing work on a collection celebrating the sixtieth birthday of the poet, Peter Riley (Hughes 2000). In 2007 I received out of the blue one of the 26 copies of a Kore broadsheet of one of his poems, produced by Philip Coleman in Dublin (Hughes 2007).[55] The poem was No 15 from *The Pistol Tree Poems*, a collaboration with Simon Marsh, which by March 2009 had reached No 57 on Great Works website (Hughes 2009).[56] When also invited by Philip Coleman to contribute a broadsheet I worked on a version of *An Alphabet for Else Here, Rolled* (Hall 2008), and included Peter in my list of twenty-six recipients. We corresponded about these exchanges of indirect gifts and then I acquired a copy of his *The Sardine Tree* (Hughes 2008), published by his own new press, Oystercatcher, and, like most of the other pamphlets in the set, featuring a reproduction of one of his own paintings on the cover. He describes *The Sardine Tree* on the Oystercatcher Website as "a poem in seven sections inspired by the life and work of Miró." One of his earlier collections was *Paul Klee's Diary* (Hughes 1995 and in Hughes 2003). His preoccupation with painters from earlier in the twentieth century was not new.

In responding to *The Sardine Tree* I commented that I had myself written a poem-sequence in the early 1970s in which Miró was a recurring presence and I sent him a copy of it. Within days my old poem was becoming another Oystercatcher (Hall 2008) and we found ourselves collaborating, as is not unusual between publisher and author in the small press world, over the back cover: I would place text over a copy of the painting used on the front. It was this that prompted the thought that we would set out on more deliberate collaboration.

The givens that we recognised were that we both write poems for pages and that we both, in very different ways, work visually, he as a painter and I as a "visual poet". So far as I knew, Peter did not conceive of his paintings as writing; rather that he did both. The paintings I had seen in reproduction did not obviously include words, though in some there are script-like shapes. I had only seen them reproduced or mediated on computer screens, but they were very obviously "painterly": produced by hand and showing trace of gestural contact with paper or other surface. My method, in contrast, was usually to produce the work on a computer, manipulating type, shape and colour by moving a "mouse" over a horizontal mat while staring at a vertical lit screen. I think we agreed that we would use these three components: page-writing (or writing as though for the page), painting, and computer-based text and image manipulation. Our channel of exchange would be the internet, through email attachments, and the transfer medium would be JPEG files.[57] Peter would make the first move.

The first image reached me as at about as 81 x 108 cms (A0 paper size, allowing for a small margin) at 72 dpi.[58] Immediately a question about scale was posed. A0 prints would be difficult to manage and this resolution would be too low. Should size become one of the rules, at least to the extent that we would treat all the image-texts as being the same height (and that they would all be in portrait orientation, though we never needed to discuss this)? Adjusting scale is relatively straightforward when working on a computer and related printers but it is as well to treat scale as a significant formal element and it makes life easier if the scale on the screen relates recognisably to the envisaged scale, though this is not always possible.

There were other elements which I could choose to respond to or ignore: variants of the colour blue; script-like swirls which evoked writing;

an implied lineation, with the suggestion of grid, that comes with so many writing forms; an overlay of text; the text—"con / script"—used very sparely, with nine letters in all, readable as either one or two words because broken over two lines. The font was Georgia, a serif font developed for the Microsoft corporation, along the lines of Times New Roman—in other words, carrying very strong reference to earlier moveable type, though specifically designed for computer screens.

The second syllable (word, line) reads "script", and is placed to the left of a script-like shape that is strongly suggestive of the capital letter A, establishing a sense that there is more than one kind of writing at work: that here script can be painted, painting can script, script can be referred to in script. And the prefix "con" opens on to various suggestions about the use of writing. Peter and I were embarking on a co(n)-laboration: we were going to be writing together, co-scribing. But a "conscript" is someone who has been written compulsorily into some obligation.[59] I was already interested in the idea of writing as a form of conscription; from its earliest days, apparently, "writing" was used to reinforce at least ownership if not broader

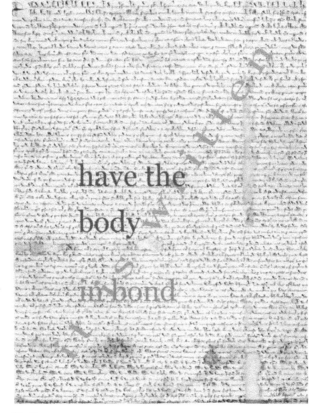

Fig 2

categories of the legally, politically or theologically binding.[60] I went in search of an easily available, possibly even recognisable, example.

The Magna Carta, or Great Chart, is often associated with the writ of Habeas Corpus ("that you should have the body"). A conscript may well ask who has her body (Fig 2). Peter responded by returning to his first painting and transforming it in ways that included reacting to the colour of the Magna Carta image, pointing more

Fig 4

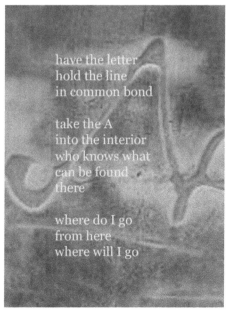

have the letter
hold the line
in common bond

take the A
into the interior
who knows what
can be found
there

where do I go
from here
where will I go

Fig 3

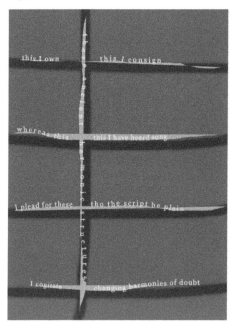

obviously at the A-like shape, and even suggesting Billy Strayhorn's tune, 'Take the A Train', so strongly associated with Duke Ellington. (Fig 3) It is one thing to take a train (indeed the A Train) into the interior but that's not what Peter "said". What is it to take a letter-line into interiors which are constructed from landfill, perhaps a landfill of discarded words and other signs.

Until this point I have taken the moves one by one, giving only my own account; another implicit rule had become that we spoke only through the exchange and not about it. Later in the exchange a found image, not shown here, from Peter, reinforced the sense of script laid on a grid and set up a whole sequence of pieces in which writing either was placed in the panels of a grid or, as in the example in Fig 4, followed the internal framing bars. Then, for the fifteenth move, Peter returned to one of his paintings, overlaying it with a single line of text near the bottom.

I wanted to respond to the disappearance of the grid—though of course the rectangular frame remains as a kind of single-celled grid and the overlaid text is strictly horizontal—and to the appearance of arcs, always implying segments of circles or indeed of spirals. I wanted to run text along them and had already been using a facility in both Photoshop and InDesign called "Type on a Path".[61] You will see that with this one (Fig 5) I wanted to add genetic conscription to the ideas already in play about political and linguistic conscription, using the familiar metaphor that DNA is a kind of script and the double helix a more complex form than a grid for setting out the "information" which continues to shape a body.

It may have been only at this point that we talked about setting a limit to the number of

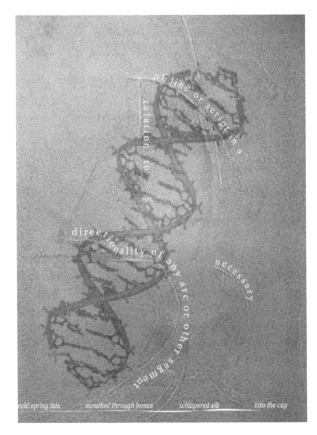

Fig 5

exchanges and also about selection and editing. We fixed on twenty as the number, did not eliminate any but did allow some editing, mostly for technical reasons, none of which involved changes to choice of words. I had been collating them in InDesign, trying out different sizes, and anticipating either or both of book publication and exhibition showing. I had been offered a residency with Plymouth College of Art that would culminate in an exhibition and that gave me access to the College's print rooms, so both possibilities were realistic.

When we reached the twentieth and were in some sort of a position to see them as a set—though we were still relying on email attachments, which made for a problem when sending more than one at a time—we discussed the obvious fact that the collaboration had not prompted any text-only pieces, even though some of them included what would amount to a full poem. Andrew Crozier, a poet, editor and small-press publisher (Ferry Press), had died on April 3rd 2008, a few days into our exchange. I had been re-reading all of his poems and I wanted to acknowledge in some way a life and work that had been very important to me. In 1976 he had published a sequence of quatrains called *Duets* (Crozier 1976; and in Crozier 1985) and there was one that I had been returning to over the years:

> bowed down by the weight of care
> while in the garden on last year's buddleia
> butterflies hover in the purple air
> something is subsiding slowly into fear

I suggested to Peter that we produce a quatrain to stand next to each image-text as an accompaniment. Apart from as homage to Andrew Crozier, quatrains had the other advantage of being short enough to encourage rather than discourage the two different kinds (at least) of reading that would now be invited. They could also be relatively small, leaving plenty of white space on page or frame. Peter suggested that we write ten each to accompany our own moves, rather than re-enact the turn-taking method we had used until then. He also made it clear that it would be a challenge to him to work in four lines, but generously took it on.[62] As an example, the following quatrain was set to the left of the image-text shown in Fig 4:

Think of script as a great order
spun out from the body of the state
stained and absorbed within the interior
like landfill. tears are always its fate.

I am writing this just over a year after we had started. There is still some unfinished business. Meanwhile the full set has been shown at an exhibition, in which the collaboration with Lee Harwood was also shown.[63] Each pair of image and quatrain was printed on A4 paper and framed simply in black. The full set was hung in three rows, with seven in the top two and six in the bottom. This arrangement allowed any of a chronological reading (top left to bottom right), a tabular one (column by column, say) or an open or intuitive reading that moved between neighbouring pieces in no directed order.[64]

I shall now describe the second collaboration, that with Lee Harwood, and will do so within a sense of contrast in context and method. If a generation of writers can be thought to have on average a ten-year span, then Peter Hughes belongs to the next (younger) generation to mine, and Lee is a slightly older figure in my own generation, whose first collection was published in 1965 (Harwood 1965), and for whom this century has already been marked with a *Collected Poems* (Harwood 2004), a *Selected Poems* (Harwood 2008a), a book of interviews by Kelvin Corcoran (Harwood 2008b), and a Salt *Companion* (Sheppard 2007). In his long list of publications are two collaborations: *Wish You Were Here*, with Tony (Antony in those days) Lopez in 1979 (Harwood 1979) and *Wine Tales*, with Ric Caddel (Harwood 1984), published in 1984 but bearing the dates 1979–81 on the cover. The first has this note on a separate page between the colophon and the body text:

> This book is a collaboration. During the autumn and winter 1977–8 we exchanged two sets of six postcards, sending the cards alternately. The texts which follow either illustrate those cards, or use the pictures as a starting point for the writing—so that we were able, indirectly, to influence the progress of each other's work.

*Wine Tales* has this in a similar position:

> Note: This book is a collaboration using the pictures on various wine labels as the starting points for our stories. All but two of the labels were written jointly, and of course the book as a whole was edited and revised by both of us.

These are two different models of collaboration, though both used "pictures" as prompts.

Lee and I have known each other, and each other's work, for over forty years, though only in the last seven years or so, following degrees of retirement, have we been able to see more of each other. During these last years we have talked and corresponded a great deal and this is relevant because of the way that conversation is a primary model for collaborating in and through words, and of course good talk tends to stay in your head and resurface,[65] especially if you are a certain kind of writer, whose ear is attuned to the speech of others. Two principles must be in place for conversation to merit its name: listening and turn-taking. Somewhere in there is the sociable mode of call and response, as long as this is not taken to represent fixed positions in ritual (or quasi-ritual) exchange. And because Lee and I talk and read each others' work there is every chance that any of our writing might, at least in part, respond to something the other has said or written. These informal, sometimes unacknowledged, collaborations happen all the time among people who converse between jobs, as it were.

We had earlier fallen into something that lies somewhere between the formal and informal as collaboration. As part of an ongoing exchange about framed texts that I make, Lee had given me a red enamelled frame, covered, except where it had been cut away for an oval picture aperture, with gold-coloured Chinese calligraphy. Since I place writing in frames and this frame was already written on, it felt important to know what the frame already "said". My ignorance of Chinese defeated me for a while and various attempts to obtain a translation failed. After a while I devised a piece that depended on a flimsy understanding of Chinese spoken dialects as using pitch (or tone) to distinguish between two words otherwise phonologically identical. Only then did it occur to me to send a scanned copy of the frame to John Cayley, poet and sinologist.[66] He recognised it immediately, saying:

Now, that Chinese. It's instantly recognizable as extracted from the most famous piece of calligraphy in the world, Wang Xizhi (321–379)'s 'Orchid Pavilion Preface'. Any even quasi-educated sino-inflected person would know what it was.[67]

When I sent this to Lee he responded with a card bearing a hand-written poem:

> Disgraced by ignorance
> we leave for the frontier
> heads bowed
> The orchid pavilion
> closed for repairs

and signed it with an improvised ideogram doubling as a monogram of L and H. At some point while this exchange was happening, I had been reading another preface, the one by Gilles Deleuze for the English translation of his *Difference & Repetition*, and because of our now ongoing conversation about ignorance, I set the following quotation within a scanned copy of the Orchid Pavilion frame and sent it to Lee, without attribution:

> We
> write only
> at the frontiers of
> our knowledge, at the
> border which separates
> our knowledge from our
> ignorance and transforms
> the one into the other.
> Only in this manner are we
> resolved to write. To satisfy
> ignorance is to put off
> writing until tomorrow
> - or rather, to make
> it imposs-
> ible.

(Deleuze 1994: xxi; my layout)

This sequence of additions resulted in a set of four which I called 'The Orchid Pavilion, a brief essay on ignorance for Lee Harwood'.[68] (Hall 2007) Rather than a full collaboration, this had been the appropriation by me of others' contributions, though, as I have made clear, the full collaboration of our conversation was behind it, and was its source and place.[69]

Two features in this near-collaboration very much apply to the collaboration that came to be called *Loose Packed*: its close relation to conversation and a tension, which I haven't spelled out, relating to "theory" or to a difference between a view of poetry as wedded to experience, to the concreteness of things, the materiality of the actually said, and one that might even look to the resources of language to question the apparent solidity of perceptual experience. This is of course a familiar opposition between empiricism and speculative thought.[70] I mentioned that I had not attributed the Deleuze text. Lee thought that I had written those words and liked them very much. I then had to reveal to him that they were from a French philosopher, out of the pit of theoretical (speculative) philosophy.

The collaboration with Lee was altogether a slower affair than the one with Peter. We had decided to embark on a collaboration long before the first text was exchanged. We talked about possibilities but didn't get going. Then Lee made a visit to the USA and fixed on two events during his time there as possible sources or lines of exploration. One was encountering in Girard, Kansas, memorials to a socialist newspaper called *Appeal to Reason* that had been produced there from 1897 to 1922, peaking at a circulation of 760,000, a remarkable figure given that the population of Girard is now under 3000.[71] This project and its title hovered over the enterprise without, I would say, in any way directing it. The other event was a visit he made to *Philip Guston: Works on Paper*, an exhibition at the Morgan Library and Museum in New York. Lee wanted to talk about the late, figurative drawings, in which Guston kept returning to a fixed repertoire of objects and figures, motivated, according to him, by this question: "What would happen, I thought, if I eliminated everything except just raw feeling and the brush and ink, the simplest of means."[72]

I did my best to make myself familiar with these drawings through book reproductions and the internet, finding that they had a prominent place in the story of the artist and in a story of US American art, with its alignments and therefore possible betrayals ("If you're not with us you're against us"). In this story, what Guston had abandoned or betrayed was abstraction. What did it mean at that point to return to the figure, to objects in relation to each other, and to a way of figuring them that could not but suggest a story, a fate, a charged scene that might be open to an interpretation? In Guston's drawings certain human figures—or synecdochic indications of himself, his wife—are often there too, objects alongside objects. Even so, there is a sense of a world reduced to props, so familiar in drawing, painting and photography, and indeed in domains of knowledge taxonomy (identification, classification). (Guston 2007) A topic was emerging and one that we found ourselves talking about persistently and never in any easy agreement.

We would take on a writing that dealt with the notion of objects, of things, and that had drawings in mind, as both reference and as other-to-writing, as another way of dealing with the world. Those drawings of Guston's would provide a context for our texts but would not be those pages, and would not be built as immediately into the process as those postcards or wine labels. We would not be the first to ask in what ways or to what extent writing could do what drawing or painting do.[73] And each of us had asked this question before.

Many of Guston's recurring objects were the tools of his painter's trade. Lee was wary of a "writing about writing" that might follow from an analogous treatment of "paper, ink and pen", a line that I had pursued in earlier writing and found myself doing again. Painting has often been allowed a celebration within its own productions of its tools and materials. The equipment of writing has changed so much recently as part of a computer-influenced broadening of writing technologies that not to attend to this can seem like an anti-empiricism, a denial of the concrete material activities—and indeed the work of others—on which writing depends. In any case, I was interested in the difference.

Where the earlier exchanges with Peter had been almost wholly through email and attachments—perhaps one or two telephone conversations, one or two packets through the royal mail—, Lee does not own a computer and chooses not to have access to one. Instead we visited each other and spent time talking and, later on, laying out what we had done, discussing possibilities with the things in front of us on a table; we sent each other letters and writings through the post; and we spoke on the telephone.

Lee made the first move, eventually sending "some fragments to start our delayed collaboration" on 18th August 2008. One feature of the collaboration was the trying out of rules to get going or to proceed, only to put them to use paradoxically, by breaking them. "Instead" below refers to an unfollowed rule. This is from the letter that accompanied the first set.

> What seems to have assembled instead is a series of fragments, scraps of language. Maybe we can use some of these? or maybe I am heading off in the wrong direction. See what you think. A mixed shuffle of our cards.

I don't think we had discussed a card-pack at that stage. By sending a set of fragments rather than a single one, Lee had established another difference in the form of exchange. This would not be a one-for-one exchange but any number that were prompted by the last received batch and by intervening reading, listening and conversation. And from very early we began to question, or suggest changes to, the ones already exchanged, whoever had written them.[74] The generation of texts and their editing became intertwined, which is often standard practice in solo writing but more complicated for a duo.

One month and a day after the first receipt, I wrote to him, perhaps still having in mind that phrase about cards, though we had been to-ing and fro-ing the "fragments" on more or less card-sized paper: "I think that there are now 43 cards. Does 52—as the standard four-suit pack, sans Joker—now beckon?"

I then went on to say:

> I suggest that we to-and-fro them a few times, and try the following rules:
>
> We each in turn make six moves.
> A move can be any of the following:
>
> a new card
>
> a removal of a card
>
> a change to a card
>
> a suggested change / removal
>
> a query
>
> a protection stake (i.e. "don't remove this one; I like it".)

All six moves could be of the same type—for example, six removals or six protection stakes.[75]

Lee responded that he had been quite unable to follow these rules. In practice, though, we had been doing all of the above, though not systematically. Many of the earlier ones, particularly some of mine that were meditations on the topic and in a different mode, had been weeded out. In my collaboration with Peter only the first of the six rules had applied until all twenty image-texts had been produced.

Already agreed was that there should be no fixed order for the cards. That presented no problem for the playing card format but needed another solution for exhibition. The decision here was to hang them (or indeed

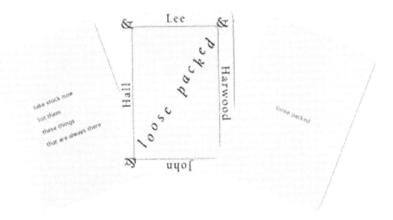

Fig 6   From the pack

shelve them) in scattered groupings throughout the gallery rather than fixed in a grid. I believe that these considerations were important to the writing and editing of the texts. The actual design and production was initially down to me as the one with familiarity with computers but we consulted at every point.

The exhibition prompted and included two spin-offs: an attempt, not yet fully successful, at a large-scale two-panelled version of two fragments (one not actually in the fifty-two), modelled on this small, domestic frame (Fig 7).

Lee had drafted sets of rules for playing *Loose Packed*, which could be included in each pack. The opening of the exhibition included an inaugural game of one form, with Lee as the dealer. Having shuffled the pack he fanned the cards out and invited guests to draw one, without turning it face-up. He then conducted a reading by asking each person with a card to read it in turn.

At a reading given at Dartington on 23 April 2009, without Lee present, another game was played, this time a two-hander, with Larry Lynch as the other player and Mark Greenwood as dealer. Cards were laid on a black music stand with a camera, linked to a projector, set over it. Each player was dealt four cards and had to choose which one of the four to read, given what, if anything, had come before. Once read, a card

Fig 7

was discarded and replaced. The game was over when there were no more cards. Of course this could be played without the camera. The point was to engage an audience in choices that might not match those of the players; in other words, to allow for layered simultaneous readings. There was little time to set this up and with more time the technical aspects could be improved.[76]

We still hope to publish the cards as packs. They may or may not include the rules.

Any sense of conclusion needs to be modest and provisional. I am talking about only two (three if you include 'Orchid Pavilion') collaborations, both of which involved me, which were very recent, and which were very different. Neither was the kind of collaboration that gets around questions of authorship any more than conversation anonymises its participants. These kinds of collaboration build response into their process of composition. In doing so, they bring reading and writing very close together. They are bound, I think, to be sites of a negotiation, through writing itself, about poetics, unless the participants start off with a completely shared view of what a poem can be. Modes and conditions of communication are probably significant. As, of course, are the different experiences and skills brought to the collaboration. They build in an obligation to the other person (or people): a decision to collaborate is a decision to make work, which is very different from awaiting an impulse to make work that is a luxury and burden for those writers whose main mode of production is in solitude.

# An Afterword to David Prior's
# Black Water Brown Water <sup>77</sup>

David Prior is a composer or sound artist who likes to work with materials that come into—or face—his music from the outside. He likes to work with others who are not—or at least not primarily—themselves musicians. He likes to work across forms, being at ease with video, with live elements, with buildings, with social spaces. He likes to respond to briefs, so that the work starts as a conversation with—or response to—the wishes of others. For a number of years he has been half of *liminal*, the company formed with his architect partner, Frances Crow. *Liminal*'s purpose is to treat sound as architectural in the broadest senses.

This work, the one in your hand, is one manifestation of a recent *liminal* project, *Black Water Brown Water*. What you have in your hand is a book, with a CD included; it is not a catalogue or a programme note and it is not a CD with a booklet in its case. It is the book version of the piece, published by a small press that concerns itself with the range of practices that can be called Performance Writing, that relate to live performance, visual and installed writing, poetry. As a book it offers itself as an experience in the first place by way of the eyes (and hands), and in particular for reading. But this is the kind of book that also includes something to hear: a CD of the sounded verbal text and of the sounds that are not verbal, and, most importantly, of the gaps between these sounds (and the way the different kinds of sounds form gaps between each other—are any of these components not themselves *liminal?*). In the pages are visual references to the setting for which the writing was first produced, for which the composition was made, because the original version was a response by *liminal* to a commission to produce "a site-specific sound piece which captures the sounds created by the island area of the [Stourport-on-Severn] Canal Basins to engage new and existing audiences and assist in their understanding of the place that surrounds them".<sup>78</sup> That version of *Black Water Brown Water* takes place as a soundwalk, in the commissioned setting. Books are portable; that's now their point. Few are now anchored to place like a huge bible chained to its lectern. But places can get into books, through writing, through images; and books can infiltrate the places in which they are experienced. When a composer has an ear not only for the sounds that provide the sonic signatures of places, but also for their economic inscriptions, for the textual memories that are channelled through them or that flow through them, then there is a writing too.

The two waters—the black water and the brown water—are the flowing "intemperate" waters of the river Severn, and the controlled, channelled waters of the Staffordshire and Worcestershire Canal. The two are separated—or joined—by five canal basins with their strong lock gates. Rivers are for the most part natural forces that have cut their own way through the surface of the land. Canals are willed by entrepreneurs, designed by engineers and cut by people who are paid for their "toil". Of course, this distinction does not hold as an absolute once engineers intervene in the courses and uses of rivers, but a heavy storm will often reassert it. Frances Crow and David Prior assert their interest in liminality, the state much discussed by Victor Turner and others of being *between*, not on but as it were *within* a border, the way that a porch-way can offer a place of transition between outside and inside. Rivers, for David Prior, are liminal ("with the liminal river, intemperate and unownéd"),[79] I think because they double as borders—supposedly fixed—and as turbulent fluxes. And in this chosen space there is another extended *limen*, the basins that separate the river from the canal, the brown water from the black.

The basins separate and join not just the two kinds of waters but also, in this piece, three—perhaps more—overlapping kinds of history: literary-mythological, territorial, and economic. These histories conjoin and separate legendary or mythological figures and biographical ones: Sabrina and Estrildis on the one side, James Brindley, the canal engineer, and his putative illegitimate son (who seems to become a daughter in the piece) on the other. Large rivers like the Severn make natural or symbolic borders, that can define where countries—England and Wales, for example—abut, and therefore re-iterate and contest their identities; canals are constructed with the purposes not of separating but of giving access to fuels and markets for manufacture and commerce, and in a way that can be controlled ("I must contain / and calm and harness"). Rivers have deities (or deific creatures like nymphs); canals have engineers. Geoffrey of Monmouth, the twelfth-century "historian" of "the matter of Britain", who provided later source material for Spenser's *Faerie Queene*,

Shakespeare's *King Lear*, Drayton's *Poly-Olbion* and Milton's *Comus*, tells us that the river Severn derived its name from a story of marital betrayal and subsequent violent jealousy: Gwendolen, the betrayed wife of Locrine, oldest son of Brutus, legendary founder of Britain, orders that both his lover, Estrildis, and his love-child, Habren (Sabrina, Severn), be drowned in the river (Geoffrey 1963: 29–32). According to Milton, she is revived by nymphs and made goddess of the river, which will carry her name (1969: 134, ll. 824–847 ).

In his researches David found a parallel of sorts with James Brindley, who may well, "despite his Quaker upbringing and otherwise blameless moral track-record",[80] have been the father of Mary Bennet's son, John, "born when he [Brindley] was apparently 'about the navigation'".

These are all thematic elements that can be read—and heard—in the piece. But plots, storylines, proper names and archetypal antagonisms can find their way into any number of narrative forms. I want to end by pointing to David's attention and aural responsiveness to his poetic sources. Just as he had to immerse himself in the sounds of the specific topographical setting, so too he attended to the prosodic sound-worlds that come with two of his principal literary sources: Michael Drayton's *Poly-Olbion*, the first eighteen books of which were published in 1613, and John Milton's *Comus*, the masque first presented in 1634, with music by Henry Lawes, when Milton was only twenty-five. A masque, as adopted by the young Milton, is a performance, with music, in which the text is divided between different voices, somewhere between characters and narrators. A soundwalk is a very different form but in David's hands allows itself some of the same stylised combination of layers, in which the verbal layer is both as naturalised and as worked as the sounds of water, of nearby machines, of walkers talking. He has the attentiveness of a cultural historian and the ear of a musician-writer. He knows what to leave out.

# *Do Not Ignore:*
## *Order-words in domestic and public spaces* [81]

Fig 1: Do Not Ignore

Many, at least in the UK, will recognise the combination of design and wording in Figure 1 and some will do so with a spasm of irritation. For those lucky enough not to recognise it, it is a quotation from and allusion to the kind of Penalty Charge Notice that is issued for a parking offence on a public highway in the UK. Other words in the notice can include "IT IS AN OFFENCE FOR AN UNAUTHORISED PERSON TO REMOVE OR INTERFERE WITH THIS NOTICE". For those on the receiving end this is a threatening and unsettling message, with details of an unwelcome fine almost certainly in the packet. The command in the negative form, DO NOT, usually in the very visible centre of these notices, is not only unsettling; it is also, I find, profoundly unsettled, not to mention authoritarian, as a language game. There is so much missing, which relies on implicit authority to fill it out. It is an order and only authorised persons can issue orders such as these. Who commands? Ignore what? Who is addressed? In practice, these answers are provided by the situation, by the context. Southwark Council in London (for example) commands; the notice itself must not be ignored; the owner or driver of the car is the implied *You*.

At the end of this article I shall offer a few other recent visual texts that I have made that also borrow the design conventions and orders of discourse of signs in public places. Before that I shall look at some examples of sources for works such as this and I shall approach these in the light of the topic of the 2010 ANTI festival—public space—and also of the declared remit of *Esitys*, a name which I am told translates as *performance*.

My visual poems tend to relate to the domains of both writing and (visual) art, but not in any obvious sense to performance. Their licence for access to a journal bearing that name lies, I hope, in the term *performance writing*, which is becoming increasingly familiar now. It is intended to offer at least a triple perspective on performance and the related term, performativity. Firstly, writing and reading are acts and events; they have to be done and to operate through time, just as other "performances" do. Secondly, the doing of reading (I'll leave writing to one side) itself does things to the bodies that read. Thirdly, writing is socially and historically contingent: on the fullest possible context of semiotic behaviour, on social traffic and interchange, on the already-written, on the being-written, on the means of production and reproduction of writing, on the means of dissemination, on who reads, on networks of exchange between readers. No writing or reading can cleanse itself of the pictures it has already seen, the songs and music it has heard, the performed stories it has witnessed. Performance writing, as a term, acknowledges that writing is embedded in almost very aspect of social, cultural and economic life; the literary is only one provenance and affiliation.[82]

Above all, perhaps, I am hoping here that the term *performance writing* will keep together the (common-)sense idea of performance associated with music, dance, theatre or live art with the idea of the *performative* developed by the "ordinary language" philosopher, J.L. Austin (1976). Put at its simplest, acts of language exert a force, some more than others. This widely influential idea was taken up by Deleuze and Guattari in *A*

*Thousand Plateaus* as "order-words":

> Order-words do not concern commands only, but every act that is linked to statements by a "social obligation". (Deleuze 1992: 79)

This allows for the useful double sense of *order* (as a verb): (1) to give an order; and (2) to behave in an orderly (socially responsible) manner. The first will always imply power and authority; the second need not—it is open, perhaps, to co-operative acts of social cohesion, to the necessity for agreed protocols in networked behaviour.

For fifteen years or so I have been particularly interested in the performativity of symbolic objects, especially photographs and cards, in domestic spaces, and have produced texts that are intended to play alongside these. ANTI Festival is particularly concerned with public space, not with the domestic, but contemporary notions of public space seem predicated on the co-existence of private spaces, of spaces with different degrees and types of privacy. These include, I would argue, the willed privacy signalled by the act of reading a book—as against a poster, advertisement or shop-window—in a public place. Does the domestic belong to the order of the "private" or is it a third order, firmly linked to coupledom, family, and the idea of "private life" (with the workplace as a possible fourth)? Within contemporary capitalist societies the home, going back at least to the home-delivery of newspapers, has become the primary receptor site for public address systems. For my purposes what is at stake is the interrelation of these differing orders of space more than their separate identities. What happens when the conventions and protocols of one are dragged across into another, either literally or virtually?

I do not myself live in a city. I live two or three kilometres outside a small town, big enough to have a handful of shops, a post office, four pubs, several places of worship and a one-way traffic system. My nearest neighbours are a five-minute walk away. The road that goes past my house has no name—at least to my knowledge—and yet it is a public highway. That means that anyone can use it but also means that its use is subject to regulation and etiquette. There are only four obvious publicly sited texts within a few metres of my front door, with one of them tucked away in the summer growth of a hedge.[83]

The first example is the name of the house, carved into a stone that is part of the wall. Names make up a significant element in public texts: places, streets, businesses (often also the names of people), buildings. In brief—because this topic of names could get out of hand—names in public places are always performatives, they "do things". In this case, the name on the wall gives a nameable identity and means of reference to a habitation, a unique address for letters and visitors, a way-mark for those passing on, a short-hand for all the associations with the domestic location, a metonym for much more than the building.

The second text is a road sign (Fig 2), a form designed to communicate instantly, with no need for conscious reading, using diagrammatic coding, a simplified pictorialism, and writing only where necessary and, wherever possible in an international code. In this case the written elements are both the number and percentage sign and the assumption of a left-to-right reading to indicate an ascent rather than descent. The red triangle on a flat base is an international convention for a broad category of warning signs. Warnings can be interpreted as commands or instructions but they are often milder and contingent: you are expected to adjust your behaviour in readiness but are not explicitly

Fig 2

ordered to. At one extreme they are indeed orders; at the other they are merely "informative". Public space must contain due warning if only to protect those legally responsible for its order.

The bottom of the slope signalled by the sign is also a sharp bend. The combination of slope and bend has resulted in several accidents over the years, mostly of cars coming downhill in slippery conditions. There is no warning sign from above about either slope or bend. Fig 3 shows the missing bend sign: no word, no equivalent of the "20%" to indicate tightness of curve.[84] In the terminology of C.S. Peirce, the thick line operates iconically, mimicking the curve in the road. The pointed end is at least in part "symbolic" within the same system of terms, relying for its indication

Fig 3

of direction on a widely held—much wider than any one spoken language community—convention; so widely held, indeed, that many would probably think of it too as iconic—though metaphorically so—invoking an arrow and its direction of flight. Various senses of direction and directionality—command and orientation—are in play.

Fig 4 is the third example. It combines the coded diagrammatic and pictorial elements of bright yellow, black triangle, jagged arrow sign for high voltage, and a simplified drawing of a falling (male) body, with two verbal phrases. The first, DANGER OF DEATH, is a warning; the second, KEEP OFF, is a command that follows from the warning and, like Do Not Ignore, the command is silently completed by the position of the notice.[85] There are two other poles in the

Fig 4

privately owned space of my garden, which also carry these warnings and commands. Who is authorised to issue such commands? The authority goes without saying.

The United Kingdom's Department of Transport calls signs that must be obeyed "Regulatory Signs". The Finnish Road Administration has a helpful set of categories: signs regulating priority, prohibitory or restrictive signs, mandatory signs, special regulation signs and informative signs. Buckfastleigh's one-way system requires Fig 5. Again, no word is needed, and the danger of transgressing such a regulation is not spelt out.

Fig 5

The other immediately local example, drawn on to establish something of a typology and also to make the point that no one has to go very far to start "reading" public space even if they live in a remote rural part, is the bunker in Fig 6, placed there last winter by the authority responsible for road safety in the area. The category is that of the label on a container that identifies concealed contents. Even though Grit and Salt are concrete nouns and not proper names, there is some resemblance between this label and signs announcing village names as you enter. An enclosed container must have a means of entry—a lid, a door, a gate, a boundary. The name-plate for the village is not only an endlessly repeatable naming ceremony; it also marks the point of entry and implies a boundary.

Fig 6

Walking northwards, there are no further words to read apart from a two-word house-name until, 200 metres up, there is a cross-roads, always a place for decisions, at least

Fig 7

by strangers; hence the multi-directional signpost, readable from all sides. (Fig 7) These are of course name signs at a distance. Far from operating as commands, they work within the logic of *if-then*: *if* you wish to get to Scorriton, *then* turn right and continue for two miles. Such signs are usually emotionally neutral, not intended to promote desire or fear, though the indications of distance can be either encouraging or disheartening and the brown signs supposedly indicate pleasurable activity. The upright words have no arrow because they point nowhere but to the very spot where they are rooted: a road junction as itself a nameable site.

The next junction in the direction to which a missing board would be pointing also used to have a post, but this, having been buried in the hedge for some time, has been removed. It marked the spot known as Five Oaks. Hockmoor Head is still a "head"—the top of a hill—and that won't change quickly. But there are no longer five obvious oaks at Five Oaks and any stranger looking for Five Oaks should not be literal about it. And it is strangers who need these signs; local inhabitants should know anyway unless they are blow-ins, i.e. stranger-residents. A road sign of this kind, before it says anything, is an official attitude to strangers. It "says"

too, that this is an orderly world: there
is a road "system" in which everywhere
leads rationally to everywhere else and
all positions are marked. You don't
have to ask; you can read the signs.
And it also "says" that a "system" looks
after the "system". Within regulatory
constraints you can even put your own
signs up. Only an *authority* can put
this one up.

Fig 8 introduces the regulatory
category of discretion or exceptionality
and explicitly refers to the notion of
"access", a key term in the regulation of
space and in the determining of what
is and is not public. A modern home,
that human container with lockable doors, is by virtue of convention and
law a place of restricted access. But then so, for practical reasons, is a
narrow road.

Fig 8

These signs, these visual texts, are all in public space, are in full view,
and they—or ones belonging to the same sets—are encountered daily.
They have a clear message, possibly enforceable by law, and must all offer
up their entirely situated meaning and purpose to a single glance, without
ambiguity, suggestiveness, multiple meaning. "Do Not Ignore", for
example, is full of potential ambiguities, suppressed by force of authority
and context.

My own pieces assume a familiarity with these signs and what they
get up to. I can make this assumption with confidence because they are
part of the everyday and belong to a category or instrumental or pragmatic
knowledge that needs to be free from the uncertainties of speculation, of
essays (trials) of thought. And it is for these reasons that I like to make
thought with them. My pieces have not (yet) been designed to be put in
public space. So far they have been in homes and a gallery. What I want
of them is that they should offers ways of thinking—of sensing—across
different *orders* of space; for example, public, domestic, literary, fine art.
And that they should offer themselves at a glance only to invite a second
and third glance, and so on.

On the following page are four related pieces:

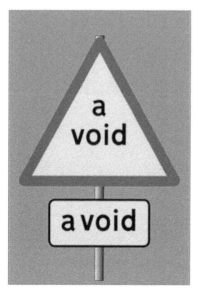

Fig 9

Fig 10

Fig 11

Fig 12

# Making It New Out of Old Hat:
## The Words in Lone Twin [86]

Three Lone Twin performance pieces, each ostensibly shaped around a task: in *On Everest* (1997), the mountain summit has to be reached through a proxy "ascent"; in *Sledge Hammer Songs* (2005), clouds must be produced from local river water; in *Daniel Hit by a Train* (2008), the deaths of fifty-three, who died attempting to rescue others, must be marked. Do these tasks need words? The last almost certainly does. The dead need to be named. But the other two are physical actions. Couldn't they be performed without—or with very few—spoken words? It seems not. All three are full of words. It is the spoken words I want to talk about, so far as possible in their relationship with the whole.[87] Words find their way into Lone Twin performances from recognisable or half-recognisable elsewheres or befores. They have this separate life. There is no need to wait until some character thinks them and means them within a relationship that is also a plot. The strongest relationships that the words in Lone Twin performances have is with other words in the same piece, in a patterning full of repetition that might be thematic, and also with the ways that words are already used out there in the world, and the patterns those have already acquired.

I might have these two relationships the wrong way round. The perfect Lone Twin script might consist entirely of the already-said. Although the already-written does play some part in this, their preference is for the spoken, for what gets said and how. This could be a description of naturalistic dialogue, as in say a Mike Leigh film. That is not their way. They assemble the already-said and put it through variations, developing their own repeatable formats and borrowing freely from existing ones. This is a writing task, and because writing can be read as well as heard I have been *reading* the words for some of Lone Twin performances or projects: *On Everest, Sledge Hammer Songs, Alice Bell* (2006), *Town Crying* (2007) and *Daniel Hit By A Train*.[88]

I have at some time witnessed all of these except *Town Crying* as live events. The only one that I had previously both seen and read was the first, *On Everest*, and this was because a copy of the "paper" which Gregg (Whelan) delivered, while Gary (Winters) walked his lengths of the performance space, was made available, along with a drink, as a way of ending the occasion. Carl Lavery has written very usefully about the business of looking at written texts of live performances, especially in the case of Lone Twin, and places his discussion in relief against the problematic of performance ontology discussed by Peggy Phelan and others (Lavery 2009). I shall side-step most of the delicacies he identifies, grateful for his attention to them. In my case, I never attended Lone Twin events with any thought of writing about them, and made no notes. This means that I was neither "an *analyst* … present at a performance", nor am I "a historian … forced to reconstruct performances from secondary documents and accounts" (Phelan, cited in Lavery 2009: 38; my emphasis). I am not trying to reconstruct anything. I am drawing on something akin to motor-memory, a reactivation by way of the text-of-the-words of a part-remembered performance of being present. The "inter-text" I draw on to do this is somewhere between recollection of the live events and the opportunity to keep revisiting the scripts, whose "liveness" can be reactivated by each visit (written texts may not be "live" but reading is). I find in the reading that I do not always remember the full *mise-en-scène* but I am always brought up against a recall of the spoken words.

Phrases, rhetorical tropes, evoked word games, rhymes, and songs— these all had their life before they entered a Lone Twin performance. They are old friends. How nice to hear them again. And then each time they are repeated there is some twist in their familiarity, in a game that builds up expectation of further returns and turns. The compulsion to repeat is a characteristic of their textual composition and performance style; it is ludic and sociable rather than pathological. In this way, any unit of the text can begin to have a life outside of any one specific utterance, setting up expectation that it will be back in some form or other. This taps into a shared pleasure in repetition that is fundamental to sociality and underlies so many cultural forms.

As an example, the phrase "in the beginning" occurs twenty-five times in the script of *Sledge Hammer Songs*, each time followed by a verb phrase in the present tense. Here are the first six examples, in four excerpts.

> In the beginning Gary—it is Gary with the beard, he is Gary The Beard—he is Gary The Beard too much, that is his failing; on the other hand I am Gregg Not The Beard, this is not a failing.

In the beginning she is her own woman, she is her own man, she is her own horse. She has a hole in her side and takes on water.

In the beginning it is so cold she throws boiling water into the air and it falls back down as snow. In the beginning it is so cold she throws some sticks into the air and they fall back down as iPods.

In the beginning he is his own man, he is his own woman, he is his own horse, he is his own Justin Timberlake. In the beginning he is a local person.

The first of these comes early enough in the performance for the opening words, delivered "outside" by Gary, still to be echoing: "Gentleman goodnight, ladies good morning to you good people of Ash Wednesday, a Wednesday full of ash. It ends here, let this be a brilliant end." The "performance" may be beginning but this beginning coincides with the ending of part of the task. Gary has been building up body heat and taking in local water and is ready to make a cloud: Gregg's end, Gary's beginning.

"In the beginning" might be the most familiar phrase from the King James Bible, occurring in two very significant contexts. It inaugurates the Old Testament: "In the beginning God created the Heaven, and the Earth" (Genesis, 1.1); and in the New Testament it opens John's Gospel: "In the beginning was the Word, & the Word was with God, and the Word was God" (John, 1.1). "In the beginning God...", "in the beginning ... word", "In the beginning Gary..." There is bathos there already. In both biblical examples, the beginning is in the past (with a difference between a completed act of creation [past perfect] and an indeterminate duration of pastness). This is the past tense of story telling ("once upon a time") or of historical explanation. The present tense tends to belong to artifice (it is not *really* the now; this is a pretend now), telecommunication ("I'm on the train"), or the immediacy of gathering and ceremony, the here and now of effective ritual ("We are gathered together here"). It is the tense of greeting, of being together, of toasting, of parting, of how things are ("it's brilliant over here, the air is cool, the sky is black and there are glasses of wine, there is no trouble, no bother, no regret and no bad language" (*Sledge Hammer Songs*). It is also used in what is sometimes called the present habitual, to deal with repeated acts, as in, "I walk to work."

Although tempted, I am not going to link all this with the references to Ash Wednesday and start claiming that this is demotic Eliot,[89] or even some kind of Cloud-man theogony. Ash Wednesday is there because the script I have was the one prepared for a performance that took place on Ash Wednesday 2003 in Leeds, and Lone Twin like to attach a performance to its time and place. There is an "in the beginning" game that is pleasurable enough without specialist scriptural or literary knowledge. The phrase is already embedded and the idea of "the beginning" already suggestive. The beginning of what? "In the beginning" is where *everything* starts. And, there, I found myself using the present tense. The beginning is now. But I am more interested in the games of variation that the phrase seems to provoke.

Take the second and fourth excerpts from *Sledge Hammer Songs* above. There is a simple variation of pronoun (from "she" to "he"), with a consequent reversal of sequence of two phrases. Each includes "horse" and in between the two, "horse", especially "female horse", has become a motif. And then the second, following the principle of repeat-and-add word games,[90] adds "his own Justin Timberlake', a name that is repeated elsewhere, once in the plural—as though Justin Timberlake is multiple, which is to say repeatable—and often as "The Justin Timberlake", as though this were a special social role, like "the priest" or "The Lord Chief Justice".

I shall not follow all the connections in detail. Almost every phrase in the quoted excerpts is a unit for repetition and cumulation, which becomes part of the weave of the spoken text. It does not matter who says what. "In the beginning" is not the only phrase that comes in with a strong separate life. The same can be said for "he is his own man", although its authority is very different. Phrases like this make up the citational relay of everyday exchange. When they are being used in completely familiar contexts, there is nothing *other* or resistant about them at all. When their situational or rhetorical context is changed, if only through repetition and variation, they become strange, are *encountered*.

For example, the word "encounter" contains "counter", in its sense of "against", but because of the importance of counting and recounting (as in story telling) in Lone Twin, I can't help hearing these other meanings too, and the way they jostle each other.[91] En-counter: in-against; coming up against. I want to get at a paradox: that I am already inside what it is that I come up against in Lone Twin's repetitions. I am inside them precisely because they are so familiar; the familiarity is benign but then so is the estrangement, much like rhyme in popular forms of poetry. The way Lone Twin perform these repetitions captures this sense of benign strangeness. The words are not utterances from within the supposed beings of their personae, but things outside them. They can speak text as though they were reading, and seem quite innocent of it; different personae can make almost identical speeches.

This is one reason why their texts can be read as *writing*, and have a self-sufficiency on the page which is beyond the instrumental purpose of providing notation for a performance or a mnemonic method for remembering one.

It is not surprising then that the words in performance can also be *heard* as writing. The performance style is one that relays the text without subsuming it into characterisation. Actors are not supposed to read their words. But there are other modes of performance, including ceremonial ones, which also foreground a material text as providing the occasion with its authority. These performances sometimes rely on an authorised relationship between reader and text, possibly involving an element of the setting and its equipment or furnishings (the lectern is an obvious example). In these modes, the primary authority lies with the *it is written* of the text, which should usually be read exactly *as* it is written, without insertion of the person(ality) of the reader. Examples might include religion's books, oaths, news, election results, and kinds of poetry.[92] Each has at least one appropriate register of delivery: modes of declamation or priestly intonation, for example. In contrast, and closer to Lone Twin, I think of the late Humphrey Lyttelton in his role as chair of the radio game *I'm Sorry I Haven't a Clue*, maintaining a disdainful arm's length from the "it says here" of the "chairman's script".[93] Disdain, whose mode is often sarcasm, is not part of Lone Twin's tonal palette. But a form of distancing is, one that reminds everyone present that the text has its separate life. No doubt *Town Crying*, with its robes, round red podium, and distributed broadsheets, provided one of the clearest examples of what I am trying to get at. More familiar in Lone Twin is the workaday clipboard. In these loud-reading modes, it is usually a role that speaks, not a character. In *Daniel Hit By A Train*, for instance, it is Geoffrey the priest, not Geoffrey who happens to be a priest. The role itself has necessarily to be performed.[94]

In this sense, Lone Twin, including Lone Twin Theatre Company, perform reading. In some cases, this is explicit. *On Everest*, for example, is the performance of "a lecture", complete with footnotes. Gregg both reads and performs reading, performs being the lecturer who reads (a lecture, the *OED* tells us, is "the action of reading aloud" [OED 1989, Def. 3]). He performs, in other words, a specific role of reading. Even where the reading is not explicit, there is something about Lone Twin's dead-pan mode of speech-delivery that plays with the solemnity of *it is written*.

### First triangle

Let me try out a diagram, a triangle, with the following three intersections: (a) performers; (b) personae (or parts adopted by performers); and (c) words spoken. It is a triangle (rather than a list of three) because all three are both joined to and separated from each other. I have not drawn it, because it can come in all sorts of triangular shapes.

In a style of performance that eschews impersonation or mimicry, a performer is, minimally, a physical appearance, carrying unavoidable genetic, social, and cultural inscriptions (including age, sex, and so on), and any qualities of movement and voice that appear also to be givens. In a style of performance that conflates performer with persona, these givens will be subjected to subtle modulations, including forms of caricature, which play up what seems already to be there.

### Second triangle

As this applies to words spoken in performance, "persona" is the effect of these modulations, in the following respects: (d) from the words a performer speaks; (e) from the words spoken to her, about her, or in her presence; and (f) from the disposition—physical, tonal—she displays towards the words she speaks, receives or overhears. This last point very much includes direction of address and attention (or lack of attention).

### Third triangle

The conventions of dialogue in naturalistic drama establish a closed circuit for spoken exchange as between characters on stage and screen. In Lone Twin duo pieces dialogue is not significant,[95] and there is always another triangle: "Gary" (g) and "Gregg" (h) form two points and "audience" (i) the third. "Audience" is a convenient holding term that fits some pieces better than others because Lone Twin can treat audience—always with immense courtesy—as a stand-in for other forms of social or public gathering, or even as participants, not stand-ins at all. The performers address each other, or one of them can address the audience, or they can do so together in a collusive public address, like a pair of television presenters facing outwards from the same sofa.

Let me try some of this out on some examples. In *On Everest*, "Gary", who is already physically present and walking his lengths, is introduced *verbally* in "Gregg's" preamble to his "paper", in the following manner: "But with time pressing on and with oxygen precious, I'll make a start on today's paper while Gary Winters very kindly continues on our five-and-a-half mile ascent to the summit of Mount Everest. Thank you, Gary."

Two points. First, something about "Gary" is brought into being by this simple mode of reference and address. Second, an audience is being addressed as though its members have come to hear an illustrated lecture on climbing Everest rather than (as well as) a performance by Lone Twin. As addressed, the audience has been interpellated[96] through repeated use of the grammatical second person ("Good afternoon and thank you all very much for coming here"), but also treated from the beginning as participating in a collective first person ("I appreciate that we have, under difficult circumstances, all come a long way to be here").[97] These are the first moments of their first piece as Lone Twin and they have set up an audience-as-performer/audience-as-persona oscillation. The audience can only *receive* words here—etiquette prevents a reply—but this is quite enough for a playful interpellation to take place into that split role.

Of course, with "Thank you, Gary", Gary's presence is acknowledged in the second person. "Thank you, Gary" is exactly one of those very familiar protocols that Lone Twin enjoy. The performance of gratitude is fundamental in social life and the way it is performed may always in part also be a performance of power relations. This one is the specific "thank you" with which a lecturer graces an assistant in public or a newscaster thanks the weather reporter—"Thank you, Matt."

This switching between third-person references and second person direct address continues, the careful courtesies of the talkative "Gregg" silently subsumed by "Gary" except when he is asked to endorse a view, or "kindly" to read the quotations and footnotes, or "help with the mathematics". Gregg's initial persona emerges through his own talk; Gary's, at this point, emerges through his benign passivity to the talk that projects on to him while he gets on with what he has to do, apparently just as serious about this project as "Gregg".

This kind of talking and not-talking establishes a dual persona that is open for variation in later pieces. Key to this is mutual address by name and the observance of elaborate social courtesies.[98] The dual persona includes a sense of the long-term friendship of co-workers, colluders (that is, co-players), who have prepared something for us.

My next examples are from the two Lone Twin Theatre pieces, in which the dual Lone Twin persona cannot be mediated by Gregg Whelan and Gary Winters as performers, and any confusion between performer/ persona now applies to a larger cast that includes women and men. At one point in *Alice Bell*, Cynthia Whelan, clearly not a man, not eighteen, and not wearing a uniform, speaks these lines: "I'm Alice's brother—I'm an 18 year old man and I'm in the police force—I'm standing here in my police officer's uniform."

Any other performer in the piece could deliver these lines; in each case, the performance effect would be different.[99] This is the same present tense of artifice that I referred to above, and which puts the opening between the "I" who speaks and the "I" represented as speaking on display, quite without subterfuge. In *Daniel Hit By A Train*, a cast of five recites and performs the fifty-three different acts of heroism. This is in large part a ceremony of naming. Nina Tecklenburg proclaims:

> I do, I see the river
> My name is Geoffrey, I am the priest
> I see the river and I see a man in it
> I do not know this man
> I try to save him
> We both drown
> This is me, in the river

When Nina says "I do, I see the river", she is answering a question that has been given ritual status by an accompanying drum beat: "Who sees the river?" "I do" is the ritual and echoic answer. Her very short speech contains only two words that are more than one syllable, "Geoffrey" and "river" ("river" appears three times). It is made up of what sound like nine very short sentences. All except one are single clauses and the exception has two simple clauses joined by an "and". Seven of the clauses start with "I". The "I" is Geoffrey the priest, not Nina. This is all we know about Geoffrey. "My name is Geoffrey. I am the priest." Geoffrey is not "a priest"; he is "the priest", the definite article implying a familiarity of bonded name and role within an invoked community. There is not a single adjective or adverb in the excerpt. The brevity of the clauses and the composition by simple clauses/sentences sets up a repetitive rhythm that works with the clausal units rather than at the level of a metric "foot". This is an extreme form of parataxis.

I assume that mine is not the only ear in the house that has this rhyme in it:

"Who killed Cock Robin?" "I," said the Sparrow,
"With my bow and arrow, I killed Cock Robin."
"Who saw him die?" "I," said the Fly,
"With my little eye, I saw him die."

And what about that kind of playground identification ("I'll be David Beckham"), not far removed from the computer game's "you are …", neither of which requires mimicry? Or the "this is me when I was three" prompted by the album of family photographs? The Cock Robin example offers the repeatable trope of question and answer—"Who did?" … "I did"—, in this case invoking similar tropes in discourses of public, forensic, or judicial inquiry, of public appointment, of marriage.[100] Such formulae are, of course, very popular in stories for very young children and were no doubt put to work by Lone Twin on the children's television programme *Boohbah*.

Not all fifty-three acts of heroism are recounted in this way, although most are. It is an inclusive device. Everyone in the category can be made to fit. I think it could be argued that most forms of story are exclusive: story requires a focus on selected characters. The list, in contrast, can be generous, and can be numbered or not. It needs to be apparent in *Daniel* that there is no selection. There were fifty-three and all will be counted.

These exchanges of words in Lone Twin pieces are verbal dances within a larger choreography. They have little to do with psychological subtlety and a great deal to do with pleasure in rehearsing the socially familiar, in a social "space" that may not be the one being rehearsed. Lone Twin are performers and poets of shared space, often shared public space. These spaces are nameable, and often are named, as the spaces where performances happen, not imaginary spaces within a performance. And these shared spaces are not just topographical or social locales. They are also shared cultural spaces, whose cultural topography has, for example in *Sledge Hammer Songs*, The Bob Dylan, The Bruce Springsteen, The Leonard Cohen, The Suzanne Vega, flowing through them, not to mention all those childhood games.

### Fourth triangle

Lone Twin's writings—their performances—endorse the pleasures of sociality. Their sense of space and sociality is quite specific, I think, positioned as a third point (l) on a triangle in which the first (j) could refer, using a shorthand here, to "private language", to all those discourses of personal life—diaries, letters, lyric poems, novels, TV "dramas"—and the second (k) to "public language", to those discourses knowingly situated in the public sphere—political, legalistic, civic. This third position is "public" in the sense of "in common", not of the *res publica*. Its modes are closer to carnival than to the political forum. Its place is common land (or common streets), and just as much it is the commonality of speaking, of popular rhetoric.

I once heard Ted Berrigan read the following poem, as though he was directing it at the previous reader, pausing for effect at the end of the first line: "It is important to keep old hat / in secret closet" (Berrigan 2007: 351). The poem as a whole catches an ambivalence, a moment of bet-hedging: it is important to *keep* the old hat but just as important to hide it, especially if you are a modernist committed to "make it new" (Pound 1934). Lone Twin seem to take a different view: their pleasure is in making something new out of all the old hat.

# Foot, mouth and ear:
## some thoughts on prosody and performance [101]

> Rhythm is originally the rhythm of the feet.
> Elias Canetti [102]

> & I took flatness as my starting point
> the line made quicker in its shorter pulse
> & slower in its flooded length
> John James [103]

Except for those who out of necessity or choice have trained their toes to do what for most of us the hand does—grasp the pen, tap the keys— what has the foot to do with writing? Even with "performance writing", where the first of the two terms might appear to invite more of the body in? For this set of speculations I start from the suggestiveness of the term *foot* as used in (literary) prosody, where it refers to "a division of verse, consisting of a number of syllables one of which has the ictus or principal stress" (OED, *foot*. n, sense II. 6).[104] My purpose is not to set out a theory or polemic for poetic metre. I want instead to use *foot* and a number of related terms as a way towards considering the reading of page-based poetry as a mode of performance.

Behind me as I do so is a poet's book on performance, Douglas Oliver's *Poetry and Narrative in Performance* (Oliver 1989), which combines waveform and spectrogram analysis of readings with metaphysical speculation about poetic stress or beat. Oliver was preoccupied with *beat* from adolescence until his last writing, the posthumously published, partly autobiographical, *Whisper "Louise"* (Oliver 2005). *Poetry and Narrative in Performance* was shaped for an academic and pedagogic context, whose modes it adopts. Other writings for different contexts reveal the strength and conviction behind the preoccupation. Here, as an example, is a brief passage from his long narrative poem, *Penniless Politics*: [105]

The music begins in each point over again, the beats that unite
the flow of melody into infinitesimal perceptions. And within each beat
the overall form is anticipated; so the past is caught up in the present:
the future breathes in the point. Here is the clue to the decent
founding of politics in a poem: that the future comes alive
now: that the neighborhood is to the world as the moment
is to the whole; unlike the politicos, poets get their world right
if the point and the flow of the whole are united in beats: all alive

now and thrilling with the future. (Oliver 1994: 36)

The poetic *foot* as such was of secondary interest to Oliver, since he saw it as
part of a "rule-governed" and "abstract" approach to poetics, an idealising
and simplifying notion of rhythm that could not be adequate to the task
of delineating the sound world of an actual reading of any given poem.
Rather than *foot*, the word that appears in the quoted passage is "beat"
(three times), and its sense is echoed (and pre-echoed) with "infinitesimal
perceptions", "point" (three times), "moment" and "now" (twice). "Music",
"flow", "melody", "overall form", "whole", are used for the medium which
the beats shape and in which they occur. For Oliver, the play of instant
and flow can give rise to an experience of time in poetry, in which the
*now* of each stress recovers the poem's own past and anticipates its future,
so that instant and whole can co-occur, and, beyond the poem, "get their
world right". For a poet like Oliver the question is both technical and
metaphysical; he wanted to know how and where within a reading of a
poem this experience takes place. Like all time-based artists, poets shape
time through their specific temporal media; in the poet's case the medium
is language, whether experienced through the intonational curves of
phrases or through the pulse of vowels in syllables.

In literary prosody, a *foot* is a rhythmically repeatable component
of utterance that contains, and is therefore more than, a beat. It relates
to syllables and lines rather than to words and sentences. It is not only
repeatable but must be repeated—at least notionally—if it is to be a *foot*,
just as a step must be repeated, even if with variation, to constitute walking
or dancing. Other elements of performed language are repeatable, and can
form part of a network of repetitions that indicates that the "message" is
performing itself more than—or as well as—its apparent ideational or

intersubjective purpose.[106] Rhyme, alliteration, assonance, for example, also work with syllables or parts of syllables.[107] Unlike these others, though, the *foot* doubles as a measuring or counting device, sometimes merely technically, at others with an attentiveness of an ear to the larger senses of measure or proportion required to get both words and world right.

Measurement of uttered language needs to be simple enough to operate at the speed of utterance and possibly to determine it (tempo). The simplest version of a metrical *foot* derives from the supposedly binary properties of its syllables: that they are either "weak" or "strong"; a *foot* must have one "strong" syllable in a patterned relationship with at least one "weak" one. Phonemes operate in a set of differences way beyond this binary pair (over forty in dialects of English) and, according to Duanmu, the number of "actual" syllables is in the thousands (Duanmu 2008: 182–206).[108] Repeating elements from a set of forty or a thousand is obviously very different on the ear from a set of two. At its simplest, weakness and strength can produce a form of alternating current, with weakness corresponding either to short or unstressed, and strength to long or stressed. This doesn't mean, in this simplified conception, that a *foot* can only have two syllables, but it does mean that it can only include two *kinds* of syllables, set up as distinct and with no gradations between, and that a strict and unimaginative adherence to this notion will need to exaggerate differences.[109]

The body operates through a number of obvious binary rhythms that may encourage this simplification: the *lub-dub* of heart-beat, the in-out of breathing, the left-right of walking. I am tempted to add one more, though it is seldom consciously experienced as a rhythm the way the others are: the rapid opening and closing vibrations of the glottis that produce voicing. Breathing and voicing are essential to speech production, whose means are the sounding and shaping of the out-breath. And any utterance has to be negotiated around the punctuating interruption of the in-breath. Depth and tempo of breathing are thus bound to prosody and syntax. Charles Olson in his 'Projective Verse' was most explicit about the connection between breathing and the line in poetry: "And the line comes (I swear it) from the breath, from the breathing of the man who writes, at the moment that he writes…" (Olson 1960: 389–90).

And what of the feet in their standing, walking, running, stepping, leaping, hopping, skipping, dancing and marching, all also bound in their energy and tempo to breathing and heart-rate? A step involves two feet; a hop, one. Three is not an option. Left, right. Or, "LEFT, LEFT, LEFT-right-LEFT", a basic chant used to keep marchers in time. The five monosyllabic words must coincide with the pivoting of the relevant foot, so two—or three—"rights" are obviously missing. Whether there are two or three depends on whether the "line", having started on the left foot, ends on the right, or whether it ends on "LEFT" and the missing "right" is lost in a "line-break". There is a simple repeatable pattern of seven (or eight) beats with a clear beginning and end. As soon as you end you begin again.[110] This is the equivalent of a line in written poetry, something that *returns* you just as syntax and meaning may be carrying you forward. The alternation of strong and weak beats is accentuated by the omission of all but one of the "rights" because, although the syllable may be omitted, the beat can't be: the right foot still has to come down in time, and responsibility for this is given over to the momentum of the moving and sounding body, introducing an important ambiguity about which of the two operations is keeping time for the other. Variation within the repetition no doubt helps produce a sense of pattern, of repeatability.

So here we have a line of four *feet* (strong-weak: ˉ ˘) and there is rhythmic repeatability at two levels: *foot* and line. Though there is accentual difference (stressed / less stressed), there cannot be a difference in the measure of the time within which each beat falls if the marching pace is to remain even. A repeated "LEFT-RIGHT, LEFT-RIGHT" does not offer a line, is an order rather than a chant, and is quickly fatiguing.

Now this is a very simple rhythm, to match the simplicity of the synchronised stepping. It uses only two words, which belong to a binary pair, and which are used as imperatives even though, technically, they are not verbs. A sentence consisting only of imperative verbs is simple and is deictic: it relies on the co-presence of the chanters in a unified activity so that there is no need to add "foot" to the order or to specify the implied "you". It is an example of a collective self-imperative, inviting pleasurable participation in self-ordering.[111]

This poetic *foot* (ˉ ˘) is known as a trochee, or choree. It is the inverse of the familiar iambic, which would require "right-LEFT" or "left-RIGHT" (˘ˉ). The Greek etymology for trochee identifies this as a "running" or a "tripping" rhythm, and choree relates to chorus and thereby to dance, so both terms imply actions of the feet.[112] In contrast, iamb derives from a Greek word meaning to "assail (in words)" and the OED has this note: "The iambic rhythm, as being closest to that of ordinary speech, was employed in Greek and Latin as the common metre of dialogue; its earliest known use is as a vehicle of invective and satire".

If "right" and "left" occupy the same duration, this is achieved by different means, as graphic representations of the sound or of the voicing patterns (switching between voiced and unvoiced sounds), such as those undertaken by Oliver, would show.[113] The initial sounds (onsets)—*l, r*— of both syllables are produced through closely related articulations of mouth and breath and are both "liquid continuants". An effect of this "continuation" is to join rather than separate onset and nucleus (vowel), *le, righ*. Conventionally, the *e* of left is "short" and the *igh* of right is "long". However, although both syllables apparently end with the same phoneme, *t*, one that stops the breath, left has an *f* on the way to the *t*. The *f* hisses breath between upper teeth and lower lip and so is another continuant, this time a fricative, and this time unvoiced—the glottis stops vibrating to articulate *f* and it does not restart for the *t*. Repeating "left" puts into play this other alternation between voiced and unvoiced, regarded by Oliver as a significant aspect of prosody. Fig 1 is a screen clip, using Audacity software, of one "line" of the chant, with the same recording represented as waveform—"the amplitude of the audio over time"—on the top row and as a sound spectrum at the bottom. In the spectrum version, high

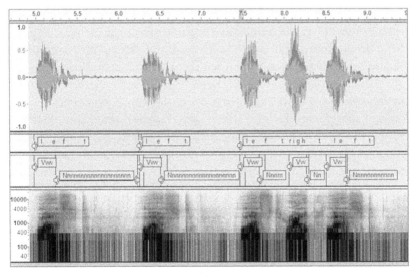

Fig 1

frequencies are towards the top and, crudely, the darker the louder. The vowels—always voiced—are loud and have the broadest frequency range; the voiced consonants are less loud and unvoiced consonants vary: fricatives and sibilants can be loud, while plosives like *t* do not rely on loudness for their percussive effect. The labels containing "Vn" and "Nn" show the alternation of voicing and non-voicing (including gaps).

What these representations cannot show, at least to an amateur such as myself, is what exactly is happening in the throat and mouth, exactly what re-shaping of the mouth cavity, what movements of lips and tongue, for example in getting from *f* to *t*—from upper teeth on lower lip to front of tongue up against front palate, just behind the teeth (in my case). What the software can show, though not all of this is easy to read off a still image, is duration of sound and gap, and their alternations. The "LEFT-right-LEFT" sequence, to the right of the figure, shows a small gap in both syllables before the *t* and that the *t* is more marked at the end of "left" than of "right". I believe that these two gaps sound very differently on the ear and feel different in the mouth (and don't careful listeners feel the sounds of speech in their own mouth?). In the case of "right", apparently hitting the *t* straight out of the vowel, my lips hardly need to change but my tongue needs time to come up against the front palate to stop the breath. In the case of "left", something vowel-like, though unvoiced, occurs between *f* and *t*. Upper teeth have to let the lower lip go, momentarily releasing the hissing breath before the tongue moves into its stop position. Treat the above not as description but as performance instructions. Repeat several times. Notice your mouth movements and listen to the *phht* sound, and also to the sound after the *t* when the stopped breath is released in a little play of tension/release. Using sound-editing software to isolate this tiny sequence of sounds and then playing them in a loop produces an unmistakably pump-like beat. These lips, teeth and tongue movements are, together with the sound they make, particularly pleasurable: *phht!* Perhaps not always uncomplicatedly pleasurable; perhaps, slowed down, deflating:

> A glow of light that wavers and collapses
> In a *phttt* of forgiving what's indifferent to it  (Riley 2000: 98)

Or what of this, from Hopkins, a poet with an explicit interest in stress?

> I am soft sift
> In an hourglass—at the wall
> Fast, but mined with a motion, a drift,
> (Hopkins 1964: 13)

In three lines there are three *ft*s, with a sonically related *st* ("fast") pulling in all the *s* sounds

If *left* and *right* are both divided into two as (1) merged onset and vowel nucleus and (2) consonantal coda, then *le*, with its short vowel, is indeed slightly shorter than *rhi*, but *ft* is considerably longer than *t*, with the effect that the sounding of left takes more time than the sounding of right.

Except in some frenetic parade-ground drill, marchers are not going to turn at the end of every line of the chant. If they did, it might begin to look like dance. And yet the OED's sense 23.e. for *line* 2. n, has this: "The portion of metrical composition which is usually written in one line: a verse'; and for the etymology of *verse*, n. this: "*versus* a line or row, spec. a line of writing (so named from turning to begin another line)". Within contemporary western writing systems we don't *turn* at the end of a line so much as *return* to the default margin or to one set for tabulation of information, say, or as prosodic notation.[114] This return-to-start either takes time or appears to. In poems this between-the-lines time, always anticipated, is a time-space, often, of ambivalence, where different decisions will have different consequences for writer and reader alike.

A Greek word for turning is strophe (στροφη). An etymological note in the OED's entry tells us that "originally the word… was applied to the movement of the chorus from right to left and [antistrophe], counter-turn, to its returning movement". It is plausible to speculate on a genealogy that traces the words—*foot*, strophe, verse, line—from dance steps timed to poetic metre (put it the other way round, by all means), in the context of larger ritual or dramatic performance, to lines stepping (tripping?) and returning across pages (or screens).[115]

In going further into the sound shapes of this very crude example, chosen because of its obvious relation to bodily feet and regular beat, I have had

recourse to some of the other prosodic features that, according to Oliver, contribute to the perception of beat or stress. Missing have been longer suprasegmental features such as intonation contours and syntax, and any subtleties of emotion and meaning, all of which even three lines from Hopkins can suggest, but which I won't follow on this occasion. I want instead to revisit the term *performance*, which I have been using until now with minimal comment. Here is the definition in Oliver's Glossary:

> **Performance** The active experience on individual occasions of creating or reading (silently or aloud) poetry or narrative fiction. As opposed to the general governing of poetic and other fictional texts by rules or generalisations about structures not specific to a single performance [...]. (Oliver 1989: xviii)

As he makes clear early in the book, this definition assumes the pairing of performance with competence, as posited in generative linguistics; and he insists on attending to the messy specificity of single performances.[116] Reader and poem both have "competence", though of a different order. Let's say that a reader has a systemic repertoire of performance judgements, knowledge and skills that can be brought to a poem; and that a poem is a network of performance potentials, running from the obvious to the undecideable. Different judgements, applied skilfully, will release different potentials, some of which just won't "work". Indecision is likeliest at moments of prosodic or syntactical ambivalence in a poem, especially where these coincide. It is easier to manage alternatives in silent reading, perhaps because the lack of external pressure, other than from the poem, can make it feel that there is time, even if at great speed, as though steering out of a skid, to change direction; or even to imagine hearing two versions simultaneously.[117] For example, are those Hopkins lines end-stopped despite the continuity of the syntax? As soon as vocalisation comes into play, a decision has to be made, perhaps in troubled awareness of the excluded options. Are there performance solutions that can catch such undecideability? Or is the quiver of hesitation, that takes place while deciding, enough? And it is not as though poets are safe from these problems in reading their own poems.[118]

In this context I am beginning to use "performance" as a generic term for a range of performance practices rather than as the conceptual other of competence. The question, with no expectation of a singular answer, can become: within a typology of performance modes, what is specific to reading? Or it could be pursued diachronically: is there a genealogy for this extraordinary mode of often solitary performance, which bears traces of song and movement, of story-telling and of communal remembering and is mistakable sometimes for modes of individual prayer? Etymology has suggested one possible line out of early Greek ritual and drama, implying a dissociation of forms of literary writing from an earlier matrix of multi-modal public ritual or performance, to the point where the dissociated form arrives at the potentially privatised and commodified space of the pages of widely distributed books. Many other writing practices manifestly retain or transform their embeddedness, but this specific literary mode that Oliver studied, and that could be called page-performance, is of its nature dual: both the silence of the text within the solitude this produces and its vocalised performance with or for others. The written score is paramount, and it has this in common with those musical practices in which scores are part of the *mise-en-scène*, and those theatrical practices in which a written score, though kept out of sight, must be followed to the letter.[119]

Oliver starts his Preface with this: "No satisfactory way has yet been developed of teaching people to hear the music of poetry" (Oliver 1989: xi). I hear the stress on "hear" (though it could also be on "music") and this suggests that the main performance modality for poetry is a kind of listening that takes place through actual or imagined sounding. Years before (1602), in his 'Obseruations in the Art of English Poesy', Campion, both poet and musician, had pronounced that "the eare is a rational sence, and a chiefe iudge of proportion" (Campion 1966: 36), and more recently and well known to Oliver, Charles Olson:

> Let me put it baldly. The two halves are:
> the HEAD, by way of the EAR, to the SYLLABLE
> the HEART, by way of the BREATH, to the LINE
> (Olson 1960: 390)

In the act of writing, hearing can be a listening *out for* and then of listening *to* the writing in its becoming; in reading, it is an act of making properly audible the soundedness latent in a given text. In the same sense that musician-performers interpret scores when they play them, this hearing is necessarily interpretative, without the need for supplementary commentary. Without the performance of reading, a text is no more than a potentiality; even to remember it is to produce a kind of performance at a distance. A reader adopts a performance mode in expectation of generic textual behaviour, laid down by prior experience. This mode may appear inappropriate to another listener, whose performance draws on a different competence set. A listening reading attempts to uncover a virtuality that is proper to the poem. In this very specific mode that I am trying to sketch, the writing is not left behind in the transformation of performance because it is the writing itself that is being performed: performed writing as writing that sounds. Very few contemporary page-based poets read from memory: the material text is part of the performance.

This soundedness is specific to any one instance. Where reading is performed audibly, an actual voice (at least one) provides a sounding. When reading silently, a voice (at least one) is imagined. This may be the reader's own; it may be the poet's remembered or imagined voice; it may also be a kind of generic "poet" voice: some voice of authority that has established how poems should be read; and some find the voice of a "character" in the text, which leads to dramatization. For others—and among these I have in mind Adriana Cavarero in her return to Kristeva's "chora" or "semiotic"—voice is not person so much as singular and sexed "body":

> Unlike thought, which tends to reside in the immaterial other world of ideas, speech is always a question of bodies, filled with drives, desires, and blood. The voice vibrates, the tongue moves. Wet membranes and taste buds are mixed up with the flavor of the tones. (Cavarero 2005: 134)

## Coda

Although the simple marching chant served other purposes, it is obviously not an example of the dual mode I have been trying to sketch. I want to end, without further commentary, with a few lines that are, from Carol Watts:

She sings. Flesh mounts up, volumes
of hot outpouring. Basalt cools in tall columns. Suddenly
there is a great surf, in rooms with distant ceilings.
Every listening ear finds itself inside the crashing. Is the
chance of exchange not quite extinguished.

(Watts 2011: 33)

# Glosses
## on and for Performance Writing

# Performance Writing: a Lexicon Entry [120]

PERFORMANCE WRITING seems to be used within three broad senses:

1 as a convenient generic term for the production of scripts or script-like texts, including play-texts and film scripts: writing for performance
2 to refer to a field of practice and enquiry in which both words are seen as in a necessarily troublesome but productive relationship with each other
3 the writing of evaluative reports on the "performance" of employees (Drewry 2003 [1989]).

I shall concentrate on 2.

The term *performance writing* almost certainly emerged in a pedagogic context as a means of identifying, naming and developing a field of study, practice and research that was open to textual practices across the arts domains, not just the literary ("creative writing") or the theatrical ("playwriting"). It was very quickly adopted as a helpful designation for modes of writing that combined and crossed different arts disciplines and discourses. These modes have included ones that relate to poetry, very much including visual and sonic poetry, book art, web-writing, performance art (live writing), sited and installed writing. The compositional strategies employed in *performance writing* were seen as drawing on one or more of visual art, performance (studies) and music, in addition to literary and dramatic page-based practices.

Far from being a precise *term* intended to describe, prescribe and proscribe specific modes, *performance writing* was meant to act also as a *name* for a constellation of existing and potential practices just then coming into view. The view was as important as the practices.

Even the grammatical status of the two words in the term is undecided. (i) A noun of action or quality (*performance*) behaves as an adjective that modifies the verbal noun (or gerund) (*writing*) that follows it. (ii) Two nouns stand side by side in dialogic proximity, perhaps with the ghost of an "and" between them or an elided "in the context of" that could work in either direction (*performance* in the context of *writing*; *writing* in the context of *performance*). There is decidedly no fixed preposition between the words such as an instrumental "for" (writing *for* performance). Other prepositions (or prepositional phrases) may hover in readiness, sometimes inviting an inversion of the noun order: *in, as, from, about, towards, in parallel with.* (iii) There is even just the possibility of hearing *performance* as a noun followed by *writing* as a present participle: performance in the process of writing.

Each of the two component terms had provided topic for argument in the second half of the twentieth century. These arguments drew on philosophy, linguistics, anthropology and sociology and were taken up in the theoretical activities around literature, visual art and performance studies. The arguments were in no way calmed or resolved—nor were they intended to be—by bringing the terms together.

Each term can appear to refer empirically to significant categories of cultural behaviour: activities unproblematically ("everybody knows") describable as *performing* and *writing*. In these terms, within the conventional evolutionary model of cultural development, performance is seen as predating "literacy" and surviving in a modified form beside it. Each category of behaviour so understood is open to conflicting understandings as either second order or first order. As second order, "performance" can be understood as akin to re-presentation—something that happens anyway can be "performed", simulated or represented; likewise writing can be thought as a representation of speech.

In contrast, both terms, following, say, Victor Turner, J.L. Austin, Erving Goffman and Jacques Derrida, can be thought of as anthropologically fundamental: the modalities of social being have to be *performed*, even perhaps in relation to what could be seen as a collective script; and cultural memory—necessary for transmission—requires a *trace*, that is, a writing.

Two variant senses of the term "performative" encapsulate this difference: "of or pertaining to performance" in a broad sense and "designating or pertaining to an utterance that *effects an action* by being spoken or written or by means of which the speaker performs a particular act" (OED, my italics).

By shifting the angle of attention, each component term can be seen as a subset of the other. *Writing*—as process—can be thought of as a performance, and can deliberately be performed—that is, played up for witnesses or other participants. The same is true of any act or event of reading (or other form of activation of text for which the term reading is inappropriate). And whether *performance* is itself a trace-making (or a tracing of an underlying "script") or is a unique, unrepeatable and unrepresentable event, moving always into its own death, has been at the heart of debates about presence and liveness.

*Performance writing* was constituted as an approach to writing practices knowingly situated within these debates. Put simply: what is it to write with the question of performance in play? What is it to perform in the face of questions about writing?

## History

The first occurrence of the term that I am aware of was in a course document for an undergraduate degree in Theatre at Dartington College of Arts, prepared for validation in 1987.[121] In this context it was being used, I believe, to invoke processes and forms of writing for and in relation to Theatre for which the term playwriting would be too specific and restricting, (i) because "play" seemed an inappropriate term for the performance mode intended and/or because "playwriting" implies a sequence and hierarchy in which script comes first and is subsequently (more or less) fixed and performance (more or less) variable in relation to the fixity of the script; and (ii) because this kind of writing could be inseparable from a collaborative process of developing or devising a performance, in which there might never be a script or a script might emerge at the end of the process.

In this specific context of "theatre", the term was deliberately invoking plural relations between processes of writing and processes of performing. A performance process that might have (at least) two outcomes—a performance event and a written text—prepares the ground for an openness to a plurality of writings, for an active engagement with *genre* as a compositional variable and for the variable output machine that is the computer.

Parallel ideas—though not yet the term—were very much in play in visual arts. All of these ideas were taken up a few years later (1992–1993) in the planning of an undergraduate writing degree at Dartington by a group that included writers with a literary background but also theatre-makers, musicians, visual performers. The proposed course title was initially to be *performance writings*, the plural intended to indicate the plurality of modes. The change was intended to avoid a positivist implication that these various writing practices could, in their plurality, already be named. There was instead to be the singular name of a field of questions or provocations in which plural practices could indeed be found to have their place.

The name was dropped as an undergraduate course title as part of a review of undergraduate work in 2002–2003 largely because of the way that undergraduate directory searches worked at the time but was retained for postgraduate work and as a frame of reference for research. Since its inception at Dartington the term has been adopted for modules or courses at a number of other institutions, usually for Masters work,[122] has provided the main title for two symposia,[123] was the topic of a feature in a performance journal (Sumner 1999), is used by arts venues to identify a mode of event,[124] is increasingly a term in critical writing.[125]

## A gloss on related terms

*Writing* as potentially inclusive of any composed *trace,* without any expectation that this trace need be confined to ink on paper or to alphabetic letter forms.

And yet any *act of writing* as necessarily specific in terms of, at least: *the writing system* adopted; the writing and "reading" *environment,* with its modes of production and participation, that rely on writing *technologies* (objects, materials, equipment, procedures, behaviours, protocols); on networks and organizations; on formal conventions with their implicit or explicit *poetics*; on social contexts of production and exchange;

*Text* as actual or potential (multiple) event (even if quotidian micro-event); as situated in social space; as having always the potential to be ambient (architectural, spatial and hence proprioceptive, visual, sonic, tactile); as already ubiquitous in immediate and mediated forms;

*Rhetoric* as a poetics of live text, a long-established discourse about composing speaking (speaking as writing).

SEE
Bergvall, Caroline (1996) 'What do we mean by Performance Writing'. http://www.carolinebergvall.com/content/text/BERGVALL-KEYNOTE.pdf. (accessed 22.12.2012)
Bergvall, Caroline (2005) *Fig,* Great Wilbraham, Cambridgeshire UK: Salt Publishing.

Drewry, Douglas (2003 [1989]) *The Definitive Performance Writing Guide*, Professional Management Spectrum Inc.

Hugill, Piers (2006) 'Love and Grammar', a review of *Fig* (Bergvall 2005) and *Via: Poems 1994–2004* (Bergvall 2005a). Jacket No 31, October, <http: //jacketmagazine.com/31/hugill-bergvall.html>

Lopez, Tony (2006) 'Poetry and Performance' in *Meaning Performance: Essays on Poetry* (Great Wilbraham, Cambridgeshire UK: Salt Publishing), pp. 73–88.

Milne, Drew (1999) 'A Veritable Dollmine', review of *Goan Atom 1, Jets-Poupee* (Bergvall, Caroline [1999], Cambridge: Rempress) in Keston Sutherland (ed.), *Quid*, Issue 4 (undated), pp. 6–8. Also at <http://www.barquepress.com/quid4.pdf>

Sheppard, Robert (2001) 'The Performing and the Performed: Performance Writing and Performative Reading', *How2* Vol. 1, No. 6. Also at http://www.asu.edu/pipercwcenter/how2journal/archive/online_archive/v1_6_2001/current/in-conference/sheppard.html_ (accessed 7.10.2012).

Sumner, Alaric (feature ed.) (1999) 'Writing and Performance', in Bonnie Maranca and Gautam Dasgupta (eds), *PAJ: A Journal of Performance and Art* (Vol. 21, No. 1). January 1999 (includes Ric Allsopp, Caroline Bergvall, cris cheek, Carlyle Reedy and Alaric Sumner), p.61.

# A Glossary for Performance Writing [126]

*Italicised words in the texts have their own entries. The list is arranged alphabetically.*

*archive*
There has been considerable interest in recent decades in art which takes on a responsibility for social or public memory. The "arch" part of the word implies that this record was an official government one. What is remembered? Who by? How is it expressed and shaped? Where is it to be found (an archive is always also a *site*). The term is often used in an expanded sense to include, for example, the body as an archive.

*assemblage*
This term refers to an approach to writing as a process of selecting and assembling (in contrast to one of "expressing"). It relates to collage in fine art practice and to montage in film making. Writings can be made by re-assembling what has already been written.

*composition*
In a performance arts environment composition is the partner and other of *performance*. At its simplest, composition is the designing, production and placing together of parts within a sense of a larger whole that they will combine to make. A distinction can be made between concentrating on *texture* and *structure*: to compose as a writer is to write within a sense of structure. The parts that make up wholes may themselves have parts, may be smaller structures within the larger structure. It can be argued that the sense of whole, which also forms the expectations of "*readers*", always relates to *genre*.

*context*
It is helpful to think of this term as one of a triplet together with *text* and *intertext*. Writers produce texts, which draw on and relate to other "texts" (*intertextual*), and which are always unavoidably surrounded and

pervaded by worlds beyond them (*context*). These are the worlds they refer to, the historical, economic, social and *cultural* worlds in which they were produced and (often very different) in which they are distributed, placed and witnessed.

Context can be treated as physical, architectural or geographical—as in attention to *site*—and as more abstractly *cultural*, as for example in the way a text relates to gender (without the author necessarily being aware of it).

### culture

This is perhaps the most debated of all the terms in this glossary. It is used here in the broad sense it has developed within cultural studies or cultural theories. At its broadest, culture is a name for those aspects of all human activity which are to do with the establishing, maintaining and contesting of values and meanings. Many have argued that *language* is the most privileged cultural medium. Since writing uses language, the different modes of writing are inescapably "cultural" in this sense of participating in the carrying and exchange of value and meaning.

### discourse

"Discourse" has a specific use within linguistics, relating to "parole" (any actual language use by speakers or writers) in a distinction with "langue" (language as a "system"). In this sense it specifically differs from "grammar" which looks at how the "system" of language operates up to the level of the generation and management of sentences. In this context *discourse* is language-in-use.

Following the lead of Michel Foucault it is used in a broader sense to refer to the institutions, networks and exchanges in—or in relation to which—a practice is located. In this sense it is similar to the term *textual environments*.

### documentation

This is a term given to an *archive* of a specific project or piece of writing. What can you do to take control of the trace left by a writing project? There is obviously a difference between documenting the processes leading to finished work and documenting the finished work itself and different forms of writing suggest very different approaches to documentation. Documentation is seen as a particular form of writing.

*editing*
This is such a familiar term that it may not need a gloss. It is a word used for those phases of a writing process which take it from first draft (or equivalent) to being ready for publication (or equivalent). For most writers this is an iterative process: each re-reading leads to adjustments (or not) which in their turn lead to a re-reading, and so on. It sometimes helps to think of editing as having two modes (some people can do them both at the same time): one which is reading and re-writing with attention to *texture* and *structure*; the other which is to do with finish—ensuring, for example, that the punctuation and spelling are as you mean them to be and you want nothing changed. Most writers spend much more time editing than producing first drafts.

*environments*
There are familiar senses of environment that do not need glossing here. In a time of new writing technologies and practices, the term "textual environment" is used to refer to the different habitats of different kinds of writing practice. An environment, in this sense, is a combination of a specific writing technology, a body of work appearing to share some aesthetic values, a network of participation and distribution and sites of debate. See also the second sense of *discourse*.

*essay*
The conventional form of expository writing (i.e. writing that explains or interprets) familiar from arts and humanities education and closely related to an article in a journal or anthology. The word relates to the French word *essayer*, meaning to try or to test, and by extension to try out thoughts. It is helpful to take from this a view of an essay as being a trying out of ideas rather than an authoritative dissemination of what is already known and decided,

*genre*
"A particular style or category of works of art; esp. a type of literary work characterized by a particular form, style or purpose." (OED)

Texts in a recognisable genre may well allude *intertext*ually, by virtue of the characteristics of the genre, to other texts within the genre. In the approach to writing known as *performance writing* no given genre is taken for granted as a starting point and therefore writers are expected to be sensitive to the differences between genres and to be able to make decisions about, as well as within, genre.

*inside writing*
This name is intended to convey a way of looking at the media and materials of writing from the point of view of practice.

*intertext*
See *context* above. "…any text is constructed as a mosaic of quotations; any text is the absorption and transformation of another." (Kristeva 1986: 37)

*language*
Writing uses language as its medium, and language was one of the great topics of enquiry of the twentieth century, not only within linguistics but also within philosophy, anthropology, psychoanalysis, literary theory and cultural theory in general. Some awareness of the terms of these enquiries, and of their implications for a contemporary writing practice, is seen as essential for practices within *performance writing*.

*learning*
Everything that takes place within the writing degrees is intended to help students learn and indeed to go on being in a position to learn long after having left. This is very different from an approach which is to do quite simply with making work. Students are given increasing autonomy in making choices, all of which should be thought of as choices for learning. Learning takes place through all of: *practice, theory, reflection, research,* awareness of and engagement in *discourse.*

*live (live treatments, live writing)*
These terms challenge the relationship between different forms of writing and of "live" performance, most particularly the assumption that by the time of *performance* the *writing* is over (no longer live). In the broad context of *performance writing* the question is usually taken to refer more to the liveness of writing than of performance. The use of the term in broadcasting has established a useful sense that the time of performance is the same as the time of witnessing and that any editing would have to

be improvised on the spot. *Live treatments* can include practices which are in effect forms of *performic editing* of the already written. *Live writing* implies an act of writing as itself a live performance. Improvised and devised theatre can often be a way of folding writing and performance into each other.

Recent discussions (for example, Auslander 1999) have questioned the clarity of any distinction between live and mediated or recorded.

*modes*

This term relates to *genre*. Within the field of performance writing it is used in two different ways to distinguish between different emphases within the writing itself. One set of modes might be more relevant than the other in relation to any given writing.

One way goes back to Aristotle (or to misunderstandings by later commentators) and distinguishes between dramatic, epic and lyric or between (i) dramatic writing for performed events; "showing" and not "telling"; (ii) narrative—"telling", whether through live story-telling or through written pages; (iii) lyric—song-like utterances, perhaps dealing with states of feeling and mind rather than with the telling of stories.

The other is of specific importance to the enquiring approach to writing at Dartington. It distinguishes between primary formal emphases within writing, as between "sonic" (writing that works primarily with the sound of language and thus relates to music); "visual" (writing that works with the visual appearance of script and thus relates to visual arts); "installed writing" (writing designed to be installed in space as a form of textual (or text-bearing) sculpture or visual installation); "live" - writing as or for *live* performance.

*performance*

Like many of these glosses, this is a very difficult term to capture in a few lines and it may be better to read the entry below on *performance writing* first. For the purposes of this glossary, the one word on its own will be treated as straightforwardly as possible.

When performance is defined in relation to writing, the most familiar understanding is that there is a two-stage operation: first a *script* is written and then it is actualised within a *performance*—a play, for example. There is a separation then between a script and any performance of that script. This does not have to be the sequence or the relationship, but it does help to catch the sense that a performance takes place in a time and place, usually with witnesses (conventionally, the "audience"). A performance is something that happens and can be attended. There are, of course, a number of *genres* of performance, not all of them *live*, including: theatre events, films, TV and radio programmes, poetry readings, story telling, conjuring acts, live art events, social rituals or ceremonies (such as marriages or funerals). These have in common a time (which may, through recorded media, be a repeatable time), a place (which might also be a channel or a medium), and a duration (of performance, though not necessarily of witnessing).

*performance writing*
This term was pioneered within the Theatre undergraduate programme at Dartington in the 1980s, adopted as the name for the new field of writing which began with an undergraduate award in Performance Writing in 1994, and subsequently more widely adopted and understood. It was intended (i) to imply a much more open range of possible relationships between writing and performance than that of *scripts* written for subsequent *performance*; (ii) to address ways in which writing itself can be said to perform (for example, animated text on screens, or visually dynamic page-based compositions—such as those referred to as "concrete poetry" in the 1960s); (iii) to open up ways for writers to think of the way that their writing can be *performative*.

*performative*
This word is currently used in two different ways: (i) in the sense of *performic*—to mean writing that is for or like performance; (ii) in the sense first established by the philosopher, J.L. Austin, in his theory of "speech acts"—to refer to the ways in which speaking or writing can be said to do something as well as to be something or to say something—writing that performs an act. This latter sense opens up a most useful set of contextual questions for writers: what does this writing do, and for whom?

*"performic"*
This coinage, which is not yet included in the Oxford English Dictionary, is a useful term for distinguishing between the two senses of performative

(above)—something that is performance-like rather than the carrying out of an act.

*poetics*
In a narrow sense, the study of poetry; in a broader sense, the *rhetoric* of all literary—or "art"—texts; it is under the heading of poetics that questions about form, *mode* and *genre* are asked.

*practice*
Practice belongs to a cluster of terms of which others are *theory, praxis, reflection, discourse* and *learning*. In this context, practice refers to the actual making of writing-work, in contrast to the reflecting about it or reading about it. Too clear a separation may not be helpful, for at least two reasons: (1) a practice without theory and/or reflection is difficult to imagine; (2) theory and reflection both have to take place—they too are "practices". In this narrower sense, practice is the making of primary writing texts.

*praxis*
This term was adopted by Karl Marx to talk about an approach to *practice* that is thoroughly informed by *theory, reflection* and *research*—at its simplest, to act after taking thought. The term is used at Dartington to indicate a desired close relationship between theory and practice—theory for practice's sake.

*presentation (assessment)*
This is a mode of assessment in which students are responsible for presenting their work to assessors and, if appropriate, an audience in a *live* situation. There are two kinds of presentation. One takes the form of an account of a completed process of work, with critical commentary. This one can be thought of as a form of performed *documentation*. The other kind is a way of showing completed work. The term is used to allow for the full range of kinds of *text* within the writing awards.

*pre-theory*
Useful *theory* is usually developed to help understand topics, structures, processes, kinds of actions and events that are by no means self-

explanatory—that are "problematic". We use the term "pre-theory" for an approach to some of these topics that uncovers a need for explanation rather that rushing in to provide one before a need is felt.

*read*
Because of the broad range of what is treated as *writing* the word *read* is often used in an extended sense to include the reception of *live performances* or films, as examples. A *script* can be read off the page and it can also be read through *performance*. Where there is no separate script a performance can, in this sense, still be "read". Anything that is "read" can be treated as itself a *text*. (It has been argued that it is reading more than writing that makes texts, for example by Roland Barthes).

*reflection*
(reflective commentary, reflective documentation)
Writers who take a learning approach to their work think carefully about what they are about to do, are doing, and have done. If care is taken about this process of thought and its articulation, it can provide invaluable and cumulative feed-back into the making of work. This is matter of careful attention to writerly and contextual decisions and their consequences. It is not necessarily *theoretical*.

*research*
Within an undergraduate programme research is used for any systematic process of finding out, whether this be for an essay, a dissertation, the exploration of a context or for a practical project. A first question is always "what needs to be found out for this task?" and a second is "what is the best way to set about doing so". The first is often simply referred to is the "research question"; the second as "research methods".

*rhetoric*
Rhetoric is an ancient term that has been revived in the last few decades: how to speak or write effectively (in any given circumstance). Rhetoric focuses on the *structure* of *discourse*, particularly persuasive discourse, and on the stylistic devices—or "tropes" and "figures"—that can be used—or not—to achieve eloquence. Rhetoric provides terms for considering both the textures and structures of any verbal discourse.

*script*

A script is a written *text* which is a form of notation for or from a performance or production in a range of performance environments. *Scripted media* are those practices (*textual environments*) which more or less rely on, or at the least allow for, a written score or script: text-based theatre, most film, much video work and television production, significant audio work and radio production. Scripts can also play a part in new electronic media.

*site*

This is often used in the phrases "site-specific" and "site-sensitive" to refer to writing which is produced (or *edited*) for a quite specific location. Some writers respond to site in strictly formal terms—responding, for example, to the shape, colour and light of an internal or external space. Others always respond to sites as places already full or social or *cultural* associations.

*structures*

The undergraduate writing awards all move from an attention to detail— putting words next to each other to make *textures*—through to attention to compositional wholes and their relation to *genres*. Structure comes from the Latin word meaning build. A builder tends to assume that building blocks are to hand, or, if they are not, that they need to be made first, having the finished building in mind.

*text*

In the triplet of *text, intertext* and *context*, text refers to the written object itself, which within performance writing does not have to be witnessed as words or words only. In Theatre, for example, a single piece of writing can manifest itself through more than one text: the script and any one performance of that script. Within the field of performance writing, the act of writing often produces multiple texts.

It has been suggested above that a text is anything that can be *"read"*. It does not have to have already been written. An act of reading can become an act of *writing* through *assemblage* and *intertext*.

*textual practices*
This term is intended to include the full range of *writing* activities that produce written *texts*, including those usually incorporated within other practices such as theatre or music or visual art.

*textures*
Where *structure* comes from the Latin word for "build", *text* comes from the same language's word for "weave", and relates to "tissue". We use texture to talk about the characteristics and qualities inherent in the ways that words are put together within sentences or other localised parts of writing. In contrast, structure is used to refer to the way that parts of a whole text are arranged in relation to each other.

*theory*
In the context of the related terms of *practice, praxis, reflection, discourse* and *learning*, theory refers to a systematic engagement with conceptual frameworks that can be used for both explanatory and generative purposes. Theory can gesture towards multiple possibilities beyond the scope of any one practice and can be used to bypass the slow accumulation of learning through experience.
See *pre-theory*, above.

*writing*
In one sense, of course, this is obvious: writing is what writers do. It is included in this list to draw attention to the fact that, in the context of performance writing—and the very wide range of writing practices included in the field—it is by no means always obvious what writing is— where it begins and ends, where it is to be found or recognised. The French philosopher, Jacques Derrida, has challenged the traditional assumptions that writing is a secondary activity, parasitic on speaking (1978). The way that he, and others, have done so, challenges writers to understand what it is they do when they write.
This entry is a marker rather than an explanation or definition.

# Xenial
## For a Lexicon on Performance training [127]

The Greek word *xenos* (ξενoσ) means stranger, who may be a feared enemy (*xenophobia*, hatred of foreigners), a benign guest, or indeed one who might become either, depending upon relations. The adjective *xenial* refers to these relations, especially when friendly, between host and guest (closely related words etymologically). Gertrude Stein said that she wrote for herself and strangers. This is to claim her writing as in part *xenial*. The term poses for training this question: how to prepare for encounters with strangers—with various strangenesses—so that work may act as either guest or in a relation.

# PART TWO

# Pedagogical sketches:

## arts teaching
## and
## interdisciplinarity

# Arts for what, for where, for whom?
## Fragmentary reflections on Dartington College of Arts, 1961–2010 [128]

## (with Simon Murray)

In the summer of 2010 Dartington College of Arts (DCA) closed after almost fifty years on the Dartington Hall Estate in rural Devon, following a passionately contested merger with University College Falmouth in Cornwall in 2008. This essay—an unfinished and open-ended collection of reflections and fragments—maps out some of the key tropes, principles and practices of this remarkable and renowned project. Charting a singular path between the liberal humanities of the university sector and the vocational training of the conservatoires, DCA explored models of learning through practice in theatre, music, performance writing, choreography and contemporary visual arts.

## Placing this writing

This essay is written by two players— with considerable help from a third[129]— in the project that from 1961 to 2010 has been Dartington College of Arts (DCA).[130] To write at this moment is to mark an ending of DCA on the Dartington Hall Estate in Devon, following merger with University College Falmouth in April 2008 and relocation to Cornwall in the summer of 2010. Merger prompted strong emotions and, in particular, speculation

> **Project**
> More or less shared desires and values, thrown forward, schematically mapped. In this case, the 'project' determined— kept determining against odds—the organisation, and not the other way round. Anyone could invoke the project against the organisation at any time. And then what could happen? This was not the organisation for a career CEO, unless circumstances were right.

as to whether Dartington's kinds of interventions in contemporary performance practices and their teaching would survive the transfer. Given DCA's rich and complex history the task in a short article is absurdly ambitious and ultimately unachievable. However, in what follows we identify a number of significant themes, tropes, principles and dispositions which we believe have characterised and marked the DCA project during its lifetime. We have no wish to offer an account which claims either closure or to be comprehensive and short fragments are merely part of a mosaic of memory and multiple practices that

> **Practice**
>
> These were practical courses. This means that people wanted to learn how to do things (or at least how to do better what they could already do). What things, though? Three possible answers, all slightly to one side: to become skilled interpreters of the canon, to become new heroes of modernism, to become skilled arts functionaries, equipped to take up already established positions in the arts 'industries'. The first continued to haunt the approach to music; a version of the second formed one pole in the main driving tension and debate of the whole project; and the third was only ever of marginal interest.

have constituted DCA at different times in its history. There is much that is missing—the role of music, for example, is nearly absent and deserves generous attention at another time. What follows attempts to articulate a sense of the rewards, difficulties, achievements, qualities, contestations and productive "messiness" that has been DCA for much of its history.

The two authors have tried to deal cautiously with their own memories, with records and with the views and details passed on to them in conversation by many others who have been involved with the Dartington project over the years. Our accounts, though, are inevitably partial since we have both, in our ways, been heavily invested in what we describe. One of us—Simon Murray—worked at DCA for the four years that included the decision to merge and re-locate, and as director of the highest recruiting field and as a staff governor, was party to policy discussions at a number of levels. The intensity of these four years put the alternatives to Dartington's approach in sharp and poignant relief. The other—John Hall—is still part of the relocated project and worked continuously at Dartington from 1976 until relocation, in roles that changed to fit the times. From 2002 he was semi-retired and at a remove from the debates and decisions about change. Before that, though, he had, as Vice Principal Academic, played a central part in making and coordinating academic decisions. In a way that would have been impossible in a larger institution, he was always combining roles—firstly directly managing the undergraduate programme, then acting for two years as launch director for Performance Writing, and finally overseeing the first three years of an integrated MA programme.

## Histories

Which history to tell? There is an institutional history, of an organisation called Dartington College of Arts that emerged into the public sector out of the private philanthropic adventure of Dartington Hall. There are the histories of various ideas of education, often characterised as "progressive" and going back at least to Rousseau. In particular there are the histories of education and training within the different arts practices taught at Dartington and the way these different histories impacted locally on each other. And then there are the art histories—the canonic accounts of what came before—and their relations to official and unofficial arts policies. For example, initially through Imogen Holst's role with CEMA,[131] and then through the estate's first Arts Administrator, Christopher Martin, Dartington's own preoccupations with developing an arts policy had become involved in the debates that led to the formation of the Arts Council of Great Britain. These anticipated the later tension between a Reithian[132] duty to make the established culture of the elite available to all and a questioning about the restricted class and ethnic base of that culture and the contempt this policy might convey for cultural forms and activities that were local or "mass". That tension offers one way of talking about where DCA started.[133]

There is no doubt that its provenance out of a private Trust[134] loosened the determinations of some of these histories on the Dartington project, licensing a sometimes idiosyncratic openness towards them. Perhaps the key historical questions about DCA are: how did it ever get started; how did it survive and adapt during all the educational changes after its inception; how was it allowed to end; what has ended and what has survived, perhaps in transformed state? It is far too early

> **Reflective avant-gardism**
> The version of avant-gardism that would not go away related to modernism's 'make it new', though out of the sense that only critical—that is, thoughtful—models of practice, that were actively enquiring into purpose and context, could begin to address the changing social situation of (at least) the UK.

to attempt to answer that last question and full answers to the others are beyond the scope of this article. Instead, we offer a few dates and some suggestive contextual detail around them.

In 1925 "one of the world's wealthiest women" married "the son of an English clergyman" (Young 1996, 94, citing "press in the USA"). This couple, Dorothy and Leonard Elmhirst, embarked on their "English experiment" (Young 1996), motivated by his experiences with Tagore in India and her wish to use her wealth philanthropically. The English experiment was Dartington Hall, which they bought in the same year. Their plan was for a kind of enlightened feudalism, which brought sociality, local economy, education and the arts together in a single social organism. Dorothy's wealth protected the experiment from a reliance on the policy constraints of external funding. By 1961, it had become apparent to Peter Cox, then Dartington's Arts Administrator, that the adult element of the educational experiment needed a public dimension. Dartington College of Arts was formed, in reliance on Devon County Council funding and on links with regional teacher education. This early connection into the teaching of artist-teachers was to leave its legacy and perhaps the hyphen is more important here than "teachers"; perhaps part of the history of DCA is the view that being an artist is inevitably a hyphenated function.

From about 1975, the College was able to end this particular dependence by offering its own nationally recognised awards through the Council for National Academic Awards (CNAA) (Cox 2002, 37–45). These—a mix of DipHEs and BAs—faced the challenge of combining the educational ethos of Dartington with the regulatory strictures of the CNAA; this was by no means straightforward, at any stage. The phrase "honours worthiness" was often taken to refer to the part played by "theory" and by "academic" writing. In the early 1980s CNAA issued a challenge to elaborate

> **Theory**
> For the project to be thrown forward, the multiple practices must also see beyond themselves, beyond their own immediate theatre of operations. Beyond know-how, what needs to be known and what needs to be thought: what thinking devices for seeing further and at greater speed than the experience alone of practice can allow.

and clarify the "theoretical underpinnings"[135] of one of the courses. This challenge was taken up most productively in formalised conversations across the departments that could be said never to have ended.

Following the 1988 Education Reform Act, DCA was alone—or certainly in a very unusual position—within the "polytechnics and colleges sector" in not acquiring assets, in the form of land, buildings and equipment, as a newly incorporated institution. These assets belonged instead to the Dartington Hall Trust, who could not be required to transfer them, and so DCA remained wholly dependent for capital development on others, most notably the Trust. Additional support it had been receiving from the local authority was cut off by the changed arrangements, making a radical restructuring necessary. This did not happen in time, giving rise to an extreme financial crisis. Many thought that the experiment was over. There were losses: of people, of the Art and Social Context course, of the fourth year of the Theatre degree, of outlying "placement" bases in Plymouth and Rotherhithe. For many this was no doubt the beginning of the end.

There were also gains, most notably in interdisciplinarity. What had been quite separate "departments" had to work much more closely together, sharing a curricular framework with common elements and much more cross-teaching (much of it drawing on the work on "theoretical underpinnings"). This may well have been the most significant development in the project in its last two decades. Research was soon to be added as a formal layer of the institution's activities and developed from the start within this ethos. In 1999 a taught MA, whose specific characteristic was the opportunity for specialist study within an interdisciplinary context, was finally established.

> **Problem syllabus 1**
>
> A syllabus constructed in part out of a bricolage of very different kinds of syllabus: what know-how, what knowledge, what instruments of thought (see Theory, above) are needed when an imagined but quite possible set of practices is situated within a problematic? The problem, because it relates to the project, can throw the syllabus beyond itself at any time.

Through prolonged debate and passionate contestation in 2006/07 an end to the geographical location of the project was decided, at a time when to many staff and students everything felt relatively secure. Just as the Dartington Hall Trust had been essential to the College's provenance, it was now critical in its ending; perhaps, more fairly, the College's unusual reliance on private landlords, with their own charitable agenda, tied its hands in responding to the need to adapt to changes in the policy and funding climate. The landlords decided that they could not provide what the College's senior management believed was needed.[136]

## Curriculum and First Principles

Before the formation of the College, the Trust had veered between, or tried to combine, two different approaches to arts education: one in which the arts are seen as potentially serving the locality and playing a full part within it through participation as well as audience consumption; the other in which it could act as a protective environment for established artists and companies to train and to develop new work. In becoming part of the national higher education system, the College was going to have to mark out a very specific approach; in retrospect, it is easy to see that there was little point in trying to do in Devon what was already being done effectively in the cities. What is already being done always has an established syllabus of sorts and, often, no apparent need to argue purpose. Dartington always had to start with an explicit purpose, design a curriculum accordingly and persuade regulators, funders and controllers of numbers that both purpose and curriculum were worthy. Significantly, this attracted teachers and researchers who were more than happy to start from first principles or to find a setting in which their own principles might be taken seriously.

## Naming

In naming its first degrees, DCA took few risks: one was called Music, the other Theatre ("theatre" rather than "drama", though). The third was much more problematic: the "Art Department" could not so simply offer an "Art" BA and its first eventual degree course sounded like a book title rather than a familiar section of the library: Art and Social Context. The term "social context" poses a problem, let alone all the relationships opened up by the "and". There was no "art and social context" syllabus to be taken down from the shelf and subtly finessed for local conditions. Later, when Art

> ***Problem syllabus 2***
>
> "But what is a problem, really? The term comes from the language of competitors who line up against each other and attempt to throw obstacles in each other's way. From here, the expression is transferred figuratively to debate: an argument posed against the perspective of the other participants in a conversation is like an obstacle. In this sense, a problem is something that impedes the progress of knowledge."
> (Gadamer1998, 25)

169

and Social Context's time at Dartington came to a premature end, "Visual Performance" was introduced. Where the first term insists that there is a *beyond art* for artists to consider, the second joins two "art" terms. Both titles at the time prompted the question: what is it? The syllabus could become a three-year attempt at answering this question from within.

In 1992 there was also Performance Writing. The word "performance" in these last two titles is in part, but only in part, a trace of local politics. With the move of Art and Social Context and the removal of a departmental structure, DCA now needed to be seen as specialising in performance practices; if there was to be anything else, such as art or writing, it needed to come in under shelter of this term. But it was much more than that too. In the case of Performance Writing, "creative writing" was bracketed because of its relatively settled relationship with literary modes and genres of practice and its usual lack of engagement with the problematics of writing as trace, as technology, as system, as performative. Writing at DCA had to define itself against and in relation to sets of practices that all involved forms of writing, including sonic, visual, and dramatic, and to acknowledge from the outset that digital technology was transforming the possibilities of writing.

## Relations between fields

Until about 1987 the departments and their courses were remarkably separate from each other, given the small scale of the organisation, and their degree courses even varied in length. The only way large numbers of students could work together was through elaborately planned "interdepartmental projects", which required temporary and sometimes reluctant suspension of at least three very different calendars. This lack of interchange had frustrated students and staff and, as HE income began to drop, it precluded what might be simple and effective economies of scale. In 1987, after agonising internal discussions, the decision was made to "modularise" and in doing so to ensure that there was the possibility for common modules (taken by all the students in a particular year, whatever their award) and for shared modules, where the synchronising of time-tables allowed options across awards.

> **Problem syllabus 3**
> "[...] , as a rule, the hallmark of the true researcher is the discovery of new questions. This is the most important legacy of the researcher: the imagination—for the main thing is to find a fruitful way of putting the question."
> (Gadamer 1998, 26)

This shift brought with it another: the curriculum itself could be viewed as structure rather than as organism. This prepared for the next step, planned for a 1991 start, which produced an agreed—some would say imposed—structure for all the degrees, with the effect that *equivalent* work would be happening at the same time in the different awards.

And so what were these equivalents? Partly what DCA graduates would need to be able to do is to work out what can be done, what would be appropriate to do in given circumstances. The work is never just the technical skills of *how to do* something that is already known; more than that, it requires the higher level skills of critical judgement about what can be done, what is at stake, who is at stake. Project conception, design and management are crucial, and with those, research and social skills. Aesthetic judgement might often also be ethical judgement. These skills and dispositions are valuable and transferable. And it is important to be able to talk projects into being. Students must have time to devise and develop work of their own. In at least one piece of practical work they must engage a context other than the institution. All of these components must be combined so that the parts feel as though they relate to each other and that they work incrementally, offering development and increasing autonomy.

For the 1991 planning of the curriculum came a further requirement: a single framework must allow for both single honours and combined honours awards. Although this requirement came from a new rescuing partner (University of Plymouth) rather than from any initial sense of internal necessity, the challenge was taken up in a way that DCA could make its own: how could combined honours help strengthen the sense of inter- and cross-disciplinarity, and, with that, an active understanding of commonalities and differences between practices? What seemed critical was that Dartington's enabling structure for combined honours should enable interplay, conversation and inflection between subjects. How could this broader base also broaden the working base of our graduates? There isn't scope for detail here about the structure of equivalents that enabled these solutions, but to take the most recent version of the undergraduate curriculum for Writing, the final "integrational" year includes the following three elements: Contextual Enquiry, Written Research Project and Critical Arts Practice, described in the Handbook as "overlapping and self-managed". The other awards also use these names. The structure of the earlier years prepares for these through combinations of seminar, workshop and project-brief teaching. The Writing handbook describing the approach to practical work at Level 1 catches some of the qualities that are very much more than technical:

> All modes of practical work will involve you co-operating with others, developing professional attitudes and collaborative skills. This practical work will be placed in a variety of settings, where you will have to respond with understanding to issues of time, place, function, occasion, audience etc. This will lead to an introductory experience for all Level 1 students into notions of collaborative work with other subjects [...] (*Writing, Writing (Contemporary Practices), Writing (Scripted Media)* UCF, Undergraduate Programme, Handbook 2008/9, p. 30.)

## Training and Anti-training

The extraordinary socio-economic project out of which DCA emerged was committed to the need for radical changes, was in no way averse to the idea of training, but equally never presumed that a useful training could be for the status quo. Almost from its beginning, the Dartington project, both within the College and across the estate, was caught up in a tension between training for specific professional practices and structured opportunities to participate in arts activities, for the values—open to debate—that such participation might realise.

> **Training**
> A teleological process with practical knowledge at the end of it and possibly a licence to trade.

Debates about training—its purpose, definition, ideological framing and practice—were rarely far from the surface as the College's curriculum developed and wrestled with the extent it needed to accommodate often unwelcome changes demanded by a higher education system increasingly in thrall to instrumental notions of learning. Arguably, one of DCA's greatest achievements over the final two decades was successfully to negotiate a position between the "discursive humanities" of the universities and the explicit vocationalism of the conservatoires. Since the late 1990s DCA received premium funding[137] for its courses which, although not quite at the level received by the conservatoires, allowed it to pursue approaches to practice-based learning which would have been rarely affordable in the universities. To justify this level of funding, DCA identified a model of learning which successfully articulated training as performance or performance-making and as a reflexive and critical practice. Here, in so far as training or skill were ever embraced as terms, they were a process towards a goal which was not known, not given and ceaselessly to be (re) invented. Noam Chomsky's pairing of competence and performance seems relevant here (Chomsky 1965): if the actual modes of performance should be left open to possibility, what are the general areas of competence that can be facilitated in the understanding that these are generative rather than fixed structures? Hostility to the most obviously limiting and closed forms of training was easy to vocalise, but students manifestly did need to feel growing competence in their performance practices. Knowing *how* to do things significantly defined their identity as practitioners, and the richness and thickness of a student's critical reflexivity was also in part dependent on this competence, as well as knowing what they might *need to know* as their practice unfolded.

Over the final decade, in the face of an increasingly instrumental learning culture, it became ever more necessary (for tactical reasons) to embrace the languages of a narrow(er) vision of training whilst protecting the integrity of the practices outlined in this essay. Often this was a slippery contestation over language rather than the substance of practice or pedagogy. Over the 50 year history of DCA the institution regularly had to chart a path in relation to skill, technique and training *between* the cultural aspirations of Dartington Hall trustees on one side *and* an increasingly instrumental framework of expectations from the state on the other.[138] As the College prepared to negotiate the regulatory structures of higher education in the mid 1970s it also had to deal with an ethos within the Trust that valued arts education as enhancement of spirituality, personal growth/development and "free" creative expression.[139]

We conclude this section with a brief "case study" that may serve as an example of the creative tensions and debate around paradigms of

> **Disposition**
> An angle of incidence, a state of preparation and readiness. The impulse ahead of action or thought. But at Dartington a disposition to denaturalize and destabilize dispositional habits. A disposition to unsettle, to keep the field of vision wide, to conversation and dialogue rather than to answers, fixity and permanent resolution. Note also its military usage as in deployment and distribution of the elements of a command within an area ...

training in a particular corner of the Dartington curriculum. *Bodyworks* courses in both Theatre and Choreography continuously posed (largely) unresolved questions around the nature of "preparation", technique and what practices should or should not be embraced by the course. *Bodyworks* in Theatre was offered only to first year students in their first semester. Between 2003 and 2010 typically four classes were run in parallel by tutors each bringing a particular practice to bear on the bodies of the students. Thus, for example, the practices and principles of Contact Improvisation, Feldenkrais, Alexander Technique, Tai Chi, Laban technique, Suzuki and strategies for play all framed classes at particular times. Towards the end of this period voice work began to play a more significant role in *Bodyworks* and the Theatre team began—though this was never resolved—to consider whether writing practices, for example, should figure equally with more obviously embodied approaches. *Bodyworks* in the Choreography programme was driven by a range of somatic practices and was taught throughout years one and two. Increasingly, for Choreography, *Bodyworks* began to play the role of a technique class as conducted in a professional dance academy.

Theatre *Bodyworks* offered a crucible for considerations and inflections around the nature and purpose of a teaching practice which students often felt was initially closer to their understanding of "training" than many of the other courses they subsequently experienced. *Bodyworks* normally received considerable affirmation from students with habitual calls that it should be extended throughout the degree. Within the team, however, there was regular discussion about the purpose *Bodyworks* should serve. Some were suspicious that we were introducing a dimension of "actor training" through the back door, others valued its role but were anxious that the movement skills learned by the students should always be pressed into the service of creative composition and devising, whilst others believed that the "readying" process that *Bodyworks* offered should be augmented by other preparatory strategies such as writing, voicework and engagement with new technologies. On reflection, *Bodyworks* also productively problematised what constitutes "skill" and "technique".[140] We believed that, at best, *Bodyworks* had very tangible consequences for improving competence, but was also a dispositional encounter which had a bearing on the cognitive and sensorial frames through which students experienced and engaged with the world. And as an afterthought, it should be noted that *Bodyworks* was also an opportunity for students to exercise the creative muscles of collaboration and to begin to rehearse the skills and strategies entailed in the multiple practices of documentation.

## Context(s)

Along with "practice" and "body", for example, *context* has been perhaps the most signed and continuously contested term within DCA's history. From the "Art and Social Context" course, achieving degree status in 1986,[141] to numerous modules in the post 2003 curriculum, "context" has been identified as a preoccupation which has driven teaching and learning and framed student practice across all fields of activity undertaken at the College.[142]

> **Out of the studio**
> "[...] bringing art practice out of the studio and closer to everyday life—achieving this in any and every way one can think of ... an awareness that context applies at many levels including the immediate context (where and with whom one works—who the work is for) as well as the wider cultural contexts in which we live."
> (Crickmay 2003: 121) Chris Crickmay was head of the Art and Social Context degree programme in the 1980s.

One modality of context—that of the immediate physical environment—offered for many a startling but seductive embrace from the first moment they arrived up either of the two driveways on to the estate. Context shouted itself as an experience which could neither be ignored nor avoided as student, teacher or visitor began to register the contours of pasture, farm, woodland, sculptured gardens, medieval courtyard, Great Hall, river Dart and countless other features of these 1500 acres which would become their studio, workshop or laboratory for at least three years. For many who worked and studied at Dartington the power and sense of topographical context became an ambiguous—and sometimes troubling—experience; one which could never be shrugged off but at best engaged with productively and provocatively. The hegemony of place as context had regularly

> **Text and context**
> "It is helpful to think of this term as one of a triplet together with text and intertext. For example, writers produce texts which draw on and relate to other 'texts' (intertextual) and which are always unavoidably surrounded and pervaded by worlds beyond them (context). ... Context can be treated as physical, architectural or geographical—as in attention to site—and as more abstractly cultural, as for example in the way a text relates to gender (without the author necessarily being aware of it)."
> (Undergraduate Programme Handbook, 2006/7)

to be challenged and questioned as students became aware that context was more multiple, complex and nuanced than suggested by the often overwhelming—and sometimes disabling—beauty of the estate.

DCA did not invent a preoccupation with context as a central concern of either undergraduate or postgraduate teaching, but it did refuse to ignore it. Indeed, DCA privileged context as a way of seeing and being in the world, as a disposition to understand phenomena never purely "in themselves", rather to recognise matters and processes as persistently and irrevocably pervaded by the economic, historical, social and cultural worlds in which they were produced. And beyond grasping the worlds which *produced* the texts of music, theatre, dance, writing or visual art, Dartington insisted that students attend also (and equally) to the worlds in which these texts were to be received, disseminated, placed and witnessed.

> **Theatre with Textual Practices**
> **Hybrid CEP**
> Traces of exchange: Theatre student, Mads Anderson, walked from Dartington to Lindebo 27 in Denmark, his place of birth. It took two months. The project, while informed by walking practices and theories, was not so much focused on the walking itself, as with his encounters and small exchanges with strangers (619 in total) along the way. Photographs of 'absences' (traces of each encounter) and a range of writing modes were composed in a small book, which acted both as a form of documentation and as an artwork in its own right. Documentation of—and as—practice. Questions around traces and markings, and an ethics of exchange—and their implications for performer/audience relationships—informed the process.

Although the College was a site of practice—of constructing art—it was an insistence on wrestling with the contexts of this making that arguably gave Dartington one of its most singular qualities. Engaging with the context of practice and its dissemination could be an often uncomfortable yet productive process—not for the good of the student's soul, or to give him/her an enhanced degree classification, but to make the work in question sharper, richer and thicker.

At different times and in different places the preoccupation with context led to embracing relationships with particular communities, regionally, nationally and internationally; with different geographical or physical spaces; and to critical engagement with the implications of social, political and cultural factors and theories. From 1991, the intellectual, corporeal and visceral concerns with context were articulated through the common undergraduate curriculum framework with its *equivalents* described above. Thus, for example, in the first semester of their final year all undergraduate students undertook Contextual Enquiry Projects (CEPs). Although these were largely solo activities—often, what in different circumstances, we might call "practice as research"—undertaken anywhere in the world, they were also sometimes collaborations across disciplines. Assessed through presentation, often with a strong performance dimension, and an analytical portfolio, these projects frequently evidenced startling journeys of imagination and geography and witnessed an astonishing "contextual" maturity and sophistication on the part of the students.

Dartington's enduring commitment to an interrogation of context through arts practice often generated tensions and unease between the laboratory or "crucible" quality of learning which the institution enabled, and the disposition to look beyond and "outside" which a pervasive concern with context necessitated. The (relative) geographical isolation of Dartington and the lure of its extensive studio resources could encourage an intense immersion in practice which, although enviable and admirable in many ways, sometimes worked against the contextualising impulse identified above.

## Themes and terms

In the conversations—formal and informal—that occupied so much time in so many different settings, about pedagogy, practice and research, a small lexicon of key terms came to mark out commonalities or productive differences. At different times they have included, apart from context and its related term, site: performance, composition, devising and improvisation (both as a set and as singular terms); practice, theory, praxis; body or embodiment; performativity, writing, discourse, inflection (and perhaps, conversation). We shall say more about two of these.

## Site(s)

We might speak of the Dartington curriculum's critical relationship to site by way of Peter Brook's much quoted remark about theatre only needing an "empty space" to establish the means of its presence. At Dartington we would simultaneously contest and affirm Brook's statement: contest the possibility that any space is ever "empty" of significance, history and trace,

**On place and walking...**

"Place is closely interwoven with a network of terms that relate to ownership and its attendant behavioural socius: proper, property, propriety, appropriate ... To walk the story is to revisit and rehearse corporeally the itineraries of a tradition that maps the complex interrelatedness of cultural spaces and identities, pasts and possible futures. ... To walk the story is to attend to landscape as inscape, and to take (a) place in the world." (Williams 1998: vi-vii; David Williams was Professor of Theatre at DCA between 1999 and 2009 and designed and led first year site course on the Dartington Estate).

but affirm the disposition that art has the potential to be made in and for any space and not simply those ascribed as "proper" and legitimate for the performance of art, music, theatre, writing or dance.

One of the first principles of the Dartington curriculum was to acknowledge the insistence of site as part of the grammar and vocabulary of performance-making. Put simply: all art is sited and that to read and respond to art necessitates understanding that the "it" of art is inextricably bound up with the materiality of its location and the range of discourses which frame the exchange between all its constituent elements. The making and reception of art cannot but be informed by its site and location. So, at Dartington a recognition of the "sitedness" of art practices was hard-wired into the curriculum from the moment students crossed the threshold. Initially, this served as an invitation and challenge for students to review their allegiance to the proscenium arch theatre, black box studio, white cube gallery, concert hall or (blank) page as the only appropriate site for the production and reception of their work. Later, more complex engagements with the multiple dramaturgies of site and elusive and ethically difficult relationships between site and "community" would be explored and tested.

Significantly, the rhythm of the curriculum, which broadly speaking alternated studio based learning with sited learning off campus, served a dual purpose which productively married pragmatism with principle. By moving students out of the College's built environment on to the estate and further afield we opened up space for other student cohorts to pursue their practice within studio, rehearsal, IT suite or seminar spaces. At any one time in the teaching calendar up to half of all undergraduate students were working outwith the main hub of the College. The rhythm of the curriculum extended the range and possibilities of site across three years of the programme. Hence in the second semester of year one all students explored site work within the Dartington estate, whilst in the same period of year two there was an obligation to make work in the context of sites further afield, for example, in Totnes, on Dartmoor or other locations in South Devon. Here the choice of location was made in order to enable the contextually engaged practice that formed the core of the particular project. In year three, working through the enabling structures of the Contextual Enquiry Project (CEP) the rest of the world literally became sites of possibility for student projects.

An important point to extract from these examples, but one which also has wider resonance for the whole of the DCA project, was that the practice-based learning enabled by the curriculum was a complex and interrelated ecology which, although robust in its pragmatics and structure, was sensitive to (and potentially destabilised by) changes and interventions from within or beyond the boundaries of the College. As with any "complex ecology" the structures of learning at Dartington could be rendered dysfunctional by any part of the system failing to understand or sign up to both the first principles which informed the curriculum and the enabling scaffolding which supported it. As in any institution, aspiration and rhetoric sometimes outpaced the reality of the experience for both tutors and students, yet at its best this was a sustainable, generative and fertile ecology of learning. An example of this was in an ambitious project (funded by an Erasmus Mobility grant) in 2008 when fifteen second-year students from across five fields went to Berlin for three months to work collaboratively on a project. Whilst for many of these students this was a dramatically productive experience, often the fine details and demands of cross- or interdisciplinary working were less successfully negotiated. Here the vocabulary and tools for collaborative practice seemed less finely honed in reality than they were in theory.

## Conversation and ending

As we near the end of our fragmented article on Dartington the very idea of "end" is sensitive and uncertain. Whilst many of the indices of "end"—for example, studios, seminar rooms and offices empty now of students and staff—are categorical and immutable, what is being preserved and reconstructed ninety miles away in Cornwall remains unresolved

> **Conversation?**
>
> Shall we cut our losses on further inclusions and just finish? End of session. Have we captured the ethos of exchange between friends (in Deleuze's sense) that has kept the project alive and changing? And the pervasive approach to learning as dialogic?
>
> Is conversation really the key term? Is it as simple as that? Because people work together and talk together—and it isn't always clear which is which—stuff happens. Because something is said, something is done. Because something is made, something is said. And so on. Including collaborations ...

and contestable. Many have argued that the project and its Dartington site are inseparable and that relocation (in this context, should we say "re-siting"?) is a euphemism for termination. Except in its most local particulars, though, the project was never Dartington's only; that is why it has attracted so many to it. Parts of it will no doubt migrate and adapt, just as they have already, with the diaspora of graduates and former teaching staff over the years.

It would be a mistake, perhaps, to turn to plans for *conserving* the project. Though it may need housing, the motivations to instigate and sustain projects of this kind will not go away, and they will be energised by just the kinds of conversation between artists, teachers and students (often one and the same) that have defined for many of us working at Dartington.

## Postscript

When we started drafting this article the climate already felt hostile enough for the kind of imaginative "anti-training" we have tried to evoke. We had not anticipated that a coalition government would, by the time we were about to submit, have more or less completed the task of turning higher education into a matter of individual investment, much like one made on the financial or housing markets. Practical critical intelligence—creative and ethical—will be desperately needed, and not just as a luxury for the wealthy. Can any future "training" close its eyes to the risks?

Fig 6 'The Dove, the Ghost, the Handkerchief Tree', directed by Karen Christopher, devised by stage 1 and 2 Theatre Students as part of the Dartington Campus Festival, June 2010, and specifically intended to mark and engage with the ending of DCA at Dartington. Photograph by Kate Mount.

# Interdisciplinarity:
## "Disciplines" and Contemporary Practices [143]

This is intended very much as a discussion paper, deliberately set at a schematic and abstract level. Behind the discussion is a question which could be very simply phrased something like this: when whole fields of practice are undergoing change and are likely to continue to do so, how can we offer a framework of teaching which helps graduates enter those changing fields with courage, energy and imagination and with appropriate skills, understandings and frames of reference? This question is too big and important to be the discussion today but it is behind it.

I want to come at it by way of a distinction which is important whenever there is a practice at the heart of a degree and that is between the practice itself—the way it is conducted and organised in a world beyond education—and the subject or discipline—the way the practice is framed and taught within institutions of higher education. I shall be using the term "discipline" more than the term "subject" mostly because I want to relate the whole discussion to the notion of interdisciplinarity and there is no useable term which relates to "subject" that has not already been put to different use by psychologists.

I am taking for granted that both practices and disciplines are institutionalised: that there are organisations which attempt to define and control them—sometimes the same organisations in each case, more often perhaps different ones. I am taking for granted too that arts practices and disciplines operate through exclusions and therefore always have their *other*, a repressed or excluded unconscious—often, of course, the "popular" or "mass" or "everyday" forms of the time. Provisionally— and with Freud, Goffman and de Certeau in mind—I shall refer to this third as the everyday.[144] I shall not elaborate, but simply have in mind that at any time, challenges can emerge to practices and disciplines out of recognitions of what has been happening in an *elsewhere*.

Between practice, discipline and the everyday there are variable distances in any given field. A crucial factor in determining the distance between practice and discipline is this: are there professional bodies who have at most specifically designed the training or at least have maintained some control over syllabuses and their delivery? In the world of performance I would suggest that some practices remain very close to education and education-based research—which in some cases seems to have considerable responsibility for sustaining them; others operate in a tension between education and industry, which is an increasingly familiar theme in discussions about education; and others finally are seen as relating straightforwardly to industrial training, perhaps training within employment.

I shall be using the term "interdisciplinarity" as a way of opening up discussion about established "disciplines" and named cultural practices, having in mind that there need be no one-to-one correspondence between discipline and practice. Theatre, opera and film are clear examples of cultural forms which draw on a number of component practices, almost any one of which can be framed as an academic discipline. "Theatre practice"—as a singular term—has to refer to a unifying or integrating practice: a practice of making coherent. Within professional practice there is usually one role which carries this unifying responsibility. The extent to which each participant also needs to understand the sense of the whole to which she or he contributes is an interesting issue, of course, for any practice with directors or conductors.

A discipline can be said to confer an intellectual unity to a range of practices. I do not myself believe it is useful to confuse the notion of "interdisciplinarity" with complex, multi-practice forms. Mixed or multi-media forms may or may not be interdisciplinary. They may be no more than an extension of the compositional palette. The issue for practice emerges when an extension of media (often through technological developments and applications), materials and practices puts into play structurally different understandings and histories of performance, composition and judgement. Where different histories abut or merge, and where practitioners and educators wish to take explicit responsibility for the consequences, interdisciplinarity is usually invoked. I shall come to this. But we still have a difference between an interplay of practices and an interplay of the "disciplines" or framing discourses within which those practices have been intellectually located. Later I shall try to provide a more detailed explanatory framework.

A number of terms have been doing business recently to name both the interplay between practices and cuts across existing practices: that old term, "new", is always useful as a prefix; in addition there has been the use of terms like "hybridisation" or "live art" or "new collaborations", where the implication is that the collaboration is across forms and not just between people. A most significant adjustment of terminology has been the adoption of the generic term "performance", which provides the "P" in the initials making up the name of CONCEPTS. This term has provided a much larger frame for thinking about practices and their relation to each other. It has certainly helped us at Dartington in England to name and develop two performance-related studies for which the term Theatre could not possibly do full service: Visual Performance and Performance Writing. As a term it can also make it easy to be conceptually lazy: why try to be precise when the catch-all term will do. It can trail with it too an easy anthropologism, the over-ready recourse to cross-cultural analogy. But these are small problems in relation to the gains. It is worth noticing in passing that the use of "performance" as a generic term has begun to displace "performance" as a fixed term in the dyad, performance / composition. Instead, the relation between the two comes to be seen as dynamic and fluid. To talk of new performance is to talk of new composition too and not just new ways of performing old compositions. For those of us who are in the business of education for arts practice, the relationship between the two sets of terminology—for which I have been using practice and discipline as shorthand—is important. We operate within two sets of practices in relation to at least two institutionalised worlds, and all the time may be conscious of a world of everyday performance practices still eluding us. How can we ensure that the educational world, with its existing institutions, resources and funds can best serve the future of performance practices—and of those compositional practices which are essential for a developing future for performance?

In Britain the term "interdisciplinarity" has begun to be used rather loosely in connection with modular or credit based courses on the assumption that an encounter with enough disciplinary fields will itself provide an interdisciplinary approach. It may well come do so for some students, but if this effect were to become widespread it would inevitably produce shifts in the sense of what makes up a disciplinary field: to what extent any of us is authorised to bring one set of knowledge to bear on another. Just as I do not see mixed-media work as necessarily inter-disciplinary, I suggest that "multi-disciplinarity" is not the same as "interdisciplinarity".[145]

Let me try out a four-term typology of approaches to the teaching of the arts as practices or disciplines. This is a matter of the primary emphasis of an approach and I shall exaggerate to make a point.

First there is the conservatoire. This takes a practice-based approach, within clear understandings of the conventions of the practice and assumptions about the "needs" of an existing profession—assumptions which are not always accurate and up-to-date. The practice implied is unproblematic; the analogies with law, medicine and engineering are clear. Let us say this aims to produce producers, subjects of a particular performance practice.

Second, there are approaches which take the field of practice as an object of study, where the assumed future practices of students are that *either* they are receiving a very useful generalist education which could lead in any number of directions *or* that they will continue as critics, scholars and educators. This approach takes the texts of a practice as givens and is usually more at ease with scripts, scores and documentation than with the processes of production or even of live consumption. As an approach it belongs to the academies rather than the practising professions. Examples include musicology, art history, literature, film studies (*about* as against *how to make*).[146]

Third, there are training establishments for contemporary representational and performance media, especially those in which production processes are industrial or "post-industrial", reliant on "state-of-the-art" technology and subject to shifting divisions of labour.

Fourth—and most risky and problematic—there is an approach which is committed to a future for performance practices but sees the forms, conventions, contexts, production methods and patterns of participation as anything but fixed in advance. What to do in these circumstances? Train for what you know now in the hope that everyone will change together? Or prepare for openness in an extreme economic version of "open field" composition? I know that this can sound like typical late-twentieth century future-talk, grandiose and full of empty posturing. I think, though, that there is a version of it which is very practical and responsible.

It is this fourth which interests me. It must take the direction of a critical awareness that can lead to practice as well as to commentaries on practice. It is all too easy to replace older canons with new, even fragmented "post-modernist" ones and leave students unable to think their way beyond what they have been given. Critical awareness must include awareness of what constitutes a practice, a discipline and their everyday equivalents, so that these can be seen as enabling rather than as restricting constraints.

This fourth category comes closest to my own key institutional motives for an interest in interdisciplinarity.[147] Other motives from within educational institutions to raise questions about interdisciplinarity include, I believe, at least all of the following: frustration at the blocking of certain collaborations or innovatory practices; the inability of institutions to respond to changes in professional practice or technological developments in the cultural industries; a disciplinary homelessness among some whose practice doesn't quite fit anywhere; a "return of the repressed"—moments of recognition of significant everyday practices; shifts in ways of conceiving theory-practice relations; tightening resources encouraging institutions to redraw a boundary around a cluster of disciplines rather than around a single one; a channelling of funding and resources down well established lines; a restrictive territorialism among teaching staff.

Some of the issues follow from decisions about how to divide up for the purposes of organisation and management an educational institution. These can only be addressed at a particular level in any given institution; they are management issues which form part of local politics and call for managed and structural solutions. As difficulties they at least have the advantage of being relatively near the surface. Below the surface, though, there are issues which cannot be accounted for in terms of easily changeable organisational arrangements. The divisions of institutions are matched, reinforced or counter-pointed with formalist divisions of knowledge and practice, which provide the focus and sense of direction for established studies; which have applications way beyond any one institution, indeed beyond the institutions of education, and which provide a constant validation for ranges of practice and discourse. Superficial changes in organisation or academic structure which ignore these established boundaries are unlikely to work very well.

When I used the word discourse then, I separated it from practice. But it is probably more useful to use the term in the more inclusive way developed by Foucault and to remember that a whole range of practices and vested interests are bound up at any one time with any systems of division and classification. I shall use etymologies of some of the key terms as a way of catching illuminating connotations; then I shall look at some of the practices which can establish and sustain disciplines and even, though more rarely, larger frames within which disciplines can inter-relate.

I want to start with the key word, *interdisciplinarity*, breaking it into three meaningful components:

inter -discipline -arity

Let's start with discipline, having in mind a sequence of nouns which descends into deeper and deeper abstraction:

disciple    discipline    disciplinarity    inter-disciplinarity

The Latin *discipulus* meant, it seems, no more than learner or pupil. The Oxford English Dictionary of 1971 gives us as its first meaning for disciple: "One who follows or attends upon another for the purposes of learning from him (*sic*)". An educational model is there already: a follower of a mentor or guru, almost certainly male. Perhaps the complementary Latin word is "magister", *master*. The OED makes clear that the primary influence in English of the word is through the New Testament—a follower of Christ. It helps if followers of the "masters" are believers.

The Latin *disciplina* can be translated as "the instruction of disciples, tuition". The OED helpfully adds, "Etymologically, *discipline* as pertaining to the disciple or scholar, is antithetical to *doctrine*, the property

187

of the doctor or teacher; hence in the history of the word *doctrine* is more concerned with abstract theory and *discipline* with practice or exercise." It could be that in relation to the teaching of practical arts *doctrine* and *discipline* have merged.

Not surprisingly, one of the meanings for *discipline* is given as: "A particular course of instruction to disciples"; and another (2) as "a *branch* of instruction or education; a *department* of learning or knowledge;[148] a science or art in its *educational aspect*".[149]

A practical arts discipline is going to be made up of at least the following components, each of which can of course be given a different emphasis:

1. a defined making (or performance) practice or a defined set of related practices, requiring a combination of technical know-how and aesthetic judgement
2. a rationale (usually implicit?) for inclusion of any specific practice in the set and for its status within it
3. defined fields of reference: what examples of past and present practice are kept in play as part of the constant defining and re-defining of the discipline?
4. a discourse or set of discourses involving judgement and value.

If I am right that a tradition of master (with all the problems of maleness deliberately left with the term) and follower is still a powerful one in arts education, we should add:[150]

5. affiliation with a *magister* (or magisters). In some cases a course or institution will define its discipline in terms of its resident Master. In other cases the discipleship is at least at one remove: a disciple of a Master becomes a Master somewhere else. In other cases the Masters will be found at a glance in the course bibliography.[151]

I would also like to suggest that in any active and healthy discipline there is always a sixth:

6. an awareness of the full intellectual and cultural context in which the discipline operates. Where this sixth applies there will always be at least one framework for looking beyond itself, which broadens the field of reference to take in related practices and informing discourses.

What about "arity", though. An "inter-discipline", which seems to me a perfectly reasonable term for, for example, contemporary cultural studies, becomes quite rapidly itself a discipline. "Interdisciplinarity" is more a pre-disposition, attitude or ethos; let's say, above all, a general attitude to the relations between disciplines. As a pre-disposition it has a motive, and as I have implied above, this is never fixed or given, and the motives of interdisciplinary pioneers are never the same as those who follow. Those who follow are disciples; disciples constitute a discipline. A key motive is often political: by which I mean no more than the wish to put knowledge to a discernible use determined by desires and needs which have their origins outside the given divisions of knowledge.

And so that leaves us with "inter". Let's go quickly to three of the many senses. In each case I shall translate "inter" as the English "between":

1. relational: as in a conversation between two people; this is dynamic and dialectical; the "inter" marks off a field of force, with constant shifting of resultants; two disciplines meet and produce a changing third (a shifting synthesis)
2. spatial: as in the English saying "falling between two stools"—i.e. taking place in the space that lies between two or more disciplines. Disciplines are historical and relatively arbitrary; there will always be gaps identified or emerging in the fields of knowledge and practice
3. possessive: as in "shared between two": "Belonging in common to or composed of elements derived from different [disciplines in our case] (OED)

These are all two-way relationships. The arts have long been familiar with borrowings, poachings or plunderings, with the illuminations which arise from the practice of analogy. These are usually one-way. I want to concentrate on the three two-way senses, though, and to catch up with a holding definition of "interdisciplinarity":

> interdisciplinarity is an approach to the organisation of learning which is as concerned with achieved and potential relationships between disciplines, with spaces between disciplines or in overlapping domains, as it is with the self-defining activities of separate disciplines.

The intended implication of this definition is that productive interdisciplinarity needs informed critical attention to disciplinarity—awareness of the field of force of any discipline which is brought into interdisciplinary play. Productive interdisciplinarity is specific—the specificity of the disciplines in play, even if they are transformed by the play, is always significant.

And so now let's try a working definition of a discipline within the arts, hesitating at the limitations suggested by etymology and metaphor:

> *discipline*: a practice (or set of practices) identified with a com/de/ partment of knowledge (or set of same) unified by the following factors:

1. a **name** recognised within academic, critical, curatorial and funding practices

2. a **history** (including a history of those who could be followed)

3. a sense of a **meta-syllabus** (against which specific approaches can be measured) (syllabus = body of knowledge; existing pedagogic conventions; assumptions about core or component practices)

4. a set of defining **differences** from other nameable disciplines[152]

5. an **organisational** presence

   a. **within** institutions (with implications for the locations, designations and loyalties of personnel)

   b. **between** institutions and their "members" (professional bodies, network organisations such as CONCEPTS, journals)

6. the gift of a specific ontological inflection: it not only **has** a name; it also **gives** a name, which is then a primary attribute of what one is: doctor, artist, musician, etc.

7. an **apprenticeship** system for potential named members, including, most significantly, a system of judgement of qualification

The concept of the discipline belongs to an organic view of education: having identified a calling or discipline, a student develops within it, building knowledge and competence incrementally until a moment arrives of initiation into a relatively achieved state, meriting the named award. There is a sense of a quantity of knowledge and competence which is *enough*. This is not the same as the level of all too visible competence in professional practice. For a practitioner what constitutes enough? Is the question ever over?

Until recently in Britain the "discipline" has been linked to a model of education which sees it as a process of increasing specialisation, with students who choose an "academic" rather than "vocational" route usually reducing their study to three subjects at 16 and to one at 18. It has often been argued that the aims of higher education have been set by the specialist guardians of the disciplines in the universities and academies rather than through any overview of the needs either of individual students or a social whole.

This is a topic of current political debate, of course. In Britain the debate tends to be complicated by another set of divisions to do this time with age; planned change seldom seems capable of consistency across the entire learning age range. A national curriculum—a politically potent working definition of disciplines, their hierarchical relation to each other, their content and how to assess students within them—is being introduced for schools, changing the sense of the autonomy of arts subjects within schools. Some reduction of the range of knowledge usually takes place at 14. At 16 our young are expected to make specialising choices. For the 16–18 year olds the debate seems to be mostly absorbed by the sense of difference between vocational training and generalist "academic" (and therefore "subject"-based) teaching—this can be viewed in some cases as a conflict between a notion of a discipline policed by academies and a notion of a vocation either actually or supposedly desired by professional and industrial interests. Much arts education is situated most interestingly between ideas of the vocational and the academic and also between historically different notions of what constitutes vocational training: traditional skills still carry with them an almost mediaeval sense of apprenticeship; new technologies require different skills and dispositions—in which any actual application needs to be viewed as an example of the possible in relation to a transitional set of contingencies. This distinction prompts a number of questions about the value of both disciplines and vocational trainings for later employment and also about their value for partial employment, for non-employment and for full participation in a sense of the future of a changing social and cultural life.

In Higher Education a significant increase in the number of participants and a reduction in unit funding has been accompanied with the development of combined honours courses, modularisation and notions of credit accumulation. At the extreme, the open-choice modular scheme enables students to achieve degrees through the aggregation of different "modules" or subject-topics; "disciplines" lose their power to impose their own sense of coherence and unity. At most, these schemes promote a multi-disciplinarity. The larger the modular scheme, the wider "student choice", the more open needs to be the conception of the totality of the student's learning. It is organisationally difficult if not impossible in large schemes for the ethos of "interdisciplinarity" to permeate the scheme; institutions, departments or faculties which more narrowly define their field have more of an opportunity to plan for interdisciplinarity. It can, as at Dartington, become an organising principle for the conception of the whole curriculum, from macro structure to design of common components. Open-choice schemes pose particular problems for conceptualising an educated practitioner.

Specific models of interdisciplinarity can be taught. It can be argued that some versions of this approach do no more than expand the subject range. This, in itself can be valuable; having the structure to identify and teach practices which lie between or which are a common domain is valuable. This will be difficult for any institution embedded in traditional disciplinarity or wholly committed to open models of credit accumulation. In the former, exploratory projects can be set up which are structured in order precisely to explore the interaction between two practices, two sets of histories. It is worth considering within either model, modules or programme components which are designed to have explicit relationships with more than one pathway or which are explicitly designed to consider difference and connectedness.

There is an interdisciplinary issue for all arts teaching which extends beyond the specifics of skills training and which certainly applies to any teaching project which wishes to address its relation to the contemporary. Put at its crudest this is the theory/practice issue. Any traditionally established discipline comes fully equipped with a body of "theory", consisting often of an established canon of reference works and authors, a critical and analytical tradition (which is probably also canonical) and a decision about specific bodies of knowledge which might be relevant. Limits of time, particularly exaggerated in practical courses, make these decisions difficult. Artists need access to other forms of knowledge. Which forms? Physiology? Psychology? Sociology? Anthropology? Philosophy? Linguistics? To what extent is there already at any one time a convenient inter-discipline, a kind of "general studies" already packaged and available, such as contemporary forms of cultural theory? All these have their disciplinary frameworks and histories. What relationship should they have with the "practice"?

When a few years ago at Dartington we were trying to re-plan all our degree work in such a way that the relationship between disciplines could be activated we set ourselves the following guidelines:

   i.  ensure that the disciplinary boundaries are seen as historically and culturally specific and therefore subject to change

   ii.  establish a continuing debate, across subject lines, about the nature of performance and composition in such a way that the debate can influence student (and staff) practice

   iii. extend the awareness in all performers of factors which affect all performance but which have traditionally been given less attention within some disciplines

   iv. encourage students, in whatever discipline, to consider compositional solutions which might involve disciplines or media other than their own

   v.  enable a sharing of bodies of information and of conceptual perspectives which have relevance to all the arts

You will see that these are very practical considerations in the structuring and planning of teaching and I shall end with a number of considerations just as practical, which in some cases will clearly repeat elements of the discussion above:

Does the academic management structure of the department, faculty or institution support or hinder the possibility of interdisciplinarity?

What is the status of those in charge of disciplines? In what fora do they debate as equals? Is responsibility for interdisciplinarity explicitly located anywhere? In an individual? In a group? Does the management structure encourage competitiveness over resources or institutional status—in other words does it work towards the defence of disciplinary territory?

At what level in the institution are educational goals set? To what extent do they allow for collaborative agreement and planning? (Interdisciplinarity will never happen by *fiat*)

How, in relation to disciplines, is space deployed?

Does scheduling work for or against interdisciplinary work? What academic considerations are brought to bear on scheduling?

Are any curriculum components shared by students associated with different disciplines? If not, why not? If there are, how were these planned and agreed? How are the possibilities of different relations to different disciplines addressed?

Are there any curriculum components which specifically address issues of interdisciplinarity and set up the debate for the students? What support does a student receive whose work crosses disciplinary boundaries? What guidelines are there on student interdisciplinary collaboration?

Do assessment procedures encourage or discourage interdisciplinarity?

There are many other issues, of course, including important ones to do with entry systems, national and international course directories and promotional literature, which are geared to established subjects and their combinations. I am going to finish at this point, though, in the hope that I have raised questions of some practical help for those keen to promote specific approaches to interdisciplinarity. Everything I have said could imply that interdisciplinarity can be as carefully planned as disciplinarity. Let me subtly adjust that in a distinction that works in English: disciplines can be *planned*; interdisciplinarity needs to be planned *for*.

# Designing a Taught Postgraduate Programme in Performance Practices: Issues for Disciplines and Context [153]

## Preamble [154]

There is one main underlying question in what follows: what can be the most productive relationships between educational institutions which teach performing arts and the various professional worlds of performance practices. I shall not be suggesting a single answer.

Three terms came into play in earlier presentations: *practice, theory* and *research*. I want to add three more and to risk some absurdly short working definitions. The three extras are: *learning, discourse* and *praxis*.

I take *practice* to refer to a commitment to an action or set of actions that, in their moment of realisation, are what they are and nothing else. Any instance of practice will owe its meaning and value to genre, convention and tradition. Even so, as *practice* it will be particular to the concrete moment of its manifestation. The decisions of practice exclude alternatives in an act of commitment. Practitioners give this specificity constant attention.

In this context I take *theory* to refer to conceptual frameworks which can be used for both explanatory and generative purposes. Theory can gesture towards possibilities beyond the scope of any one practice and can be used as a fast track to bypass the slow accumulation of learning through experience. Generally speaking, criticism does not belong to the world of theory, though it is likely to draw from it.

*Discourse* is a useful term for remembering that there is a much wider frame of talk—of all kinds, including, most importantly, gossip—which is inseparable from any field of practice. These forms of talk will include received wisdoms about what is thought to be worth knowing. This is where criticism is more likely to belong. Many university departments have little to offer in the way of theory but are rich in discourse.

By *research* I mean no more than a systematic question-asking and finding-out in relation to either practice or theory. A research task can be timed to last an hour and it can be a lifetime's project.

And finally *praxis*, that term that is one of our remaining debts to Karl Marx: bringing all of the above to bear on each other in a strategic practice. Or, to put it more simply, to act after having taken thought.

I add *learning* as a reminder that this, rather than concrete "practice", is the primary purpose of all educational institutions. What should be learnt and for what purpose is not addressed, of course, simply by importing the term.

## Introduction

I am going to be using very recent and as yet relatively untested experience of planning, developing and beginning to implement a new master's programme to talk about issues for postgraduate approaches to arts learning. In particular I want to open up thoughts around the following:

1. Questions of purpose
2. Questions of level and starting point
3. Relations of named and established subject fields with emerging practices
4. A triangle of terms: practice/ theory/research
5. The role of academies in relation to contemporary practice
6. A programme structure to address these issues

I state them now not because I shall be moving systematically through them one by one, but for the opposite reason. I want to be able to move around them more freely.

## The Dartington context

I am going to approach these questions by way of something of a case study of the development in the institution where I have been working for some time: Dartington College of Arts, located in the rural South West of England. I shall offer a sketch of the context so that you can judge how much of what I have to say is quite specific and how much has a more general application.

Dartington is small, specialist and necessarily focused. All of its work relates in some way to contemporary performance arts. It has an undergraduate body of about 430, which is unlikely to grow significantly over the next few years, given current UK funding policies. These undergraduates are divided between Music, Theatre, Performance Writing and Visual Performance, with some also giving a proportion of their study to Arts Management.

There are about 25 research students, studying towards PhDs or MPhils. This number has been growing steadily over a five-year period. Many of these research projects have a practical component.

The number of salaried academic staff is in the low 20s. Nearly all of these are, in the current jargon, research-active—either as practitioners or as more conventional researchers or, in a number of cases, both. Each year, well over a hundred others, mostly practitioners, also make teaching contributions.

Dartington College of Arts is now very much part of the Higher Education world of the UK. This was by no means always the case. It emerged out of a project in rural social regeneration modelled on that of Rabindranath Tagore in India. A wealthy couple, Dorothy and Leonard Elmhirst—she from the United States, he from a different part of England—bought a depressed rural estate in the 1920s and set about a restoration intended to restore the local economy and the social and cultural environment as well as the buildings. They wanted to bring together in one place work, education, arts and a shared concern for the environment. They did not want these to be separate from each other. They wanted all of them to be part of communal interaction. Their view of the potential of arts activities within communal behaviour was not at all at odds with their espousal of and support for some of the key modernist painters, dancers and theatre makers from both sides of the Atlantic. To some of these they gave, quite literally, a home—and indeed more than a home, a work base. Michael Chekhov had a studio to work in; the Joos-Leder Dance Company had a dance studio specially designed for them.

Dartington was thus a place where the practice of the arts had priority over their teaching, though always, and I shall elaborate on this, in a way in which the two were seen to need each other. It was assumed that the practice—process as well as product—was for others. Teaching, of course, is always in one sense for others, though quite how "Other" will vary considerably since there is usually a strong motivation to transmit what is already known in order to ensure that the next generation is the "Same". In times of change the arts can mark a battle ground between this investment in the Same and Other.

The mission of the College stresses "personal and social value". When in sound-bite mode, we use three other headings to characterise our approach as:

- An interest in emerging practices and forms
- Pragmatic, theoretical and strategic concerns with context
- A concern with interdisciplinarity, borderline disciplines, and practices without clear disciplinary homes

**The Dartington MA and the notions of practice and learning**
We have just started a taught MA. A single framework offers routes to five different awards, all relating in some way to performance practices. This includes an approach to Arts Management for practitioners. The programme is aimed at and designed for practitioners—either recent graduates wanting to establish a practice or more experienced practitioners who want a structured opportunity to reflect on their practice and extend, develop or transform it, or perhaps even to change direction, to cross a disciplinary boundary. Because the research programme was already in place we were able to think carefully about the different purposes and values of a taught Masters and a research-based MPhil. Although there is a difference in status reflected in the varying investment in time, we wanted to see them as different kinds of opportunities, not just as steps on a single ladder. Researchers must have a clear project from the outset and be prepared to work it through on their own with supervisors as support and the institution—its staff, students, activities and facilities—as a sustaining environment. Taught Master's applicants want the opportunity for (re-)orientation, for examining their own motivation, for exploring methodology and for spending some time working in close proximity with others. With the MA we wanted to create a context in which the MA students would be actively helped to become a primary resource for each other.

I have said that the programme is aimed at and designed for practitioners. When we say "practitioner" at Dartington we mean reflective and autonomous practitioners—people who make their own work and expect to take responsibility for it. We also assume that for this kind of practitioner the process of learning is never over; their practice will continue to develop and adapt; and except in respect of quite particular skills, there will be no neat division between "training" and "application".

This kind of artist learns on the job, always.

More specifically we are trying to reach people who see their practice as fully contemporary and who are prepared to engage strategically with the context in which their work will be made. This is not a kind of practice that has well established career structures. These are always in the process of emergence and transformation. We expect people to be active in making work—and in helping to shape the contexts and conditions for that work—rather than more conventionally being equipped to "find" work.

There is a theme here which still challenges many of us: how to square a conviction that in times of change the arts must be part of the activity which shapes a future and at the same time keep touch with the everyday values and activities of that time. This too is where "context" comes in.

There is another theme I would like to pick out: connections between arts, learning and forms of sociability. All arts have their craft or skills dimension. In some traditions this dimension is very prominent and its learning sometimes jealously guarded. In relation to another kind of arts learning there is a doubleness which I would like to stress. Let me say that participation in arts activity—of whatever kind—is always both a particular way of being and acting in the world and also a very particular way of knowing it. The *learning how to* which is involved in the acquisition of craft or technical skills always also opens up on to a further set of possibilities, touching on the body's practices and knowledges. I am not trying to suggest that these openings are always consciously taken up. Far from it. Many practitioners are content to see themselves as technicians and aim perhaps at technical virtuosity. But for others there is this interplay between technique, medium, form, context, cognition, social intervention, where a change in any one aspect is likely to demand a change in at least some of the others. This interplay can never be over—another reason why practitioners of this persuasion are condemned to being "life-long learners". It isn't a choice. The packaging of competences and knowledge, which can name a moment of completion, is never for them. A new motive will demand a new skill, a new skill suggest new formal possibilities, and so on.

What I have tried to sketch here is an intertwining of *learning how to, learning through* and *engaging with*: a consciousness perhaps that form is knowledge and that this knowledge is always a practice, an event, an action in the world. As knowledge it always has substance, form and context. This cannot be precisely spoken in another tongue, nor perhaps, precisely, in another place. It can be spoken *about*, but that is another matter.

It has been my experience that the practitioners who fit the category I am trying now to sketch not only go on learning. They also can't help "teaching": they are often very good at it and find multiple ways of doing it. Because their own learning engages with the *how to* in relation to a *what* and a *why* and a *with what effect*, they tend to engage with responsibilities way beyond any narrower definition of their own practice. A rich notion of context is part of their activity. They see their work, perhaps, as not only *for* others, but as *with* or even *from*, others. The preposition I have left out is *about* others. That is far less relevant in my view.

## Purpose and motivation

I hope that it is becoming apparent that I am circling questions of *motivation* for practice and learning and how this might connect with postgraduate learning in performance practices. Without clarity about motivation, decisions about structure and curriculum content are vacuous.

Up till now I have assumed that the most important motivation is that of the practitioner him or herself. This accords with the image of the driven artist that has been with us at least since romanticism. Other motivations are now also assumed, relating to other so-called stakeholders in national educational projects. It is as well to name them. It is one clear way of deciding who or what a programme is for. Let's say, at speed, that these other stakeholders include parents, employers, professional bodies, educational organisations (at all of regional, national, institutional and inter-institutional levels), funding bodies, and those strange partners in the practice of the state, civil servants and politicians.

It is worth stressing that this is the separable list of stakeholders in the (higher) educational process. If we ask the same question about stake-holding in the performing arts we find ourselves in an even more complicated and speculative discussion. I shall leave the question hanging.

In many cases parents are extending the time of support for their daughters and sons, and want it to be worth it. It would be challenging indeed to design a postgraduate course around the presumed wishes of parents as a category. The category of employer is relatively straightforward in relation to the specialist needs of the cultural industries but much less clear within the loose web of not-for-profit activity where so much emerging contemporary practice finds itself. The clearer the connections with employment, in its conventional sense, the clearer also the role of professional bodies.

The educational context is complex. I shall pick out one or two features or relevance to this paper. The specialist focus and scale at Dartington removes one layer of problems: any new programme is going to be consistent with the declared institutional mission; tension between satellite and centre is much less likely. Other issues we cannot avoid. Despite a number of years of widespread modularity and a national statistic showing that now nearly 80% of all UK applicants for first degrees apply for programmes of study involving more than one subject, the notion of the subject is still a guiding principle behind funding, recruiting directories and academic quality assurance. It is risky to step outside the canonic roll call of academic subjects either by proposing a new one or by taking up an interdisciplinary position that looks across more than one border. Emerging practices often do not fit neatly within these established categories.

Finally in this rapid survey, there is the combination of funding regimes and government policy and the way that these can be brought together to act as a filter on student numbers. Currently "employability" as a criterion is likely, in the UK, to crop up in most funding-related documents. This of course encourages programme design in fields where this notion can be addressed relatively unproblematically. At least within the arts this might also encourage short-termism—a failure to address newer and more open notions of employment and patterns of work in the future. It might also fail to address important questions about the roles that participation in arts activities can play *in relation to* the world of work without always being seen as part of it. Issues of cultural policy need more headings than "employment". It helps if governments and their funding agencies have an understanding of the values of arts activities that goes beyond the notion of immediate "employability".

Earlier I invoked one current slogan for educational policy, "life-long learning", and implied at least that in my view any postgraduate programme should fit into a sense of a learning continuum, or of multiple learning continua, with possibilities of very different points of departure.

The second familiar category I want to invoke is Continuing Professional Development. I have already suggested that highly motivated practitioners will find ways of going on learning whether or not they undertake formal programmes of study. This is an internal drive, which will inevitably also be stimulated by contextual changes, some of which may well suggest the need for updating of skills and knowledge: in new technologies or new discursive fields, in response to manifest social and cultural change in the community, or to understand changes in cultural policy, for example. Where opportunities exist, individuals who recognise these needs in themselves can deal with them in piece-meal fashion if they so wish. A master's programme with its own logic of coherence may not be the answer. Even so, it seems to me, any taught postgraduate programme has to be positioned in relation to this heading. What are the development needs of practitioners? To what extent can practitioners be told what these needs are and to what extent do they need a structured opportunity to find their own answers?

It is at this point that I want to address the question of *post- what?* Postgraduate awards are by definition for people who already have a first degree. In practice this has proved true of our first intake at Dartington, though, in common with many other institutions it is not the degree as such that matters to us; it is what it signals, what it might say is already in place. Any applicant who can demonstrate the qualities without actually having the qualifications would be more than welcome.

So what are these qualities? Some of them are of course generic and lead towards those debates about "graduate attributes". For example, an honours graduate is expected to know how to learn within the protocols of higher education—how to shape and organise a discursive enquiry; to be at ease with the notion of "theory"; to be disciplined in the management of learning time; to have a working awareness of the western divisions of formal knowledge; and to have been initiated into at least one academically defined subject field. Graduates with conventional arts, humanities or social science degrees, may, through their first degree studies, have become highly motivated to extend their study *of* or *about* into a practice. The degree itself will not indicate their ability to make this transformation. In many cases they will already have made an independent start and will have work to show for it and that work might be sign enough, one way or the other. I would be interested to know of postgraduate conversion courses designed specifically to effect this transition. There could well be a demand. Many gifted school students are still steered away from practical arts activity in favour of conventional studies whose practice is geared to the essay.

Where the first degree has been in a practical arts discipline there are other expectations. It certainly should indicate that the graduate could operate within a nameable practice. The award itself may say relatively little about the status and identity of this practice for the individual. There is a profound difference between having marketable skills and having a sense of being a practitioner with an established or emerging sense of direction. It is this latter that we are after. This is not something that a first degree can be expected to confer on all graduates. Nor is it something that has a direct correlation with class of degree. The aims and orientation of the particular degree programme will be pertinent and so of course will the motivations—again—of the graduate.

*What is my practice?* Or *what does my practice seem to be becoming?* These are very valid postgraduate questions. They need a structured environment in which to ask them.

## Types of programmes in the arts

A minute or so ago I referred to the orientation of a programme. I want to come at this term by way of two slightly different typologies: one derived from the *Review of Postgraduate Education* published by the Higher Education Funding Council for England and others in May 1996 and still referred to in the UK as the Harris Report; the other, one that I have been using for a few years now.

Harris included the following types for master's programmes: "professional and practice related", "preparation for research" and "deepening subject knowledge". The first indicates a clear link between a programme in an academic institution and the assumed needs of a profession. In the UK at least this type might also be taken to imply a link with at least one professional body, perhaps even recognition by a union. An award may double up as a licence to practice. The other two imply a greater likelihood of a closed academic loop in the sense that academic institutions are still the privileged homes of research, at least in relation to arts activities. "Subject knowledge", when set in distinction to practice, is also an academic concept through and through, I would argue.

At Dartington we found these types useful provided they were not seen as mutually exclusive. We decided that we were addressing all three listed above. Practice, research and subject knowledge are all relevant for a particular kind of practice, one that embraces theoretical modes of enquiry and values certain discursive practices. More pragmatically, the combination acknowledges that the academies are now very significant players in the supporting framework for contemporary practice: many practitioners have academic roles, either as teachers or researchers or both. "Employability" for an increasing number of practitioners will at least include the thought of employment within education.

The second typology I am going to use is mostly descriptive but is also intended to be useable as a simple orientation device. There are three types. These too will, of course, be found to overlap in practice.

**Type 1**: programmes designed to train practitioners for known and established practices: conservatoires, acting schools, degree level training programmes related to employment in the cultural industries. The motive for such study is vocational. These programmes must be career-related. They risk being designed around an inevitably very low success rate measured in terms of successful career rather than academic qualifications.

This type relates to the Harris category of "professional and practice related". The assumption is that the profession is an established one with known forms of practice. It is likely to be geared to the known rather than the unknown—in some cases so known that the repertoire belongs to the heritage industry.

These are for obvious reasons the kinds of programmes which need to work closely within an understanding of the needs—or supposed needs—of employers.

**Type 2**: programmes designed predominantly as studies *about* practices or at least the formal outcomes of such practices—their related bodies of scores, texts, scripts, histories and commentaries. This approach tends to be doubly text-based. It studies texts and it results in the production of secondary—that is, discursive—texts. It relates to the Harris type of "deepening subject knowledge". The key issues here are:

What assumptions underlie the designation and definition of the subject field? How is it bounded?

What is the object of such study? Towards what practices does it lead? I am surprised how seldom this question is asked—how little examination there seems to have been of the privileged practice of the essay (of which this paper, is of course, an example).

Historically this form of study has always been better equipped to deal with texts as already there, and by implication with some sense of a canon. Its innovations, where they exist, are more likely to be in relation to its own discursive instruments—methodological or conceptual—rather than with forms of practice.

Type 3: there are programmes which share with Type 1 that they are practical but differ in that they are not preparing students for known and established practices. The approach tends to look for a balance between technical training and conceptual and strategic awareness. They tend to have a strong reflective and theoretical component which is geared to practice just as much as to discursive commentary.

This is where Dartington sits and where any programme concerned with the idea of making—rather than interpreting or studying *about*— will find itself. The issues here are many. If neither "known and established practices" nor already named subject fields are the key determinants of the frame, there is a real difficulty in setting limits and a risk of arbitrariness in pedagogic decisions about skills, bodies of knowledge and frames of reference. There is the opposite risk that other considerations, including validation principles and methods and institutional and national quality assurance frameworks, will exert negative pressure on approaches which are inevitably open-ended since they emphasise questions and motivations and try to avoid institutionalising solutions.

## Parts and whole / subjects and frame

A key issue of principle as well as of design is in the naming of wholes and parts and of the relative status of whole and part. At Dartington we have gone for a solution along the lines of "specialist study in an interdisciplinary context". We tend to name versions of the parts and arrange validation procedures to turn those names into awards. The "whole" is then a meta-structure, aimed at effecting interaction between the parts. So for our MA we do have a name for the whole: Performance Practices. This is not a name for any award, though. The structure of the MA, with a taught Part 1 (representing one third of the credit value of the whole), and supported independent study and practice as Part 2 (the remaining two thirds), is very much designed to bring all students across subjects together for both theoretical and methodological study, for developing a shared critical language and for developing means of supportive and collaborative activity. A subject narrows down the skills range and a body of knowledge. A subject is seen then as a platform for practice and enquiry which crosses over into a neighbouring boundary or finds itself, as it were, in an epistemological and pragmatic no-place, between boundaries, itself not bounded.

When someone fills in an application form they have to choose one of five subject boxes to tick. A high proportion finds this choice difficult to make. Is their practice better placed in relation to Visual Performance or Devised Theatre? Where should a writer who comes out of a fine art education go? Continue the writing practice in relation to the visual art discourses of Visual Performance or bring that art training to bear on a focused attention to textuality? Of the seven of our own graduates who were accepted on to the MA, three crossed over from their undergraduate subject to another one: one from Theatre to Visual Performance, one from Music to Visual Performance, one from Theatre to Performance Writing. Another applicant, not a Dartington graduate, after being accepted on to Performance Writing, wanted within a day or two of starting to relocate herself within Devised Theatre. Roughly half of all applicants have said that they wanted to tick more than one box.

This is likely to remain an unresolved issue for some time. In relation to contemporary practice, existing subject fields no longer operate either as guilds or clear ontological frames offering "natural" recognition of belonging. Fit is in many cases approximate, suggesting that for practical purposes these taxonomies are always obsolescent. For an independent study MA this need not be an issue. The skills and conceptual curriculum could be tailored to individual need, as with a practice-based PhD. Taking responsibility for a syllabus or—to put it another way—for providing the second term in a dialectic, forces an issue, and brings tension and challenge.

At validation one panellist invited us to consider flipping the solution: naming the award after the whole and allowing for options within that, perhaps showing up in brackets after the award name. We were clear. Our interest in interdisciplinarity and cross-disciplinary work required the discipline of a discipline, the defining of a field.

## (In)conclusion

All of these considerations are still live for us. There is no one magical solution that will address all of them in one blow. Academic structures are always constraining—sometimes creatively so—and the scheduling constraints of combining part-timers with full-timers are considerable. What we have tried to do is create an environment in which reflective practitioners have the opportunity to question their own sense of direction and learning need, reflect productively on questions of methodology, engage with contemporary cultural discourse, pursue a relevant research question and develop their work in a context which gives permission to concentrate on learning from practice and from peers.

I started by saying that the design is as yet untested. We are seven weeks in. The questions are complex but the design solution needs to be simple. It is too early to say how well our very simple adopted structure will deliver what we want of it.

# *Review of* The Anxiety of Interdisciplinarity 155

Alex Coles and Alexia Defert (eds) (Vol Two of *de-, dis-, ex. Interdisciplinarity: Art / Architecture / Theory*) 168 pp., (London: BACKless Books and Black Dog Publishing, 1998.

Reviewing this book for Performance Research poses a problem that the book itself might be expected to help solve. If "performance" is a name for a contested interdisciplinary field of contemporary cultural practices, here is a book whose title finds no single name but which commits itself to an "interdisciplinarity" in relation to Art / Architecture / Theory. What should a review do? Take this designated interdisciplinary field as quite other, to be viewed over the hedge as it were? Consider if there are issues that can valuably be researched in relation to performance that are entangled—"imbricated" as Barthes or his translators might say—with issues considered here? Gauge correspondences? Or look at general issues for attempting to establish or operate within interdisciplinary fields? Each of these questions implies not just a different review but different models of interdisciplinarity.

At the time of writing, this series of "volumes"—carefully not referred to at any point as a journal—has reached Volume Three. "Interdisciplinarity" appears in both this volume title and the series title, suggesting that it is the key topic, not just a mode of operation. There are other aspects to the layering of titles that snag. At least two of the dislocated prefixes are open to ambiguity and, after reading the collection, make me wonder what happened to "inter-" and "post-". And this interdisciplinarity is quite specific: Art / Architecture / Theory. Given the discussion that goes on within the pages it is surprising that so many troublesome unities can be invoked in the title. Perhaps two anxieties for interdisciplinarity should be (1) the temptation to essentialise its contributory disciplines and (2) the fragility of any shared understanding of what is meant by the term. Are we to expect a concern with hybrid or collaboratively cross-disciplinary fields of practice? Or an attention to the named component fields that draw on the discourse of the others? Will architecture be treated as though it were "art" and if so what would that mean? Or is this really about theory and practice—the conjunction of disciplines from these two larger domains? And so on—the questions could continue.

Of all the unities implied in the titles the most troubling of all to me is that last: Theory. Have we reached a point where Theory is a discipline, where there is a canon of primary texts or authorities (in a medieval sense) marking out the field? Perhaps by now an interdiscipline of cultural theories has fully achieved disciplinary status. A fairly short bibliography could be elicited or inferred from this collection and it is an increasingly familiar one. There are noticeable absences: anthropology, for example; Bakhtinian/Volosinovian approaches that insist that language is nothing if not context bound and is only encountered as "speech"; J.L. Austin's approach—recently most productively applied by Judith Butler—that attends to what signification does, not just what it is alleged to say or mean; and lastly, the line of theorising of the everyday, associated most notably with de Certeau.

The volume is topped and tailed with two interviews, forms that on the face of it give an opportunity for editors to fix an agenda but which in practice are usually subverted by the authority of the interviewee. In this case, neither interviewee is particularly interested in giving detailed responses to questions about architecture, the main focus of the volume. The first is Julia Kristeva; the second, Hal Foster. The first article is by Rosalind Krauss, like Foster a Professor of Modern Art and editor of October. These three all have an authority that extends beyond the disciplinary fields cited above.

What I am circling is this question of a discipline, what it is, what any of us can do with it, and what can we do without it. The articles in the collection allude to but never directly confront this question. Julia Kristeva very helpfully relates the issue both to her own individual intellectual trajectory and to the pedagogical aspirations of an educational institution. Her early ambitions to study nuclear physics or astronomy were not realisable in the political context for her family in Bulgaria at the time. I suspect that many connect with that: for any individual a discipline is as likely to be a response to contingencies as to a call of destiny. One way or another choices are made—or land upon us—which locate us in divisions of practice and knowledge-labour which are already very much in place. Some of these take years of initiation during which we take on—at least to an extent—an identity that belongs to the specialism. It is not just something we know about or know how to do; it is what we are.

These specialisms are both epistemological and pragmatic. They are to do with what it is felt necessary to know, what form that knowledge should take, how it should be acquired, what is pertinent and what is impertinent. Knowledge is a set of institutional and individual processes so that there are always performances, practices, involved. Putting it crudely, how do you do knowledge? By "making art"? By designing buildings for others to construct, use, walk past unknowingly or knowingly to comment upon? By adding directly to the genre pool of knowledge—for example through writing articles or reviews?

No one can do all of this, know of all of this. Disciplines are in part melancholy responses to the unavoidable trauma of ignorance. Both Kristeva and Foster point out how much work is required in an interdisciplinary approach; there is so much less that you are allowed not to know. This might make the anxiety attributable to interdisciplinarity more burdensome but it would need arguing. Why be interdisciplinary, why "do" it? This question of motivation is all: what gaps or flaws in the divisions of knowledge and practice, in the defining of boundaries with immigration control, drive you this way?

There are modalities, technologies and institutions of knowledge— for its acquisition, storage, transmission, its economic status. These are historical; these change. A "discipline" is every bit as much to do with networks of vested interests as it is with "pure" differences in topic, angle of knowledge, career. The so-called "knowledge revolution" has not yet had a profound effect in this respect. The new technologies of knowledge do not operate on the same categorial principles that produced the current array of "disciplines"; nor are they likely to be respectful of the current systems of authority that protect the boundaries.

A structure of disciplines represents a massive investment in specialisation. An anxiety of specialisation, unless it is approached as a platform for any number of adaptations or transformations, is the threat of anachronism, of pertinence becoming impertinent overnight. Both Kristeva and Foster touch on this. The last words of Kristeva's interview are these: "Thus, let us learn to draw again." (21) Foster expresses a related anxiety about "what might serve as a medium in a post-medium age" (168). There is a specialised sense of discipline here: the craft or trade discipline.

The other contributions to *The Anxiety of Interdisciplinarity* are focused on instances, appearing to operate within the brief of "art / architecture / theory" rather than addressing the general problematic in a more systematic way. A number of themes do emerge and more than once I had the experience of an article later in the collection providing a response to questions raised in my reading of earlier ones.

Appropriately for a publication addressing interdisciplinarity, some different discursive modes are used. Apart from the interviews, the prevailing mode is the theoretically informed art-historical article, but there is also a sequence of six photographs of institutional interiors by Candida Hôfer and a piece by Howard Caygill which combines photography with a more open form of narrative commentary interspersed with theoretical meditation.

The Rosalind Krauss piece is a republished 1977 article that uses a discussion of Peter Eisenman's Houses to plot a narrative leading to the emergence of the post-modern. In a lucid explication Krauss characterises formalism as the rendering of the transparent into the opaque (Compare Julia Kristeva: "In many ways theory is pursued because something is hidden behind the visible. But we need the visible side of the equation first". (21)); structuralism as "the dispersal of unities into a field of differences" (45); and then, finally, the post-modern as the expression of differences "without positive terms" (50). Operating powerfully on this is an interesting contradiction: the importation from literary theory of an expanded notion of text in relation to predominantly visual discourse— that architecture is not only a "language" but is in the main a visual one. There is an attempt (this is 1977, remember) to explore the notion of subjectivity in relation to architectural space but it is constrained by the chosen linguistic model and by reliance on phrases like: "The work of art pictures more than its own contents; it also pictures its beholder". (47)

Who is the "beholder" in relation to a house? In this article the house is treated—and perhaps was by the architect—as a sculpture, as an "object" in a subject-object relation. This is a decontextualised house, as it were isolated in a gallery, not pushed up against other houses in social space where people get on with their lives. This is also the effect of Hôfer's black and white photographs of institutional interiors—with one exception empty of people and therefore of the immediacy of institutional function. As soon as people move through spaces like these the geometry is disturbed. This emptiness troubles the point of view but in these photographs—unlike the Robert Smithson piece described in another article—technically there is one. Site lines are organised perspectively: as beholder I am outside emptiness; I am excluded but I am excluded from nothing.

The counterpoint this offers with the first paragraph of Louis Martin's article on the architect, theorist and teacher, Bernard Tschumi, is an example of the sequencing I referred to above: "The project was based on the statement that the success of urban life depends on the relationships established between peoples, ideas, objects" (61). This article concerns itself with architectural practice as cultural and political strategy. Tschumi lends himself to the book's thematic in a number of ways. He was fully aware of the theoretical preoccupations of, for example, the Tel Quel group, was aware of their attempts to incorporate architecture into semiological theory, saw architecture as an expanded discursive field with actual buildings as only a part and, according to Martin, was prepared to extend Derrida's privileging of writing over speech :

> Just as Derrida had replaced speech with writing, in arguing that architecture was a form of writing anterior to textual writing, Tschumi proposed to replace writing with architecture. (80)

This particular article touches usefully on one of the possible mechanisms for—and forms of—interdisciplinarity: "transposition". Can you transpose a theory of language to the practice of architecture? If you do so are you acting on an intuition in productive analogy or are you assuming—as Saussure did at first with his famous anticipation of semiology as a meta-discourse subsuming linguistics—that there is a meta-discourse or perhaps an Ur-theory from which others can proceed:

> Thus the logic of language appeared to be the primordial symbolic material from which to start in order to understand other signifying practices. (Kristeva, 4)

I take "transposition" to be itself an analogy taken from musical composition and arrangement. Analogy is the more general conceptual device: to what extent can we treat these as alike? Analogy assumes equivalence. Homology assumes structural identification rather than equivalence—that there is a deeper structure underlying different forms.

Some compositional concerns across arts practices seem to me to be homological rather than analogical. These can be intuited fairly rapidly. A compositional trick is to start by saying, for example, what happens if I treat this poem as though it were a piece of music, as though it were a visual image, and so on? This kind of discussion raises questions about the productiveness of certain interdisciplinary or cross-disciplinary strategies.

The article by Timothy Martin on Robert Smithson moves straight in on a parallel between Lacan and Smithson in their conceptions of a split subject. There is no indication given that either had read the other. The article relies on two careful explications of work by Smithson against the notion of the split subject, of binocular (split) vision, the desire of the subject to see the gaze and the idea of an architectural unconscious. This involves detailed accounts of the lost Enantiomorphic Chambers and of the lecture on the Hotel Pelanque in Mexico. Both are accounts of refusals of any kinds of unity or happy closure. The Hotel Palenque is a long way from Eisenman's Houses.

Beatriz Colomina's piece on another house, that of the Eames couple, is anecdotal, descriptive, unusual in this context in not appearing to need to validate itself through theoretical exegesis. The Eames shared something with Tschumi in viewing architecture as part of a larger game—according to Colomina in their case a "life-style" game—and something with Smithson in a playful interest in what could, borrowing his phrase, be called "de-architecturisation".

The final piece—apart from the Foster interview—is the dual text (perhaps not dual; perhaps as in the other articles the photographs are illustrative?) by Caygill of a visit to Naples deliberately undertaken in full knowledge of the powerful superstitions already at work on the place itself and on the place as site of the kinds of tourism that the author wants both to acknowledge and outwit. It is an engaging piece whose photographs could not be more different from Höfer's. These don't record "architecture"—instead his Cageian game catches buildings that get in the light and that in doing so are usually shaded or blurred—the blur of passing without attention to form. What is avoided is the projection of a narcissism on to building. The text is kept unified through the discursive (talkative even) presence of the author. Though this is a kind of practice that genuinely muddles "theory" and "practice", there is no doubt which is the dominant mode.

Like the Höfer piece, the work is recent (1997 in this case). The work discussed in the articles can be dated as follows: Eisenman Houses—dates not given; probably mostly 1960s; most of the references to Tschumi activities are 1970s and early eighties; the Smithson references 1965 and 1969; the Eames house, 1949.

What do these dates tell us? Perhaps that so much intellectual discourse operates within an inter-temporality in which a speaking subject supposed to be split calmly views across time texts which stay still long enough to annul the threatening anxiety of their fragmentation?

# *Notes*

*Author's Preface*

[1] The poet was Kris Hemensley and the date somewhere in the mid-70s. I had finished a draft when Kris was invited onto the editorial board of the Australian journal for which the piece was intended and this was felt to introduce a conflict of interest.

*Thirteen Ways of Talking About Performance Writing*

[2] This lecture was given to all first year undergraduates of Dartington College of Arts on Tuesday 22nd November 1994. This was the inaugural term for a new undergraduate degree called Performance Writing. The lecture was one of a series of "definings" of the subject fields at Dartington. The other fields at the time were Arts Management, Music, Theatre and Visual Performance.

[3] At the time of first writing, the plan had been for two colleagues, Caroline Bergvall and Melinda Drowley, to be performing a task of writing behind me. Caroline missed the occasion but the anticipation that she would have been there remains in the text.

*Performance Writing 1994–2004 (a talk)*

[4] As part of the 2004 Exeter Text Festival, Mark Leahy and Deborah Price curated an exhibition at the Phoenix, Exeter, celebrating the first ten years of Performance Writing at Dartington. The Exeter exhibition was open between 30th April and 16th May 2004. I was asked to give a short talk about Performance Writing at the opening. This is a text of what I remembered of the talk a few days later. (The exhibition moved to the Gallery, Dartington College of Arts from 20th–30th May 2004 and then from 10th–14th November 2004 to the Fine Arts Gallery, George Mason University in Washington DC.)

*Performance Writing: twenty years and still counting*

[5] To appear in the special Performance Writing issue of the *Journal for Writing in Creative Practice* (Issue editor, Jerome Fletcher) in 2013.

[6] As it happens, according to the Wikipedia entry "most of the stars in Orion are thought to be physically associated with each other". According to the same source, though, "There are alternative ways to visualise Orion". http://en.wikipedia.org/wiki/Orion_(constellation). (accessed 30.10.12).

[7] By "we" here I mean both the initial mixed disciplinary planning group and those involved in teaching and talking the project into operation. (1: 42, 148)

[8] To what extent could it be asked of any text whatsoever, not is it an advertisement, but what is it advertising? This may also be a question about the co-option of the desire which, in writing, runs in syntax and prosody every bit as much as in reference and proposition.

[9] Variants of Cultural Studies were increasingly adopted by arts schools from the late 1970s as suitable "theory" for contemporary practitioners.

[10] Perhaps initially largely through cris cheek. Caroline Bergvall uses the term "with caution" in Bergvall (1996). It came to be used as one of the "five modes" within the curriculum, the others being visual, sonic, digital and page-based.

[11] While Derrida's expanded understanding of writing was productive for performance writing, those of us interested in uses of the voice as materially significant within performances of writing were resistant to wholesale dismissals on the grounds of a supposed "metaphysics of presence" that preoccupation with voice could represent. See 'Dedicated to Derrida' which appears as a postlude in Cavarero (2005: 213–241).

[12] In the early 1990s, the influence was still strong of a number of poets who had responded to debates about the performativity of language as political through and through by identifying themselves, or allowing themselves to be identified, as L=A=N=G=U=A=G=E poets. They were of course by no means the first poets to recognise the social forces that were implicit in the far from innocent or exclusive medium of their trade. The critical—and even more so, the polemical—writings of some of them very much informed the early thinking about performance writing more, I think, with exceptions, than did their own poems.

[13] *Performance Research* devoted a themed issue to this topic. (*Performance Research, On the Page*, 2004)

[14] As I write, a merger is planned between Penguin Books and Random House, two very large producers of printed pages. The motivation for the merger is explicitly given as the threat to paper print of corporate e-book distribution. Every effort has been made for Amazon's Kindle to simulate the experience of reading pages, as though a change in one dimension need not affect the others. This is a classic instance of skeuomorphism, in the sense of a form (gk. *morphe*) originally designed for one "vessel" (gk. *skeuos*) being adapted with minimum change for another.

[15] Now Falmouth University.

[16] This term refers to the budget allocated by the European Union to assist the development of regions whose GDP is under 75% of the Union average. Previously this was known as Objective 1 funding. Nothing in the objectives for the funding, administered through the ERDF (European Regional Development Fund) and the ESF (European Social Fund), refers directly to arts or education, though "research and innovation" are signalled within the ERDF's terms.

[17] Results lead quickly to Bergvall (1996), Allsopp (1999), cheek (no date) and Clapham (2010) as well as to Falmouth and Dartington pages.

[18] See (1: 148–9) for a list emerging in 2006.

*Sentenced to*

[19] Published in *Performance Research* Vol 1, No 1 (Spring 1996) pp. 98–102. With thanks to the publishers: http://www.tandfonline.com/toc/rprs20/current.

[20]      Good my lord,
You have begot me, bred me, loved me. I
Return those duties back as are right fit,
Obey you, love you and most honour you.

[21] In J. L. Austin's (1976) sense of "performative" speech where an utterance does something as well as says something. All sentences are located *between* people and necessarily enact or propose a form of relationship. Syntax is inseparable from these constant enactments. In any performance, especially in any form of live performance, a sentence may be *either* between performers (actors) *or* between a performer and audience. Of course, it is seldom *either/or*; it is more usually both.

[22] Not, of course, the only one to trust. Not even the only one to have difficulties with her (grammatical) inheritance. A whole other article could look at the Fool's sentences and their forms of address: the unlocated pronoun removes some risks from truth-telling.

[23] "She squints down" rather than the instruction, "Squint down" or even "Get her to squint down".

## Performed through

[24] Published in *Performance Research* Vol 2 No. 1 (1997), pp. 68–72; first given as a paper at the first Performance Writing Symposium, held at Dartington College of Arts in April 1996. With thanks to the publishers: http://www.tandfonline.com/toc/rprs20/current.

[25] See Bourdieu (1992), especially 'Authorised Language' and 'Rites of Institution', pp. 107–126.

[26] This discussion owes itself very obviously to J.L. Austin's *How to do things with words* (1976) but also to the Bourdieu discussions referred to above.

[27] I am intending to develop these thoughts on personal pronouns in a later article. (1: 70–74)

[28] See Benveniste (1971: 101–112) and my own previous article in this series (1: 53–60).

[29] For a different list, see Gertrude Stein's 'Poetry and Grammar' (Stein 1971: 125–147).

[30] In the original talk, I had left "or" out. Fiona Templeton suggested afterwards in conversation that it should be there. Of course!

## Missing Persons

[31] Published in *Performance Research*, Vol 3 (Spring 1998), No 1, pp. 87–90. With thanks to the publishers: http://www.tandfonline.com/toc/rprs20/current.

[32] Jespersen's, and later Jakobson's, term for personal pronouns and other words like "here" and "now" which rely for their specific meaning on the instance and context of each speech event in which they occur. (Jakobson 1995: 386–389)

[33] Skeat's (1993: 542) gloss on "converse" includes this: "to dwell (lit. to turn oneself

about)". I like the suggestiveness of both aspects of this—dwelling in language and turning oneself from *you* to *I*.

[34] In a much quoted moment, Jacques Lacan, thus: "...there is no speech without a reply, even if it is met only with silence, provided that it has an auditor...". (1977: 40)

[35] The title of the long-running (1977–98) BBC Radio 4 Programme, *Does He Take Sugar?*, catches the effect of this exclusion.

[36] "The addressee, however, is included within a book's discursive universe only as discourse itself." (Kristeva 1986: 36)

[37] A revised version of the cited article was incorporated as a chapter into Riley 2000a under the changed title of 'Linguistic Unease' (56–92).

## Not Showing

[38] This symposium, planned by Caroline Bergvall, took place at Dartington College of Arts on the 19–20 January, 2002. Participants were asked to prepare a note for the symposium's web-page (no longer accessible) and an intervention—rather than a structured paper—within the proceedings. Both of my contributions are included below.

[39] If I recall correctly, all participants had been asked to name ahead of time two "items" that could act as points of reference in the symposium's discussions and to provide a brief written commentary on their pertinence, to be read ahead of the symposium.

[40] At the time of preparing this note for publication, a copy of this print can be viewed at http://digital-libraries.saic.edu/cdm/printview/collection/jfabc/id/2729/type/singleitem. See also Finlay 1998.

[41] Cassell's *Latin Dictionary* of approximately 1905 divides *privo*, *privare* into "a bad sense" and a "good sense": "to deprive of" and "to free from". Both Skeat (1993: 371) and the OED gloss the "deprive of" variant as "to bereave", with the past participle, *privatus*, giving us private. A privileged person could then be someone either deprived of or liberated from the benefits and restrictions of law.

[42] I was thinking of his notion of hegemony, which he uses and considers on many occasions throughout Gramsci (1971).

## Reading Illegible Pages

[43] Published in *Performance Research*, Vol 9, No 2, 2004 (ed. Ric Allsopp and Kevin Mount), pp. 15–23, along with the supplementary piece below. With thanks to the publishers: http://www.tandfonline.com/toc/rprs20/current. The photographs in Figs 1 and 2, taken at the exhibition at the Fine Arts Gallery, George Mason University (see Note 4 above) by Nicky Matthews-Evans, replace the images in the original.

[44] "When you see a word, you cannot help but read it." (Harley 200: 150)

[45] "The antiabsorptive does not so much prevent / absorption as shift its plane / of engagement—forcing / a shift in attentional focus." from 'Artifice of Absorption' (Bernstein 1992: 76).

[46] "Writing is not on paper, like a flat projection upon a screen, but it is *in* the paper, as it were." Robert Sheppard (in Cobbing and Upton, 1998; no page numbers)

[47] The blank and the black pages in *Tristram Shandy* are both highly legible—one to be filled, the other a graphic version of "Alas, poor Yorick". Images of these can be seen on the Glasgow University Library website (Sterne 2000). The image of the blank page (147) shows that it is not blank at all. The text of p.148 shows through, to my eye just below legibility.

[48] Jacques Lacan's reply to M. Valabrega, when he has just said, "In consequence it is the forgetting of the dream that is the obstacle", "It isn't the obstacle, it's part of the text." (Lacan 1991: 126). Or Gertrude Stein: "it is wonderful how handwriting which is illegible can be read, oh yes it can". (cited in Perloff 1998: 264 and Dworkin 2003: xviii; Stein's proposition appears in Stein 1939: 155. The Dworkin citation—and inclusion in the bibliography—was mistakenly omitted from the originally published version of this article).

[49] N Katherine Hayles discussing Roland Barthes *S/Z* in Hayles (1990: 188): "Barthes concludes that "literatures are in fact arts of "noise"" and declares that this "defect in communication" is "what the reader consumes".

[50] Steve McCaffery in Cobbing and Upton (1998).

[51] How new? *Tristram Shandy* was first published between 1759 and 1767; Joanna Drucker's *The Century of Artist's Books* was published in 1995.

## Reading a Polished Page

[52] This reading doubles as a postscript to the article on reading illegible pages above and as a commentary on a photograph by Tanja Dabo inserted in the same issue of the journal. The handwritten page appeared as p. 92; the whole printed text is in the DVD included with the issue.

## Two Textual Collaborations

[53] This essay was prepared as a paper for a seminar in the Performance Writing Field Research Seminar Series, Dartington campus, University College Falmouth, May 5th 2009. The colours and lack of contrast in some of the images used in the talk made it difficult to transfer them into monochrome; some have had to be left out. A version of the paper is planned for publication in a projected web journal to be called *Divergence* (ed. Keith Jebb).

[54] Of course I could not begin to enumerate all those who have contributed to the work, the vast majority of them unknowingly: just think of all those authors of InDesign software.

[55] "Since November 2004 I have edited and produced a series of broadsheets out of the School of English, Trinity College Dublin, called *Kore Broadsheets*. [...] The series will conclude with Broadsheet # 26 in 2009, at which point all 26 broadsheets will be installed as part of a permanent exhibition in the Oscar Wilde Centre for Irish Writing." (Philip Coleman, on http://en.wikipedia.org/wiki/Orion_(constellation). (accessed 13.5.09). Each broadsheet was restricted to twenty-six copies.

[56] Since published by Shearsman Books (Hughes 2011).

[57] Most digital camera and computer users will be familiar with the file format known as JPEG. The letters are, apparently, an acronym for the committee that set the standards for a particular method of coding and compressing photographic images (The Joint Photographic Experts Group). JPEG is by no means a good format for undertaking a collaboration in which the quality of text reproduction is an issue:

> JPEG is *not* as well suited for line drawings and other textual or iconic graphics, where the sharp contrasts between adjacent pixels cause noticeable artifacts. Such images are better saved in a lossless graphics format such as TIFF, GIF, PNG or a raw image format.
>
> JPEG is also not well suited to files that will undergo multiple edits, as some image quality will usually be lost each time the image is decompressed and recompressed, particularly if the image is cropped or shifted, or if encoding parameters are changed [...]. (http://en.wikipedia.org/wiki/JPEG, (accessed 1.5.09)

[58] Dots per inch. This is a way, often viewed as imprecise, of measuring graphic "resolution". 72 dpi is regarded as perfectly adequate for images on the internet but it does not provide the quality for any enlargement, especially if there is text in the image.

[59] "The very first one also spoke to me about CON-NING a script, & the Italian sense of "con" - i.e. images con (with) script. Lots of meanings there, as you say, drifting in & out of focus." Email from Peter Hughes to the author, responding to a draft of this article, 29.4.2009. And this from Lee Harwood: "Another possible reading of "con script" can also be that script is a con, a confidence trick. This reminded me of how years ago Eric Mottram pointed out how Melville's story 'The Confidence Man' was an accurate image of a writer. A writer has to have confidence to do what he or she does, but equally the work created is in a way a con(fidence) trick." Letter to the author, (2.5.09.

[60] On ownership, see, for example, Fischer 2001, 22.

[61] Photoshop and InDesign are the names of software programmes distributed through Adobe Systems Incorporated and both forming part of the Adobe Creative Suite, with the intention that material can be moved between the programmes—and others such as Illustrator—to take advantage of the facilities and strengths of each. As its name implies, Photoshop is geared to visual images (the computer's equivalent of a photograph). InDesign is better for manipulating text. The "Type on a path" facility allows a user to set type to an existing "path", already defined, without having to manipulate the position of letters one by one. It relieves text from the usual textual grid at minimal labour costs.

[62] Collaboration can push collaborators into doing what they would not otherwise do. This is one of its attractions and also one of its risks.

[63] *Artifice & Candour* (Hall 2009).

[64] The sequence has since been published in book form (Hall 2011).

[65] I like to think that there are at least four interlinking "places" in "the head" where word-memories remain charged and active: as "tunes" (in other words in the same place as songs); as concepts; as narratives or narrative-like shapes still connected to the body

that narrated them; and as linked to picturing. Some readers will see that I have slipped in a fourth to add to Pound's melopoeia, logopoeia and phanopoeia (Pound 1971, 25–26).

[66] Some of John Cayley's work can be seen on his website at: http://www.shadoof.net/.

[67] Email to the author, 26.2.2007.

[68] I had allowed "orchid" to drift into "orchard" and I found that this had happened a long time ago. The caption on the Litter Magazine site is "Orchard Pavilion". I thank Lee Harwood for pointing this out.

[69] The collaboration didn't end there. Lee worked on a poem he called 'Frames', which became another Kore Broadsheet and which continued the "conversation". (Harwood 2007)

[70] And one that is given a corrective in that same Preface by Deleuze: "Empiricism is by no means a reaction against concepts, nor a simple appeal to lived experience. On the contrary, it undertakes the most insane creation of concepts ever seen or heard." (Deleuze 1994, xx)

[71] See, for example, http://www.spartacus.schoolnet.co.uk/USAappealR.htm (accessed 1.2.2013).

[72] Cited in the museum's website, which does not give the source. In his letter of 2.5.09 Lee Harwood cites Guston as saying that he got "tired of all that purity. Wanted to tell stories."

[73] There is the word for this, or for one aspect of it, kept alive from Greek rhetoric: *ecphrasis* or *ekphrasis*. Etymologically this implies a "speaking out" and, by extension, a kind of ventriloquism which allows the silent image to appear to speak. In the introduction to his *Museum of Words* James A.W. Heffernan identies a competition (which he also sees as gendered) between the power of literary words to give speech to the mute image and the enviable eloquent stillness of the image (Heffernan 2004, 1–8). Ecphrasis, as a term, does not extend, it seems to me, to the preoccupation with "the life and work" of a visual artist, where "work" implies the whole body of work and not just a single image. Some very recent writing that takes in the biographical circumstances of painters as well as specific images must include Basil King's *Learning to Draw/ A History* (for example, King 2005 and 2009) series and his *77 Beasts* (King 2007), and Kelvin Corcoran's engagement with Roger Hilton (Corcoran 2005 and 2008).

[74] "In all and after all the exchanges, revisions, etc. I felt I almost lost sight of who wrote what." (Lee Harwood, letter to the author, 2.5.09.)

[75] Letter to Lee Harwood, 19.9.08

[76] My thanks to Darren Perry and Adam Loveday Edwards for the set-up.

*An Afterword to David Prior's* Black Water Brown Water

[77] This afterword appeared in *Black Water Brown Water*, a book with CD. Totnes: Acts of Language, 2009.

[78] http://www.stourporttown.co.uk/Final%20Arts%20Booklet.08rev.pdf (re-accessed 1.2.2013)

[79] "Unownéd" comes into the text from Milton's Masque, known as *Comus* (Milton 1969: l.407), where it is applied to the young woman who is temporally out of the surveillance, and therefore possession, of her brothers and father who co-own her chastity.

[80] A private note from David Prior.

## Do Not Ignore: order-words in domestic and public spaces

[81] First published in *Esitys* 3: *Performance Writing*, (Helsinki), 2010. ed. Pilvi Porkola and Johanna MacDonald, pp. 8–13.

[82] For fuller discussions of performance writing, see other essays in this volume (1: 25–44, 146–160).

[83] Do sociologist and market researchers yet use a standardised measure of public text-density as an indicator of wealth and social status? I would guess, for example, that an urban context with a low public text density would be one with wealthy residents.

[84] Downloaded from http://www.dft.gov.uk/trafficsignsimages/imagelist. php?CATID=4 (UK Crown copyright)

[85] When a referent relies on the context rather than surrounding text (such as in the use of the words *here* and *now*), this is known as deixis in linguistics.

## Making it new out of old hat: the words in Lone Twin

[86] Published in Williams, David and Carl Lavery (eds.). 2011. *Good Luck Everybody: Lone Twin – Journeys, Performances, Conversations*. Aberystwyth: Performance Research Books.

[87] I shall not especially consider either sung words or "cried" words in performances such as *Town Crying* (2007), although some of what I say can apply equally to them.

[88] My thanks to David Williams and Lone Twin for letting me see working copies of performance texts.

[89] Here are some of the temptations. The pub scene at the end of the Game of Chess section of 'The Waste Land' puts to work familiar repeated phrases from everyday life and ends:

> Goodnight Bill. Goodnight Lou. Goodnight May. Goodnight.
> Ta ta. Goodnight. Goodnight.
> Goodnight, ladies, good night, sweet ladies, good night, good night.
> (Eliot 1936: 67)

That is in my ear when I hear "Gentleman goodnight, ladies good morning". And I have almost cited "In my beginning is my end" from 'East Coker' (Eliot 1959: 23), which also includes the following passage, piling up a list of examples to indicate comprehensiveness, just as Lone Twin do, or Whitman did, or Ginsberg did. Of course, this is not uncommon.

> O dark dark dark. They all go into the dark,
> The vacant interstellar spaces, the vacant into the vacant,
> The captains, merchant bankers, eminent men of letters,

The generous patrons of art, the statesmen and the rulers,
Distinguished civil servants, chairmen of many committees,
Industrial lords and petty contractors, all go into the dark,
And dark the Sun and Moon, and the Almanach de Gotha
And the Stock Exchange Gazette, the Directory of Directors (Eliot 1936: 27)

[90] The one I remember was, "In my suitcase I packed…". Each player in their turn must start "I packed my suitcase and in it I put…". The first player completes the sentence by naming an item, the second player repeats what has been said and adds another item and so it continues, until someone can't remember all of the objects that have been mentioned or gets it wrong.

[91] The two senses of "counter" have two quite different derivations: one from the Latin *contra*, the other from *computare*, suggesting "to think with" (and of course offering the modern "computer"). As the *Oxford English Dictionary* explains, "tell" was formerly the "ordinary word" for the business of counting as in 1,2,3. (OED 1989, Def. 1a) Strikingly both "count" (in "recount", "raconteur", "give an account") and "tell" ("tally") suggest a strong connection between number and narration.

[92] "By contrast, the poets whose readings I have most admired have tended to become depersonalised; listeners learn to tolerate not-knowing in a referential sense through the poet's toleration of a space of not-interpreting about the poems". (Wilkinson 2007: 153)

[93] *I'm Sorry I Haven't a Clue* was first broadcast on BBC Radio 4 in April 1972. Following the death of Humphrey Lyttelton in 2008, there was a pause before it was revived under different chairs.

[94] Many readers will recognise a debt to J.L. Austin's theory of speech acts in these paragraphs (Austin 1976).

[95] Nor is it in *Daniel Hit by a Train*. There are some exchanges in *Alice Bell* that take on a form of dialogue.

[96] I am using interpellation in the sense established by Louis Althusser in 'Ideology and Ideological State Apparatuses'. (Althusser 1971: 171 –86)

[97] The link between "persona" and the grammatical notion of "person" seems far from fortuitous. I have written elsewhere about pronouns in "performance writing" (1: 70–74).

[98] I see this courtesy as extending to the mockery directed by "Gregg" to "Gary" in *Sledge Hammer Songs*. No offence is taken. Everyone recognises the tradition of comic duo that is being evoked, including the players (that is to say, the players' style "performs" recognition).

[99] In the recent tour of the *Catastrophe Trilogy* (2010), Cynthia's role was played by Guy Dartnell.

[100] For example, "Who gives this woman to be married to this man?" It is the bride's father who is supposed to say, "I do." Or these lyrics, from Cole Porter (1956): "Who wants to be a millionaire? I don't. Have flashy flunkeys everywhere? I don't."

*Foot, mouth and ear: some thoughts on prosody and performance*

[101] Published in *On Foot*, eds. Carl Lavery and Nicolas Whybrow, *Performance Research Journal*, Vol. 17, No. 2, April 2012, pp. 36–41. This version of the paper contains a few extra lines that were edited out of the journal to provide a neat fit with the page. With thanks to the publishers: http://www.tandfonline.com/toc/rprs20/current.

[102] Canetti 1973: 34

[103] James 2011: 39

[104] I shall italicise "foot" when using it in its prosodic sense and leave it in regular font when it refers to "the lowest part of the leg below the ankle" (OED).

[105] For other examples, see Oliver 1979, 1990 and 1992.

[106] Or to use the now very familiar terms from Jakobson (1966), that the "set" of an act of speaking or writing is on the "message" and that the mode is therefore "poetic".

[107] The obvious parts of syllables are phonemes, the sounded equivalents of letters. Phonologists also divide a syllable into three segments: onset, nucleus and coda. The nucleus is necessarily a vowel. See, for example, Fabb 1997: 30–33.

[108] According to the notion of "distinctive features", phonemes are indeed produced through combinations of binary switching choices: for example, nasalised / not nasalised. Poets can put these alternations into play and the voice / unvoiced distinction is very important in Oliver's account.

[109] The OED's definition of foot (above) implies that a foot can only have one "ictus" (a blow) or "principal stress". This allows for any number of weaker stresses within a rhythmic "division". It does make troublesome, though, the notion of *feet* without a strong syllable (such as pyrrhus or dibrach, ᵕ ᵕ) or with more than one (such as spondee, – –) unless these are seen as ways of describing metrical variation within a line whose main metre is otherwise set.

[110]
There was a man called Michael Finigan,
He grew whiskers on his chinigin.
The wind came out and blew them in ag'in,
Poor old Michael Finigan, begin ag'in. (Opie 167: 31)

[111] Of course the social implicature may not be so simple. I have approached this topic in an article on road signs and my own appropriations of their mode within visual texts (1: 115–122).

[112] "Speak the speech, I pray you, as I pronounced it to you, trippingly on the tongue; but if you mouth it, as many of our players do, I had as lief the town-crier spoke my lines." (Shakespeare 1970: Act 3, scene 2, ll.1–4)

[113] Though equipment for the analysis and manipulation of acoustic recordings is much more accessible now than it was at the time Oliver was experimenting, I have not yet been able to "apply two electrodes to the glottis" (Oliver 1989: 14) to register shifts between voiced and unvoiced.

[114] Some computer keyboards still have a key marked Return, a reminder of the need for "carriage return" at the end of every typed line. For continuous prose, this return is

managed automatically by word-processing software, but paragraphs, lists and poetic lines still require "hard returns".

[115] In contrast to *verse* and *strophe*, *stanza*, which appears to have entered English at a much later date than *verse*, relates to "stand" and indeed to an Italian word for "room". I take the stasis implied by the term to refer to the fixed metrical pattern of lines within a "verse"; the pattern stands still, while the component lines move. My thanks to Nicolas Whybrow for nudging me back to this distinction.

[116] Noam Chomsky (Chomsky 1965) paired the terms in this way; the correspondence with Saussure's much earlier pairing of *langue* (system of language) and *parole* (putting language to use through speaking) is obvious (Saussure 1974).

[117] Oliver uses the example of the slowing down of time when steering out of an impending car accident (Oliver 1992: 277).

[118] Charles Olson, for example, after stumbling in a reading of his own poem, responded like this: "I have this problem with scoring, it's more difficult than music. Like one writes music one doesn't play it. That's that problem with this kind of performing situation. I'm not, I'm not, I'm not—I'm Beethoven!" (Olson 2011: 10)

[119] The conditions imposed on performance by the Samuel Beckett estate are perhaps the best known example of the latter.

## Performance Writing: an entry in a lexicon

[120] Published in *A Lexicon: Performance Research* Volume 11, No. 3. September 2006. pp. 89–91. London: Routledge. (With thanks to the publishers: http://www.tandfonline. com/toc/rprs20/current.) Many of the secondary terms alluded to in this entry are dealt with more fully in the following essay in this volume.

[121] The actual author of the phrase may well have been Ric Allsopp, one of the editors of this issue of *Performance Research*, a journal whose title also leaves the grammatical status of performance undecided.

[122] Including Aberystwyth, Lancaster, Scarborough School of Arts (University of Hull).

[123] First Performance Writing Symposium, Dartington, April 1996 (Bergvall 1996); Second Performance Writing Symposium, *In the Event of the Text*, School of Theatre, University of Utrecht, Holland, 1999. (Both organised by Ric Allsopp and Caroline Bergvall.)

[124] For example, New Langton Arts, San Francisco.

[125] For example, Hugill 2006, Lopez 2006, Milne 1999 and Sheppard 2001.

## A glossary for Performance Writing

[126] This glossary was developed in 2003 in conversation with colleagues at Dartington College of Arts for use in the teaching of writing and performance writing. I particularly thank Ric Allsopp, Jerome Fletcher and Redell Olsen for comment and contribution. The original version had many references to specific teaching modules and assessment tasks within these degree courses, Most of these have been removed, though some more general references have been retained in case they are of use.

*Xenial (an entry in a lexicon)*

[127] Published in 'A Lexicon of Training Terms' in *Theatre Dance and Performance Training*, Vol. 3, Issue 3, 2012, p. 398.

*Arts for what, for where, for whom? Fragmentary reflections on Dartington College of Arts*

[128] Published in *Theatre Dance and Performance Training*, Vol 2, Issue 1, ed. Jonathan Pitches and Simon Murray, March 2011, pp. 54–71. Only one of the several photographs included in the original context has been retained here.

[129] See below for a note on the two players. Our thanks also go to Catriona Scott, Director of Taught Programmes (2000–2004) and Associate Director of Theatre (2004–2010), who has given us considerable help in writing this account. Our thanks also go to Peter Cox, without whom there almost certainly would not have been a Dartington College of Arts, for his knowledge and memory; to Kate Mount for allowing us to use her photographs; and to Kevin Mount for advice and for providing prepared photographs and art work.

[130] We shall use DCA to refer to the institution, Dartington College of Arts, and Dartington, a term full of ambiguity, for the wider project associated with Dartington Hall.

[131] The Committee for the Encouragement of Music and the Arts was founded "informally" in 1939 and established by royal charter in 1940. According to Peter Cox, Holst was "one of Sir Walford Davies' CEMA Music Travellers, working her way through the South West of England", who was given a home and a brief on the Dartington estate. (Cox 2002, 11)

[132] John (later Lord) Reith became the first Director General of the BBC in 1927. Reith was driven by a belief that public service broadcasting had an overriding duty to educate—and hence improve—the masses.

[133] Michael Young's account (Young 1996, 239 and passim) suggests that there was never a coherent arts policy—nor indeed an education policy—on the estate as a whole. It seems that in the early years of the Dartington Hall experiment, there were two competing approaches: the sponsorship of already valued avant-gardist practice (for example, Kurt Joos and Michael Chekhov) on the one hand; educational or community based approaches, as exemplified by Imogen Holst, on the other.

[134] The Dartington Hall Trust was established by Dorothy and Leonard Elmhirst as a registered charity in 1935 and has run the Dartington estate since that time.

[135] This phrase was mis-typed at the head of a paper prepared for Academic Board by John Hall as "theatrical underpinings", a notion that at the time was more likely to be understood than a "theoretical underpinning".

[136] In this brief sketch, the Elmhirsts and their Trust play a very significant part, as would, if there was time for more detail, a story of often precarious negotiations with regional and national bureaucracies. The contributions of the Elmhirsts to the local economy and cultural life, together with their very conspicuous good works, almost certainly meant that experiments in education were viewed more favourably in the early days.

[137] The Higher Education Funding Council for England (HEFCE) commissioned a report, *Funding of specialist performing arts institutions* (HEFCE 99 / 41), from its Performing Arts Review Panel on "future levels of funding for the specialist performing arts institutions". There was a favourable outcome for Dartington. This first recommendation in the Executive Summary indicates an attitude to training and its purposes: "to recognise that the provision of performing arts training in preparation for a career in professional performance is high cost, or very high cost and should be funded accordingly".

[138] The title of the BBC 1972 *Man Alive* programme about Leonard Elmhirst illustrates this point: 'A Job is not Enough'. That "enough" should be emphasised. The Elmhirsts manifestly did not disdain jobs, even if they themselves did not need one, at least in the conventional sense.

[139] One of the Trustees most identified with a view of the arts contrasting with the prevailing ethos of the College was John Lane. The author's page on the *Resurgence* website tells us that "He lectures and conducts workshops on the subject of the arts and spirituality worldwide". (Resurgence) The Trust's own website has this: "The spirit of Dartington is hard to capture but the aspirations which continue to inform the work of the Trust may be expressed as a respect for the natural world; the encouragement of human creativity, artistic, intellectual and practical; the promotion of learning by doing; and the attainment of the highest standards of performance and execution in all the activities undertaken or supported by the Trust". (Dartington Hall Trust) The ideological differences discerned between College and Trust are discussed on the Save Dartington website. (Save Dartington)

[140] Our example, though touching on Choreography, is from Theatre; we know that this question of technique or skill is one that is specific to each of the disciplines taught at Dartington. In Music, the equivalent to *Bodyworks* might be instrumental tuition. At DCA, as elsewhere, this became an increased tension with every reduction in unit funding. The closest to *Bodyworks* in Writing were first-year modules still called Inside Writing, in which "language" is treated as the equivalent of a performer's body, to be explored both conceptually and practically and in ways that ensure that concept and practice engage each other.

[141] The DipHE course Art and Design in Social Contexts was underway from the late 1970s.

[142] The text in the box headed Text and Context is from a glossary of key terms in an undergraduate handbook, originally drafted (by John Hall) for a revalidation of the Writing degree in 2002/3. That it could later be adopted for the programme-wide handbook indicates how shared and established the term had become. An edited version of the full glossary is included in this volume. (1: 151–160)

*Interdisciplinarity: "Disciplines" And Contemporary Practices*

[143] Published in *Dreams and Reconstructions: Conference Papers (from the 2nd Concepts Conference, Held in Oporto, Portugal, April 1995)*, edited by Gerald Lidstone and Noel Witts (Leicester: Concepts, Department of Visual & Performing Arts, De Montfort University, 1996).

[144] I am thinking of Sigmund Freud's *Psychopathology of Everyday Life* (Freud 1975); Erving Goffman's *The Presentation of the Self in Everyday Life* (Goffman 1959), and Michel de Certeau's *The Practice of Everyday Life* (Certeau 1988); More recently there has been Alan Read's *Theatre and Everyday Life* (Read 1993).

[145] A genuine multi-disciplinarity—within the sense of discipline that I shall be elaborating—is probably inevitably also interdisciplinary for any given individual. A single "module", however effective in its own terms, is unlikely on its own to initiate anyone into a discipline.

[146] In relation to Theatre, I am not sure whether the name always makes the approach clear. Is there, for example, a distinction along these lines between Theatre and Theatre Studies?

[147] I admit freely, though, that I have others. No established disciplinary field matched my own practice as a poet. As a student who already wanted to write I signed up to study literature, which is the study of the already written within quite specific genres. That is important to writers, but their field of reference always extends way beyond the written *as literature*. What were writers reading and studying? No disciplinary field defined this. This has not altogether been a disadvantage.

[148] "Branch" is reassuringly positive; as a metaphor it is organic: branches grow on trees, in this case on the tree of knowledge. The image gives knowledge a powerful natural and unified presence—growing and changing but only just. Imagine if the dictionary had referred instead to a slice of the knowledge cake, or indeed a shelf in the knowledge cupboard (I understand that the German word *fach* is a compartment, shelf or drawer). It is helpful to get behind some of these metaphors which still lurk in our terms. What is useful about the metaphor of shelf or drawer is that it implies one of those storage systems which is at the same time actively a classification system. The drawer, for example, can bear a name; and anything can be put into it as long as it fits either or both (a) the shape of the drawer; (b) the name. As a "compartment" a drawer or shelf differs from a "department"; the first is spatial or topographical; the second is organisational.

[149] The typographical emphasis is mine.

[150] There is a telling overlap between "discipline" and the other word which is often used in the English language to do the same job, at least within education: "subject". Strikingly, control and power are associated with both terms:

| | | |
|---|---|---|
| 1 disciple—follower | \| | subject—under the power of |
| 2 discipline—branch of learning | \| | subject—branch of learning |
| 3 to discipline (to control, chastise) | \| | to subject—(to exercise power over) |

[151] Where discipline is defined by discipleship it is likely that there will be resistance to any forms of interdisciplinarity which are not sanctioned (at least in spirit) by the Masters.

[152] Or even from the indiscipline of the activity which has not yet claimed an academic name. Think of the different modulations of the term "music", each implying a different range of inclusions and exclusions.

*Designing a taught postgraduate programme in performance practices*

[153] Published in the Proceedings of the conference: *Further and Continuing Education of performing artists in the Nordic Countries—a Nordic Task* (Videre og affernddanneelse for scenekunstere I Nordern; Oslo: Norway 12th–14th November 1999, pp. 77–85.

[154] This preamble is a written version of a short spoken commentary aimed at linking the paper with some of the presentations of the previous evening.

*A review of* The Anxiety of Interdisciplinarity

[155] Published in *Performance Research* Vol 4, No 3 (Winter 1999), pp. 103 –106. With thanks to the publishers: http://www.tandfonline.com/toc/rprs20/current.

# Cited works

Abraham, Nicolas and Torok, Maria. 1994. *The Shell and the Kernel: Renewals of Psychoanalysis*. trans. Nicholas T. Rand. Chicago, IL: Chicago University Press.

Allsopp, Ric. 1999. 'Performance Writing'. in *PAJ: A Journal of Performance and Art*, Vol. 21, No. 1, pp. 76–80.

Althusser, Louis. 1971. *Lenin and Philosophy and Other Essays*. trans. Ben Brewster. New York and London: Monthly Review Press.

Auslander, Philip. 1999. *Liveness: Performance in a Mediatized Culture*. London: Routledge.

Austin, J.L.. 1976. *How to do Things with Words*. Oxford: Oxford University Press.

Bakhtin, M.M.. 1986. *Speech Genres and Other Late Essays*. trans. Vern W. McGee; ed. Caryl Emerson and Michael Holquist. Austin, TX: University of Texas Press.

Beckett, Samuel. 1963. *Happy Days*. London: Faber & Faber.

— 1984. *Collected Short Plays*. London: Faber and Faber.

Benveniste, Emile. 1971. *Problems in General Linguistics*. Miami, FL: University of Miami Press.

Bergvall, Caroline. 1996. 'What do we mean by Performance Writing?'. http://www.dft.gov.uk/trafficsignsimages/imagelist.php?CATID=4. (accessed 16.11.2012).

— 1996a. *Éclat sites 1–10*. Lowestoft: Sound and Language.

— 1999. *Goan Atom 1, Jets-Poupee*. Cambridge: Rem Press.

— 2005. *Fig*. Great Wilbraham, Cambridge: Salt Publishing.

— 2005a. *Via: Poems 1994–2004*. Rockdrill CD #8. Optic Nerve, for London: Contemporary Poetics Research Centre, Birkbeck University of London.

Bernstein, Charles. 1992. *A Poetics*. Cambridge, MA and London: Harvard University Press.

Berrigan, Ted. 2007. *Collected Poems*, ed. Alice Notley. Berkeley, Los Angeles, CA and London: University of California Press.

*Beyond Text*. No date. Website. Arts and Humanities Research Council (AHRC), UK: http://www.beyondtext.ac.uk.

Bourdieu, Pierre. 1992. *Language and Symbolic Power*. Cambridge: Polity.

Campion, Thomas. 1966. *The Works of Thomas Campion*. ed. Percival Vivian. Oxford: Oxford at the Charendon Press.

Canetti, Elias. 1973. *Crowds and Power.* trans. Carol Stewart. Harmondsworth: Penguin.

Carroll, Lewis. 1993 (1865). *Complete Illustrated Works.* London: Chancellor Press.

Cavarero, Adriana. 2005. *For More Than One Voice: Towards a Philosophy of Vocal Expression.* trans. Paul A. Kottman. Stanford, CA: Stanford University Press.

Certeau, Michel de. 1988. *The Practice of Everyday Life.* trans. Steven Rendall. Berkeley, Los Angeles, and London: University of California Press.

cheek, cris. No date. 'Reading and Writing: the Sites of Performance' in *How2*, Volume 3, No. 2. http://www.asu.edu/pipercwcenter/how2journal/vol_3_no_3/bergvall/cheek-reading-writing.html (accessed 16.11.2012).

Chomsky, Noam. 1965. *Aspects of the Theory of Syntax.* Cambridge, MA: MIT Press.

Clapham, Rachel Lois. 2010. *(W)reading Performance Writing : A Guide.* London: Live Art Development Agency. http://www.scribd.com/doc/35778372/W-reading-Performance-Writing-A-Guide-2010-by-Rachel-Lois-Clapham# (accessed 16.11.2012).

Cobbing, Bob. 1999. *kob bok.* Buckfastleigh: etruscan books.

Cobbing, Bob and Upton, Lawrence, (eds.). 1998. *Word Score Utterance: Choreography in verbal and visual poetry.* London: Writers Forum.

Corcoran, Kelvin. 2005. *Roger Hilton's Sugar.* Nottingham: Leafe Press.

— 2008. *Backward Turning Sea.* Exeter: Shearsman Books.

Cream. 1967. *Fresh Cream.* Hamburg: Polygram. (CD).

Crozier, Andrew. 1976. *Duets.* Guildford: Circle Press.

— 1985. *All Where Each Is.* London and Berkeley: Allardyce, Barnett.

Deleuze, Gilles. 1994. *Difference & Repetition.* trans. Paul Patton. London: The Athlone Press

Deleuze, Gilles and Felix Guattari. 1992. *A Thousand Plateaus: capitalism and schizophrenia.* London: Continuum.

Derrida, Jacques. 1976. *Of Grammatology.* trans. G.C. Spivak. Baltimore, MD and London: The John Hopkins Press.

— 1978. *Writing and Difference.* trans. Alan Bass. London and Henley: Routledge and Kegan Paul.

Drayton, Michael. 'Poly-Olbion: The Fift Song' in *The Poems of Michael Drayton Volume, Two.* ed. John Buxton. Cambridge, MA: Harvard University Press.

Drewry, Douglas. 2003 [1989]. *The Definitive Performance Writing Guide.* Professional Management Spectrum Inc.

Drucker, Joanna. 1995. *The Century of Artist's Books* . New York, NY: Granary Books.

Duanmu, San. 2008. *Syllable Structure: The Limits of Variation*. Oxford: Oxford University Press, 2008.

Dworkin, Craig. 2003. *Reading the Illegible*. Evanstown, IL: Northwestern University Press.

Eliot, T.S. 1959. *Four Quartets*. London: Faber.

— *Collected Poems 1909–1935*. London: Faber.

Fabb, Nigel 1997. *Linguistics and Literature*. Oxford and Malden, MA: Blackwell.

Finlay, Ian Hamilton. 1998. *Evening Will Come They Will Sew the Blue Sail*. Edinburgh: Graeme Murray.

Fischer, Steven Roger. 2001. *A History of Writing*. London: Reaktion Books.

Forced Entertainment. 1995. 'Speak Bitterness' in *Language Alive one*. Lowestoft: Sound and Language.

Freud, Sigmund. 1975. *Psychopathology of Everyday Life*. trans. Alan Tyson. Harmondsworth: Penguin.

Frisch, Max. 1962. *The Fire Raisers*. trans. Michael Bullock. London: Methuen.

Gadamer, Hans-Georg. 1997. *Gadamer on Celan: Who Am I and Who Are You? and Other Essays*. Albany, NY: SUNY Press

— 1998. *The Beginning of Philosophy*. trans. Rod Coltman. New York, NY: Continuum

Geoffrey of Monmouth. 1963. *History of the Kings of Britain*. London: Dent.

Goffman, Erving. 1959. T*he Presentation of the Self in Everyday Life*. Harmondsworth: Penguin.

Gramsci, Antonio. 1971. *Selections from Prison Notebooks*. ed. and trans. by Q. Hoare and G. Nowell Smith. London: Lawrence and Wishart.

Guston, Philip. 2007. *Works on Paper*. ed. Michael Semff. Ostfildern, Germany: Hatje Cantz.

Hall, John. 1996. 'Sentenced to' in *Performance Research, Vol 1, No 1*, pp. 98–102; and (1: 53–60)

— 1998. 'Missing persons: personal pronouns in performance writing', *Performance Research* Vol 3 No 1: 87–90; and (1: 70–74)

— 2006. 'Performance Writing' in *A Lexicon: Performance Research Journal*, Vol 11, No 3: 89–91; and (1: 151–160)

— 2007. 'The Orchid Pavilion, a brief essay on ignorance for Lee Harwood'. in Litter Magazine: http://www.leafepress.com/litter1/johnhall/index.html.

— 2008. *Thirteen Ways of Talking About Performance Writing*. Plymouth: Plymouth College of Art and Design; and (1: 23–41)

— 2008b. *The Week's Bad Groan*. Old Hunstanton: Oystercatcher Press.

— 2009. *Artifice & Candour* (exhibition). Plymouth: Viewpoint Gallery, Plymouth College of Art, 11–23 March.

— 2010. 'Do Not Ignore: order-words in domestic and public spaces', *Etysis 3* (Helsinki): 8–13; and (1: 115–122).

Halliday, M.A.K. 1979. *Language as Social Semiotic: The social interpretation of language and meaning*. London et al.: Edward Arnold.

Harley, Trevor. 2001. *The Psychology of Language: from Data to Theory*. 2nd edition. Hove: Psychology Press.

Harwood, Lee. 1965. *title illegible*. London: Writers Forum.

— 2004. *Collected Poems 1964–2004*. Exeter: Shearsman Books.

— 2007. *Frames*. Dublin: Kore Broadsheets, #19.

— 2008a. *Selected Poems*. Exeter: Shearsman Books.

Harwood, Lee and Richard Caddel. 1984. *Wine Tales: un roman devin*. Newcastle Upon Tyne: Galloping Dog Press.

Harwood, Lee and Antony Lopez. 1979. *Wish You Were Here*. Deal: Transgravity Press.

Harwood, Lee (with Kelvin Corcoran). 2008b. *Not the Full Story: six interviews by Kelvin Corcoran*. Exeter: Shearsman Books.

Heffernan, James A.W. 2004. *Museum of Words: The Poetics of Ekphrasis from Homer to Ashbery*. Chicago, IL: University of Chicago Press.

Hayles, N. Katherine. 2002. *Writing Machines*. Cambridge, MA: MIT Press.

— 1990. *Chaos Bound: Orderly Disorder in Contemporary Literature and Science*. Ithaca, NY and London: Cornell University Press.

Hélène Cixous. 1991. 'The Author in Truth' in *Coming to Writing and Other Essays*. trans. Deborah Jenson. Cambridge, MA: Harvard University Press.

Hopkins, Gerard Manley. 1964. 'The Wreck of the Deutschland' in *Gerard Manley Hopkins: A Selection of his Poems and Prose by W.H. Gardner*. Harmondsworth: Penguin.

Hughes, Peter. 1995. *Paul Klee's Diary*. Cambridge: Equipage.

— 2003. *Blueroads*. Great Wilbraham, Cambridge: Salt Publishing

— 2007. No XV from *The Pistol Tree*. Dublin: Kore Broadsheets, #17.

— 2008. *The Sardine Tree*. Old Hunstanton: Oystercatcher Press.

Hughes, Peter (ed.). 2000. *April Eye: Poems for Peter Riley*. Cambridge: Infernal Methods.

Hughes, Peter and Simon Marsh. 2009. *The Pistol Tree*. Great Works: http://www.greatworks.org.uk/poems/ptp/ptp1.html (accessed 25.4.09). (since published as Hughes 2011)

— 2011. *The Pistol Tree Poems*. Bristol: Shearsman Books.

Hugill, Piers. 2006. 'Love and Grammar', a review of Bergvall 2005 and Bergvall 2005a. *Jacket No 31*, October. http: //jacketmagazine.com/31/hugill-bergvall.html (re-accessed 01.02.2013)

Jakobson, Roman. 1966. 'Closing Statement: Linguistics and Poetics' in Sebeok, T. A. (ed.) *Style in Language*. Cambridge, MA: MIT Press, pp. 350–377.

— 1995. *On Language*. Cambridge, MA and London: Harvard University Press.

James, John. 2011. 'Pimlico', in *In Romsey Town*. Cambridge: Equipage.

Karton, Joshuam, ed. 1983. *Film Scenes for Actors*. New York, NY: Bantam Books.

King, Basil. 2005. *Twin Towers, from Learning to Draw / A History*. Austin, TX: Skanky Possum.

— 2007. *77 Beasts: Basil King's Beastiary*. East Rockaway, NY: Marsh Hawk Press.

— 2008. *Learning to Draw / A History: In the Field where Daffodils Grow*. New York, NY: Libellum.

Kristeva, Julia. 1986. 'Word, Dialog and Novel'. in *The Kristeva Reader*. ed. Toril Moi. New York, NY: Columbia University Press.

— 1987. *Tales of Love*. trans. Leon S, Roudiez. New York: Columbia University Press.

Lacan, Jacques. 1977. *Ecrits: a Selection*. trans. Alan Sheridan. London: Tavistock.

— 1991. *The Seminar of Jacques Lacan, Book II*. trans. Sylvana Tomaselli. New York and London: W.W. Norton and Company.

Lavery, Carl. 2009. 'Is there a text in this performance?'. in *Performance Research* Vol14 No. 1: 37–45.

Lopez, Tony. 2006. 'Poetry and Performance'. in *Meaning Performance: Essays on Poetry* (Great Wilbraham, Cambridge: Salt Publishing. pp. 73–88.

McCrum, Carolyn. 1978. *The Soup Book*. London: Magnum Books.

Milne, Drew. 1999. 'A Veritable Dollmine'. in Jacket 12 (http://jacketmagazine.com/12/milne-bergvall.html) and Keston Sutherland (ed.), *Quid*, Issue 4 (undated), pp. 6–8.

Milton, John. 1969. 'A Mask (Comus)' in *Poetical Works*. ed. Douglas Bush. London: Oxford University Press.

Murray, Simon and John Hall. 2011. 'Arts for what, for where, for whom? Fragmentary reflections on Dartington College of Arts, 1961–2010'. in *Theatre Dance and Performance Training*, Vol 2, Issue 1. pp. 54–71. Routledge, Taylor and Francis. (and 1: 164–181)

O'Hara, Frank. 1972. *Collected Poems of Frank O'Hara*. ed. Donald Allen. New York, NY: Alfred A Knopf.

*OED (Oxford English Dictionary)*. 1989. 2nd edn, CD-ROM. Ver. 3.1 (2007). Oxford: Oxford University Press.

Oliver, Douglas. 1979. 'Even poets have beliefs about poetic "stress"'. in *Grosseteste Review*, Vol 12, pp. 12–32.

— 1989. *Poetry and Narrative in Performance*. London: Macmillan.

— 1990. 'An island that is all the world' in *Three Variations On The Theme Of Harm*. London: Paladin, pp. 37–109.

— 1992. 'Three Lilies', in *Poets on Writing: Britain, 1970–1991*. Denise Riley (ed.). Basingstoke and London: Macmillan, pp. 276–282.

— 1994. *Penniless Politics*. Newcastle upon Tyne: Bloodaxe Books.

— 2005. *Whisper "Louise"*. Hastings: Reality Street.

Olson, Charles. 1960. in *The New American Poetry*. Donald Allen, (ed.). New York: Grove Press and London: Evergreen Books.

— 2011. *Charles Olson at Goddard College April 12–14, 1962*. Victoria, TX: Cuneiform Press.

Ong, Walter. 1982. *Orality and Literacy: The Technologizing of the Word*. London: Routledge.

Opie, Iona and Peter. 1967. *The Lore and Language of Schoolchildren*. Oxford and New York: Oxford University Press.

Paterson, Mary and Rachel Lois Clapham. No date. *Open Dialogues: Critical Writing on and as Performance*. Website:http://www.opendialogues.com/ (accessed 16.11.2012).

Pattison, Neil, *et al,* eds. 2012. *Certain Prose of* The English Intelligencer. Cambridge: Mountain Press.

*Performance Research*. 2004. *On the Page*. ed. Ric Allsopp and Kevin Mount. Volume 9, No. 2. London: Routledge.

Perloff, Marjorie. 1998. *Poetry On & Off The Page: Essays For Emergent Occasions*. Evanston, IL: Northwestern University Press.

Porter, Cole. 1956. 'Who Wants to Marry a Millionaire'. *High Society*. Warner Brothers Records.

Pound, Ezra. 1934. *Make It New*. London: Faber.

— 1971. How to Read. New York, NY: Haskell House.

Prynne, J.H. 1993. *Not You*. Cambridge: Equipage.

— 2001. *They that have powre to hurt; A Specimen of a Commentary on Shakespeares Sonnets, 94*, Cambridge: Privately published.

— 2005. *Poems*. Fremantle: Fremantle Arts Centre Press & Tarset: Bloodaxe Books.

Read, Alan. 1993. *Theatre and Everyday Life*. London and New York: Routledge.

Riley, Denise. 1997. 'Is there linguistic guilt?', in *Critical Quarterly 39. 1.* pp. 75–110.

— 2000. 'Outside from the Start'. in *Selected Poems*. London: Reality Street Editions.

— 2000a. *The Words of Selves: Identification, Solidarity, Irony*. Stanford, CA: Stanford University Press.

Saussure, Ferdinand de. 1974. *Course in General Linguistics*. ed. Charles Bally and Albert Sechehaye; trans. Wade Baskin. Glasgow: Fontana / Collins.

Searle, John. 1969. *Speech Acts: An Essay in the Philosophy of Language*. Cambridge: Cambridge University Press.

Shakespeare, William. 1963. *King Lear*. ed. Russell Fraser. New York: Signet Classics.

— 1970. *Hamlet*. ed. Bernard Lott. London: Longman.

Sheppard, Robert. 2001. 'The Performing and the Performed: Performance Writing and Performative Reading', *How2*, Vol. 1, No. 6. Also at http://www.asu.edu/pipercwcenter/how2journal/archive/online_archive/v1_6_2001/current/in-conference/sheppard.html (accessed 7.10.2012).

Skeat, Walter W. 1993. *Concise Dictionary of English Etymology*. Ware: Wordsworth Editions.

Stein, Gertrude. 1936. *The Geographical History of America*. New York, NY: Random House.

— *The Autobiography of Alice B. Toklas*. Harmondsworth: Penguin.

— 1971. 'Poetry and Grammar' in *Look at Me Now and Here I Am: Writings and Lectures 1911–45*. ed. P. Meyerowitz. Harmondsworth: Penguin.

Sterne, Lawrence. 2000. http://special.lib.gla.ac.uk/exhibns/month/oct2000.html (accessed 11.10.2012).

Sumner, Alaric, feature ed. 1999. 'Writing and Performance', in Bonnie Maranca and Gautam Dasgupta (eds), *PAJ: A Journal of Performance and Art,* Vol. 21, No. 1.

Watts, Carol. 2011. *Occasionals*. Hastings: Reality Street.

Wilkinson, John. 2007. *The Lyric Touch*. Great Wilbraham: Salt Publishing.

# Index

Milton Keynes UK
Ingram Content Group UK Ltd.
UKHW051538160424
441254UK00002B/178

9 781848 613171